VGM Professional Careers Series

CAREERS in

COMMUNICATIONS

SHONAN NORONHA

FOURTH EDITION

VGM Career Books

New York Chicago San Francisco Lisbon London Madrid Mexico City
Milan New Delhi San Juan Seoul Singapore Sydney Toronto

Library of Congress Cataloging-in-Publication Data

Noronha, Shonan F. R.
    Careers in communications / Shonan Noronha. — 4th ed.
       p.   cm. — (VGM professional careers series)
    ISBN 0-07-143735-5
    1. Communication—Vocational guidance—United States.   2. Mass media—
Vocational guidance—United States.   I. Title.   II. Series.

   P91.6 .N67   2004
   302.2'023'73—dc22   2004007911

1 2 3 4 5 6 7 8 9 0 DOC/DOC 3 2 1 0 9 8 7 6 5 4

ISBN 0-07-143735-5

Interior design by Robert S. Tinnon

This book is printed on acid-free paper.

This book is dedicated to my mother,

Mary Felicitas,

who has inspired me with her passion for good movies,

her fascination with creative imaging, and

her enjoyment of a story well told

in any medium, and

to the loving memory of my father,

Dr. A. B. C. Noronha,

who appreciated the immediacy of radio news,

enjoyed sports broadcasts of cricket matches, and

understood the power of the printed word.

CONTENTS

FOREWORD

The subject of the book you are about to read is a revolution as profound as any that has shaped the modern world, from industrialization to the spread of computing.

And the revolution is still under way. Today's communication technologies are changing the way we talk, think, and relate to one another and also the way we work. Whether the field is journalism, film, photography, television, video, radio, advertising, or public relations, old practices are adapting to new necessities in virtually every area of our lives, from corporate offices and government agencies to schools, hospitals, the uniformed services, houses of worship, and even private homes.

In dealing with such change, in which little seems constant except the certainty of further change, the great challenge facing current and future employees is: How do I prepare for my career? This is, of course, a question young people ask themselves as they look to their first "real job." Surprisingly, it is also a question now being asked by experienced workers who may be on their third, fourth, or even fifth "real job."

New and incumbent workers alike face the same issues in building careers in communications, especially when technologies, the economy, and the conditions of work are changing as rapidly as they are today. Experienced fifty-year-old workers still remember the more measured pace of work when the speed of office typing pools and postal delivery schedules chiefly determined how quickly communication took place.

Today's employees are more likely to work collaboratively over the Web with people all around the world, and they sometimes feel that work moves too quickly. Equally important, the economy has changed: Typing pools are long gone, and an increasing amount of work is now handled offshore. Young people approaching this environment don't have the same memories as older workers, but they confront the same question: How do I prepare for jobs that may not yet have been invented?

So what do I, a fifty-something employer, have to say about preparing for that new job in communications? In one sense, it's simple—prepared employees are capable learners, people who can repeatedly extend their knowledge and learn about new topics, possibly even topics never heard of before. Prepared employees adapt what they know to new environments and accept the challenge of creating new ways to do things.

When I find such employees, I know that they will flourish on our staff when they enter the job as well as ten years down the road. Capable learners, although useful to employers, are also employees who have prepared themselves for careers that will be interesting and rewarding.

Preparing to be an employee capable of learning new things is part mindset and part hard work. But, essentially, it comes down to three simple yet complex tasks:

- Become an expert. Know what you know as well as anyone can know it. Be passionate, whether you're in a technical position such as designing communications equipment or in a nontechnical role such as marketing. Either way, know your job from top to bottom.
- Don't box yourself in. Know enough about other things that you can see how and where your expertise best applies. If you are going to participate in new endeavors, you must be able to see beyond your own knowledge, even if you already know what you know better than anyone else does.
- Hone your communication skills. Be able to communicate to others what you know and how it works. Almost all communication takes place in teams or with customers, so, if you want to move the team or the customer, you must be able to communicate. And don't forget to listen! Whether you're dealing with a team member, your boss, or a customer, truly listening will take you farther, faster.

This advice works for me as I continue to prepare for my career, just as what I'm doing now will be different tomorrow, and again next year. This advice will also serve young people who will still be in the workforce long after I've retired and gone off sailing my boat. But even on my boat, I'll still be learning new things. Today more than ever, no one can live without continual learning. I know that I can't.

RANDAL A. LEMKE, PH.D.
Executive Director,
International Communications
Industries Association, Inc.

PREFACE

It is with great pleasure and excitement that I present this revised and updated edition of *Careers in Communications*. The past two years have been challenging for professional communicators looking for work and for the companies seeking media talent. In such a short time, so much has changed in the ways we produce and deliver messages.

The career of a professional communicator is focused on crafting and deploying messages and conducting two-way communication with specific audiences for defined purposes. Mass media such as print, radio, television, cinema, and, in recent years, the Internet, are used to inform, entertain, teach, persuade, and engage audiences. As a consumer of these messages, you probably appreciate information you receive in a timely and responsive fashion—local weather and traffic reports, for example. Thousands of media programs are being created for training, education and edutainment, and distributed via radio, television, and the Internet, or on audiocassettes, videocassettes, CD-ROMs, DVDs, and digital networks of all kinds.

We are all aware of the media's power in influencing our purchasing, political, and cultural decisions through advertisements, advertorials, commercials, and infomercials. Many people who enjoy a good TV show or movie, music video DVD, 3-D video game, or even a virtual reality exhibit sometimes wonder how these programs are made and are curious about career opportunities in the media.

The creative crafts attract many people to this industry. Others are lured by the power of influencing large audiences and the celebrity status that goes along with it; and many revel in the excitement of working with dynamic new technologies.

New communication technologies are having a positive impact on productivity levels in business, education, and government organizations. As more companies and institutions use the various media to stay competitive, the demand for professional communicators with specific skills and disciplines increases.

The new media technologies have also led to many new job titles. In just a few years, job titles such as online editor, audio digitizer, and database marketer, and even new industry niches such as Internet radio, digital cable, and virtual reality have moved from the pages of science fiction novels to the job marketplace.

DYNAMIC INDUSTRIES

The media industries are constantly in motion, and communications professionals must keep abreast of developments. Significant changes in any one of the media industries have an impact on the others. Work styles and employment opportunities are also affected. The following topics and detailed information in this book will give you a head start on keeping current:

- The impact of the latest technological developments on each of the media arts—for example, electronic imaging in photography, digital nonlinear editing in video, and 3-D animation in film—and how they are changing the outlook for career opportunities in each field.
- The current challenges posed by major trends such as file sharing on the World Wide Web, the consolidation of media company ownership, the flight of production and other work overseas, and the blurring of traditional boundaries between content and advertising. Also covered are shifts and changes in the marketplace caused by new production and distribution technologies such as Internet radio, desktop video and audio editing, and HDTV.

- The opportunities created by the recent growth in industry segments such as cable TV, satellite radio, and game production.
- How women and minorities are faring in the communications industry, and some key resources to help further their career development.
- A selection of updated online resources in each field, carefully chosen to provide you with varied viewpoints and access to the best education, networking, and employment opportunities.

Careers in Communications covers the technologies and industries involved in content creation for media such as print, broadcast, audio, multimedia, and the Internet. It addresses the skills that a professional communicator may need for the writing, design, production, presentation, or distribution of content in a wide range of media. You will find a comprehensive picture of the major communications disciplines and the opportunities for meaningful employment that each provides. It includes chapters on journalism, photography, film, radio/audio, television/video, multimedia, advertising, and public relations. Although your initial interest in using this book may be one particular topic, it will serve you well to browse through the chapters on other media. Because most jobs in the communication industries are interrelated, having a comprehensive view of the other disciplines will enhance your opportunities, no matter what path you choose. You will also find a wide range of resources—websites, associations, schools, publications, and recommended readings—that will help you get to the heart of the matter.

I hope that this book will provide valuable assistance to those who are just starting out on a career in this exciting field, and that it will give working professional communicators an expanded view of their career opportunities.

PREPARING FOR A CHALLENGING CAREER

Although "eyewitness" amateur video occasionally does make it onto national TV news, and low-budget films like *The Blair Witch Project* sometimes hit it big at the box office, careers in the field of communications call for professional skills and long-term commitment. Professional writing and the design, production, and presentation of multimedia content are a science and an art that must be learned and fine-tuned through real-world experience. For example:

- Good news reporting requires research, interviewing and writing skills, as well as journalistic integrity.
- Top-notch photography demands knowledge of the fine art of visual composition, the science of light, the timing of human emotion, and the use of image manipulation software such as Adobe Photoshop.
- Film and video production call for visualization and storytelling expertise, as well as project management and people skills.
- Radio requires training in speech, theater or drama, and audio technologies.
- Video game creation calls for an understanding of everything from animation techniques to the principles of character development.
- Multimedia program design requires an understanding of human-machine interaction as well as the techniques of information mapping and the art of storytelling.
- Successful advertising campaigns require good market research, superior creative skills, strategic campaign planning, and a knowledge of the synergistic capabilities of every medium.
- Public relations today calls for creative thinking, industry knowledge, determined optimism, and superior writing skills.

And, most of all, anyone who hopes to succeed in these exciting, creative, and very competitive fields must have a lot of talent, tenacity, and dedication.

GETTING THERE IS HALF THE FUN

Mass media communication studies at most colleges are organized into the following tracks: journalism, film, broadcasting (includes radio and television), and advertising and public relations (PR). Many schools also offer multimedia, computer graphics, and Internet studies as specialization areas. Several undergraduate schools require students to opt for a specialization in one of these disciplines after taking introductory courses in mass media theory and principles. I have known many students who have found it difficult to select a specialization area or have had to drop out of the one they first selected because they lacked an understanding of the demands of working in that area. I hope that *Careers in Communications* will help aspiring professional communicators identify where their strongest interests lie and where their talents can best be applied for enjoyable, gainful employment.

It's never too early or too late to opt for a career in communications. Young people who want to get a taste of the real world of journalism or other content production disciplines have a wealth of opportunities. Children's Press Line, for example, teaches and empowers young communicators by enabling them to take part in the work of real journalistic interviewing teams.

For more information, visit www.cplmedia.org. Likewise, adults who have substantial life experience can find numerous opportunities to acquire media-specific skills or to experience firsthand the excitement of being part of a team of professional communicators. Community colleges and university extension programs offer inexpensive hands-on learning in every discipline from computer animation to TV production. You can find hundreds of community media centers that provide free or low-cost training and access to a variety of communications media, including the Internet and public access cable television, through the Alliance for Community Media. For more information, visit www.alliancecm.org.

CATCH THE WAVE

Throughout this edition, I have referred you to useful websites. I encourage you to use the Internet for everything from researching your story ideas to keeping abreast of the issues and concerns facing your chosen discipline and the entire communications industry. Professional communicators must continually improve their online research skills. And you can have fun doing it, especially when you are trying to learn more about the new media. You may stumble upon a fantastic animation, an audio file of some strange new music, an incredible video clip, or just an inspiring new idea or interesting piece of information.

The majority of us who work in the media are doing what we love and enjoying almost every minute of it. So if you haven't yet decided what you're going to be "when you grow up," check out careers in the communication arts. You may get hooked while viewing the DVD "extras" on the making of your favorite movie, playing a video game, reading about a great filmmaker, watching a 3-D artist at work, or even taking a camcorder to your next neighborhood event. If you're really lucky, you too may catch the wave of an adventurous, creative, extremely rewarding life.

ACKNOWLEDGMENTS

The success of every mass media communication program depends, to a large extent, on good team work. Throughout my career and to date, I have been fortunate in working with professionals who are excellent team players. I owe them a very special "Thank You." My deep and sincere gratitude to all those mentioned here and to many others who have enriched my professional life. Many thanks to:

- John Rhodes, a communications consultant who specializes in the deployment of new media, for his insights on the applications of emerging technologies—also for being a career-supportive husband and serving as technical consultant and my collaborator on so many interactive media productions;
- Paul Schneiderman, owner of two MotoPhoto stores, and Associated Press photojournalist Bebeto Matthews, for their update on working in the photographic industry;
- Norry Niven, Emmy award-winning director and a partner of Stone Core Films, for his insights on directing commercials; and James Tusty, president of Mountain View Group, for his thoughts on what it takes to work on corporate productions;
- David Campbell, a principal of 4-D Media Group, for his input on the multimedia business, and also for the learning, sharing, and

synergy we enjoyed while producing our first consumer CD-ROM;

- Independent publicists Sofia Alayon, Scott Heath, Carrie Lombardi, and Debra Mercado for their insights on careers in public relations;
- Dr. Alan Richardson, professor in the Department of Telecommunications at Ball State University, Indiana; and Dr. David Ostroff, professor of Journalism, University of Florida at Gainesville, for their useful advice on internships;
- Staff members at several organizations who assisted me in compiling the reference material that is an essential part of *Careers in Communications*. I am grateful, in particular, to the research and library staff of the National Association of Broadcasters, International Communications Industries Association, and Public Relations Society of America;
- My patient and perceptive editor, Monica Stoll, and production manager, Rena Copperman.

For munchies and crunchies, chocolates and flowers; for large doses of humor, and for much-needed TLC, all credit goes to my network of family and friends, with a very special "Thank You" to:

- My mother, Mary Felicitas, for being a constant source of inspiration; my sister Sirikit, a movie buff with whom I've "thumbs-upped" several lesser-known great films; my nieces, Kara and Bianca, for rekindling my joy in storytelling; and the "Noronha Cast" of Jean, Antonio, and Avertano, for cheering from the sidelines;
- My sister Simkie and her family, Anand, Joy, and Natasha Sarkar; and my cousins in the D'Souza, Alvares, Pinto, Lobo, Mascarenhas, Menzies, Pereira, and Paes families for their joy and pride in my work;
- Meena Advani, Shailendra Kashyap, Julie Lemos, Mariola Mendonca, Hemi Jashnani, and Isabel Cuso and their families for their continued interest in my work although they are thousands of miles away;
- Jerry and Candice Landress, Michela Halpern, Roy and Julianne Singh, Janet and Richard Cross, Chatur Advani, Rupa Iyengar, and Karen Dautresme, for support and encouragement when it was needed most.

Finally, for those who inspire, challenge, and provide the best reason to write this book, many thanks to:

- All my students, for their countless questions and boundless enthusiasm for all these cool media;
- The kids—John, Matthew, Faith, Lindsey, Maya, Heather, Natalie, Kanaga, Nouara, Karim, Chelsea, Nikita, Carina, Eli, Zachary, Nicole, Frankie, Raymond, and all the others with whom I enjoy creative thinking and interactive media projects using the new digital tools.

THE EVOLVING GLOBAL MARKETPLACE

Today's sophisticated mass communications systems enable us to deliver information faster, to more locations, and with greater impact than ever before. The convergence of computer, telephone, television, audio, and data networking technologies is leading the digital revolution in mass media technologies. We take for granted media events that were impossible just a few years ago, such as simultaneous "live" television and Internet coverage of news events, as they are happening, almost anywhere in the world.

People everywhere are demanding more information of every kind, and media outlets are serving it up on a daily basis. From weather and traffic news via satellite television and radio to entertainment and education programs on DVD and the Internet, mass media production and distribution are increasing, and media companies are flourishing. This growth has created an unprecedented demand for people with the skills and abilities to communicate effectively using words, pictures, and sounds. At the same time, audiences are becoming more critical and demanding, and media organizations that fail to meet these demands are succumbing to the intense competitive pressures of the evolving global marketplace.

MARKET DEMANDS

In business and government, people seek up-to-the-minute market data and other information that help them to make decisions. Employees need training to acquire critical skills, and executives need help in analyzing the flood of information that confronts them every day. Managers review online demonstrations and view live multimedia presentations before making important decisions. At all levels, organizations must keep members and employees informed and motivated through every available channel of communication. Customers, stockholders, and other constituencies also demand accessible, up-to-date information.

Entertainment is the fastest-growing market segment in the booming communications marketplace. Sales of movies and special-interest DVDs, computer and video games, and books and magazines are at an all-time high. Even the music industry, beleaguered though it is by file sharing and piracy, continues to grow in new and unexpected directions. The rapidly expanding international market seems to have an insatiable capacity for American culture of all kinds—films, games, music, and TV programming.

This tremendous need for a continuous flow of information and entertainment products is creating many new career opportunities for communications professionals who are trained in both traditional and new media technologies.

WHAT PROFESSIONAL COMMUNICATORS DO

A career as a professional communicator involves the crafting, production, and distribution of messages to specific audiences for defined purposes through a variety of mass media channels. These channels may include print, television, radio, multimedia, the Internet, and others yet to be named.

Print It

Newspapers, magazines, books, and other print publications convey information to large audiences, both in hard-copy form and on the Internet. The production of print materials requires journalists, writers, editors, photographers, graphic designers, and people skilled in the printing process, which includes prepress imaging, press checks, and binding. Print media companies also employ advertising, publicity, sales, and marketing professionals who know how to increase subscriptions and the publication's circulation as well as increasing book sales. Most print-based media companies now publish their content on the Internet, which requires the services of Webmasters and other multimedia specialists.

The Big Show

Traditional electronic media such as film, radio, and television also employ journalists, writers, researchers, and editors. In addition, they hire a host of creative and skilled people such as videographers, video editors, 3-D designers, music producers, animation artists, and lighting directors. They also employ people in technical areas such as tape duplication, disc replication, and audio, video, and information technology (IT) engineering. Electronic media have embraced the Internet to an even greater extent than print media organizations and have greatly expanded the demand for Web-based communication skills.

Aspiring professional communicators need to specialize in one of the disciplines. No matter what the field—journalism, film, broadcasting, advertising, or even game creation—each uses special techniques and technologies for the creation and distribution of messages. Those who seek to attain positions of greater responsibility must develop management skills as well as an understanding of the emerging synergies among diverse media and methods.

The Functions of Communications

Words, sounds, and images are currently the means by which communicators convey messages to their audiences. Each message is intended to serve one or more of the four basic mass media communications functions: to inform, to educate, to persuade, or to entertain. Communicators must be adept at the techniques of writing for each specific medium and knowledgeable about the production of other media elements, such as graphics, animation, sound, or video, that make up the message.

Professional communicators work in all sizes and types of media organizations including publishing firms, radio and TV broadcasting companies, advertising and PR agencies, and even large theme park and entertainment conglomerates. Media organizations outsource specialized work to independent production companies. Some of these production companies specialize in graphic design for the print media or shoot and edit commercials for television, while others produce software for the game market or create interactive websites for a variety of clients. These production companies hire communications graduates, including writers, photographers, videographers, animators, producers, and programmers. In addition to media and production companies, career opportunities for professional communicators exist in all types of organizations—business and industry, government agencies, education, and nonprofit institutions.

DEVELOPMENTS IN TECHNOLOGY

Advances in computer, audio, video, and networking technologies are changing the ways in which we meet today's mass media communications needs. Developments in Internet-based technologies and the recent growth of Internet usage have provided professional communicators today with perhaps their most powerful tool—one that can combine all the other media elements into a single channel of almost unlimited potential.

One unexpected result of the growth of the Internet has been a blurring of the boundaries between advertising and editorial content. Thousands of websites deliver opinion and fact along with E-commerce links, often with little regard for the reader/viewer's need to understand the relationship between them. Even the websites of reputable journalistic organizations frequently offer direct purchasing links for products or services that they review or cover. This blurring of intent and accountability can make it difficult for consumers to differentiate between messages that are influenced by commercial interests (e.g., advertorials or infomercials) and "real" editorial content.

For this reason, aspiring communicators need a basic understanding of the essential differences of messages presented as editorial content, opinion, and advertising, as well as relevant regulations, legal compliance issues, and ethical considerations.

Just in Time

Electronic publishing systems are reducing the time and costs of publishing a wide range of material. The more elaborate and expensive systems are being used for higher-quality image reproduction and text-intensive, high-volume production of newspapers, magazines, catalogs, and websites. Affordable personal computer-based systems allow users to combine text and graphics into print and Web pages. Corporations and institutions are also using these inexpensive systems to produce reports, newsletters, and other information that can be distributed on internal networks (intranets) and on the Internet.

Digital imaging and computer graphics are two of the fastest-growing segments of the visual communications industry. Today's computer imaging software and hardware tools allow us to capture, create, manipulate, store, and retrieve images with artistic flair, flexibility, and speed. From digital cameras to intelligent software applications that can produce any image that can be imagined, these new tools have greatly enhanced the presentation of business information and democratized the power of visual communications.

Computer animation systems enable producers to add astounding digital effects as well as increased impact to their messages. Readily available systems enable the creation of new visual worlds and the transformation of existing objects into strange new forms. With high-end systems, one can explore three-dimensional space and even create virtual reality environments. Billions of dollars are being spent on computerized images today—some for business, but most in commercials, film, and other entertainment media.

Digital video has developed rapidly and has placed new and improved tools, from affordable 3-chip digital cameras to microcomputer-based editing systems, in the hands of the producer. The miniaturization of video cameras and recorders has taken video and television into remote corners of the world. Low-cost digital recording and editing systems have brought broadcast-quality production within the reach of even small organizations.

Advanced TV systems such as high-definition television (HDTV) are evolving at a rapid rate and hold out the promise that the near future will see widespread, high-quality, affordable networked video production, editing, and distribution capabilities.

Satellite, cable, and Internet technologies have made it possible to target messages to specific viewers through the mass media. The revitalization and growth of cable and satellite television has led to specialized programming such as all-news, all-sports, and even all-food channels. Direct broadcast satellite (DBS) networks are also making a significant contribution to the free flow of information across national boundaries.

Developments in digital telecommunications have led to the greater use of teleconferencing technologies such as audio, audiographics, Webconferencing, videoconferencing, and interactive computing for greater business productivity.

No longer is creativity in film and TV production constrained by the limitations of the equipment. Today, it is limited only by the imagination of the artist or communicator.

To a person considering a career as a professional communicator, this means that the tools of the trade to create virtually any message and reach any audience already exist. One needs to learn how to use them and to develop an understanding of the scope and limitations of each. Too often, students of communications, in attempting to master the technology, overlook the more important challenge of understanding the process. It is our task as professional communicators to keep abreast of the full range of technologies available and of the capabilities of each to improve the quality of our messages and the communication process we engage in with our audiences.

As new applications of media technologies emerge, so also will new jobs and career opportunities. People who are imaginative, flexible, and energetic will be able seek out and find many exciting new opportunities in communications.

THE CHALLENGES OF NEW TECHNOLOGY

Although the new technologies are providing professional communicators with powerful tools, they are also putting greater demands on them and changing the very nature of many media jobs. Sophisticated systems enable communicators to work with speed and ease, but also create different standards of performance. The concepts of "deadline" and "quality" take on new meanings.

The race for fast-breaking news stories has put enormous pressure on wire services and newspapers. Computerized typesetting and quick-printing presses have pushed newspaper deadlines close to the early hours of the day for morning papers. That, in turn, has made the work of reporters and editors more demanding, in terms of both the number of hours they spend on the job and the pressure to get up-to-the-minute information. Internet delivery of breaking stories is also increasing the pressure on everyone involved in the daily news reporting business.

Desktop publishing systems are adding to the tasks of reporters, who are now expected to do a lot more editing and layout work on their stories. The move toward electronic publishing by many publishing companies is also leading to the elimination of some jobs in typesetting and printing. Some newspapers and magazines have computerized page layout and pagination capability that enable editors to prepare the publication for the printer, thereby eliminating layout positions.

Modern technology is demanding more skills from today's communicators. In the past, typing was the only technology-related skill required of print journalists.

Today, however, skills in a word processing program as well as the ability to edit and copy fit in a page-layout program are necessary. In addition, journalists, writers, and other content providers must have good Internet-based research skills. Aspiring professional communicators will do well to gain skills in basic computer graphics programs as well as familiarity with other production and distribution technologies such as the World Wide Web and CD-ROM.

New applications of microwave and satellite technologies to electronic news gathering (ENG) have revolutionized the broadcast newsroom. Many television ENG crews take portable cameras and microwave transmitters right into scenes of action, where the broadcast journalist proceeds to conduct live interviews.

A nearby mobile van equipped with a microwave transmitter and antenna receives the signal and transmits it back to the TV station. The miniaturization of satellite transmission technology has made it possible for reporters "embedded" with the troops to cover developments during a war even as they happen.

Along with this technology comes the pressure to disseminate news without any delay. Radio and TV newscasters and reporters must be quicker thinkers, writers, and speakers today than ever before.

FANTASY VERSUS REALITY

One of the biggest illusions about the field of mass media communications is that it is glamorous. Films about the power of television and the apparent glamour and excitement of the business may be responsible for these illusions. The tremendous attention and celebrity that TV reporters enjoy make broadcast journalism one of the more popular career choices of young people even before they finish high school. Another misconception is that a career in mass media communications does not require intellectual abilities as outstanding as those required for medicine, law, or engineering. This may be due to the fact that admission to communications programs is usually not very competitive—and that media people are rarely portrayed in films and TV dramas as intellectual giants. This simplistic view of the demands of the communications professions sometimes attracts indecisive minds to the field. They are often lured by the Hollywood glamour, the excitement portrayed in films like *All the President's Men*, the charisma and apparent influence of network TV anchors such as ABC's Peter Jennings, or the exciting on-air personality of a favorite talk-show host.

Although the mass media communications industries do offer the excitement of a broadcast studio, a movie set, or glamorous foreign locations, only a few end up enjoying a public or glamorous career. The media professions are very competitive, challenging, and demanding. In some areas, such as film and television, it is quite difficult to break in. Any career in this industry calls for a well-rounded education and a strong sense of commitment. Working as a professional communicator can bring you job satisfaction and financial rewards. You must, however, invest some time in proper career planning and training. The chapters that follow will provide you with a picture of each field of practice and will help you identify the type of work that will best suit your unique talents and ambitions. Beyond that, this book is intended to serve as a practical guide to those seeking a position in the business.

CHAPTER 2

JOURNALISM

The world of journalism is much wider than that of a few national newspapers and scores of tabloids. American journalism has come a long way since colonial days when newspapers served as organs of commercial and political information. Today, the term *journalism* is applied to throw-away shoppers found at supermarket doors, to prestigious publications such as *The New York Times*, and to TV news operations such as *60 Minutes* and the *NBC Nightly News*.

First Amendment rights and the democratic political environment of the United States have contributed to the uninhibited growth of the news media in public and private communication. The United States can pride itself on supporting the largest mass media system of any country in the world. The media in turn have generated millions of jobs and become major industrial forces that support the nation's economy.

The "fourth estate" today includes not only newspapers but also wire services and syndicates, radio and television, and trade and business publications, yet the role of journalism remains the same: to report and interpret information to the general public or to some specific subgroup. However, the nature of the industry has changed considerably due to socioeconomic changes and technological innovations.

The invention of new technologies has changed the nature of the journalism industry, making it an increasingly sophisticated and complex operation that requires a wide range of skills. Journalism has come a long way since the days of commercial printers who single-handedly published newspapers, and of one-person radio stations operated from private homes. Today, even many small-town newspapers and radio stations employ advanced production technology and the services of professionally trained journalists and skilled production people.

The demands of contemporary society have expanded the role of journalism. Newspapers and broadcast stations provide a great variety of services today.

Besides reporting and interpreting news, they also entertain their audience with a variety of feature material. Newspapers, magazines, and broadcast stations are constantly competing with each other to capture the audience because this is crucial to their advertising revenues and sales.

The socioeconomic structure of the United States today has added new functions for journalists. Organizational demands have created thousands of company and institutional publications that offer far more than the mimeographed newsletters of yesteryear. Publications targeted at internal and external communication have become an integral part of most organizations today.

The evolution of journalism into a massive industry has resulted in a number of related jobs in production, circulation, advertising, publicity, promotion, and management. Newspapers and broadcast stations employ specialists in all these areas. The number of allied jobs in news organizations has increased substantially in recent years, but many job seekers are unaware of these career opportunities.

Still, aspiring journalists dream of being like Bob Woodward, Carl Bernstein, Walter Cronkite, or Barbara Walters. However, the harsh realities of a highly competitive market and the stresses and strains of an extremely demanding profession stand between them and greatness. Although full-time staff positions are decreasing in American journalism due to the decline of major daily newspapers, advancing technology and the ever-changing needs of society are opening up new avenues every day. Those who are innovative, creative, and aggressive can still find a place in the exciting world of journalism.

Journalists today face two major challenges, one old and one very new. Issues of professional ethics and integrity have challenged journalists for hundreds of years, but the recent revolution in the way that news is gathered and distributed has created a crisis of conscience for many in the field.

Journalistic Ethics

The instantaneous nature of modern mass media increases the competitive pressure to be first with a big story. This pressure, combined with the public's insatiable appetite for full disclosure regarding important issues, has created an ethical minefield for modern journalists. Examples of some of these dilemmas are: Should newspapers publish confidential defense documents a month before a criminal trial, possibly jeopardizing the defendant's right to a fair trial? Can a reporter participate in a demonstration without compromising objectivity? What are the proper ways to report and identify leaks and "rumored" information? What should a newspaper do with confidential files that contain the names of HIV-positive people? Journalists in forums such as the Ethics Committee of the Associated Press Managing Editors are actively discussing these and dozens of other ethical issues.

Editorial Integrity

Ensuring that editorial content is always clearly distinguished from advertisements and special advertising sections such as advertorials, in print publications as well as electronic editorial products, is a constant challenge to journalists in many areas. The American Society of Newspaper Editors has a "Codes of Ethics" page on its website (www.asne.org) with links to the codes of ethics pages of newspapers, news organizations, and associations. Read the ethics code of your favorite news source to get an idea of what is covered. The guidelines, as you are probably aware, have not been universally adopted and do not cover every new twist of the electronic "pen." Several factors, such as the blurring of the lines between editorial and "paid for" content on the Web, contribute to the many gray areas in the new journalistic virtual landscape.

TECHNICAL SKILLS

Journalists of the future will be expected to possess online research and other computer skills that once were the province of librarians and graphic designers. Anyone working in the editorial field today must possess desktop publishing skills. At a minimum level, the ability to proofread, copy edit, and copy fit in a page layout program such as QuarkXpress is becoming a requirement. Online search tools such as Google and Yahoo are becoming essential to the daily work of journalists, as is the ability to evaluate and filter the flood of information available through these and other channels. To get acquainted with the various databases, go to www.spireproject.com. Strong research skills and proficiency in the use of databases like Lexis-Nexis can make the difference in getting your first job.

The Technology Advantage

The publishing industry is leveraging today's technological developments for increased productivity in production as well as audience reach. On-demand publishing is reducing warehousing costs while meeting the needs of customization.

As a research tool, the Internet provides aspiring journalists with instant access to more data today than was available to the staff of a major news organization just a few years ago. Thousands of newspapers, magazines, and institutions are accessible through the Web, and millions of opinions and firsthand reports are posted on newsgroups and personal pages from individuals all over the world.

On the other side of the screen, anyone with an opinion or factoid to offer has the opportunity to reach an audience of millions through the very same newsgroups and websites. New, powerful, and inexpensive electronic publishing tools from such companies as Adobe and Microsoft make it easy for journalistic entrepreneurs to get into publishing.

As paper, press, and distribution resources become less of a factor in building an audience for a publication, publishers are becoming even more aware of the value of reputation, independence, and credibility. At the same time, these core journalistic values are increasingly besieged by the competitive pressures of the wired media marketplace.

Journalism is a demanding profession, and the more you learn about it, the better prepared you will be to manage your career as a journalist. The organizations listed below address some of the challenges discussed earlier in this chapter and also offer guidelines and other supportive information to enrich the professional work of journalists. Explore their websites to get a comprehensive picture of the field. Read what working journalists say about the challenges they face in their day-to-day work.

Several websites, including those of universities with journalism programs, offer excellent information about how to forge a successful career in journalism, creative writing, and the publishing field at large. A number of these organizations offer distance learning programs with online courses of study. The following websites contain useful information with links to other selected sites that also list sources for scholarships, internships, and awards of excellence:

- American Journalism Review (www.ajr.org). This website presents a wealth of information and resources, including writing aids and other websites that offer a range of reportorial aids from guidelines for searching the Internet to tips on using public opinion polls.
- Center for Communication (www.cencom.org). The center is committed to bridging the gap between the communications industry and the schools that offer courses in the media arts. Each year, it offers more than 50 seminars that cover all fields of communications and all aspects of working in this industry. The website enables students to tap into the seminars via audio-streaming and transcripts, as well as offers valuable career tips and strategies.
- I Want Media (www.iwantmedia.com). This website, which focuses on media organizations for media professionals, links to major newspapers and other media-related businesses. It also serves up links to media jobs.
- NewsLink (www.newslink.org). Here is a great gateway to international news services and publications. Its JobLink enables journalists who are job seekers to post standard ads at no charge if submitted online.

- Poynter Institute (www.poynter.org). The institute's online mission is to provide "everything you need to be a better journalist," and it does a great job. Tip sheets are a series of articles on extremely useful topics. Use the website's search engine to locate links to the articles.
- Project for Excellence in Journalism and the Committee of Concerned Journalists (www.journalism.org). This project is an initiative by journalists who seek to clarify and raise the standards of American journalism. Its journalism tools are organized by the various media, including print, TV/radio, and online.
- Writers Store (www.writersstore.com). This website is designed not for journalists but for writers. It provides information for writers in all genres and formats. Journalists who also aspire to be creative writers will find useful articles and resources.

WHERE THE JOBS ARE

For many graduates of journalism schools or departments, a job in journalism means reporting or even investigative reporting. Unfortunately, reporters make up less than one-fourth of the staff at most newspapers. The market is very competitive, and entry-level jobs at newspapers are hard to get. Enterprising candidates look beyond newspapers for a career in journalism. Wire services, syndicates, magazines, and radio and TV stations offer reporting, writing, editing, and other related jobs.

Newspapers

In the United States, thousands of daily and weekly newspapers employ hundreds of thousands of professionals.

Large and medium-sized newspapers have the following departments: news, editorial, advertising, production, circulation, and business. At smaller papers, these functions are often combined, and the same person may handle several of these responsibilities.

Jobs in the news department include those of reporter, rewriter, feature writer, columnist, critic, and photographer. Entry-level jobs of researcher and messenger are also available at large dailies. The editorial department consists of city editors and section editors who are responsible for the selection and assignment of stories, editorial writers who write articles that state the paper's position on issues and events, and copyeditors who process the copy for publication.

Newspaper advertising departments employ people in the classified and display advertisement departments. Both use copywriters, salespersons, advertising managers, and national sales representatives.

Production department personnel select materials and suppliers for the printing of the newspaper and may also supervise in-house printing. Jobs here range from production assistant (or traffic assistant) to production manager or production director.

Circulation departments, which are responsible for the distribution of the paper, employ circulation assistants, collection managers, and circulation managers at different ranks.

Wire Services and Syndicates

Wire services, popularly known as the "wholesalers" of news, have traditionally been full of opportunity for people seeking entry into the world of journalism. Many people start out as part-time correspondents or "stringers" for Associated Press (www.ap.org) or United Press International (www.upi.com), the nation's leading wire services. Such stringers often go on to serve as full-time correspondents and bureau chiefs, both at home and abroad. Although most wire service foreign bureaus are headed by Americans, many reporters, copy readers, rewriters, correspondents, researchers, photographers, and photo editors are local hires from the respective countries. Some examples of the content offered by syndicates can be found at these websites:

Classified Guys (www.classifiedguys.com)
Knight Ridder/Tribune Information Services (www.krtdirect.com)
Reuters (www.reuters.com)
United Feature Syndicate (www.unitedfeatures.com)
Universal Press Syndicate (www.amuniversal.com/ups)

Syndicates, which supply features, columns, cartoon panels, and comic strips to newspapers and magazines, require the talent of experienced journalists. About a dozen major syndicates and more than a hundred smaller ones supply packaged entertainment and educational material.

Magazines

The magazine industry provides interesting and rather lucrative jobs for thousands of people looking for an alternative to the daily pressure and rigor of newspaper journalism. Magazines provide more room for creativity for writers, editors, and artists.

Magazines employ editors of different grade levels. The entry-level position is editorial assistant or researcher. Assistant editor, associate editor, senior editor, and executive or managing editor follow. These employees are responsible for selecting and processing the magazine's content. They review manuscripts and assign stories based on ideas they have developed. On small magazines, they also serve as rewriters and copyeditors. Staff writers, art directors, and photographers are also key links in the editorial chain.

Magazine advertising departments offer the positions of sales assistant, sales representative, sales manager, and advertising manager. This department makes or breaks the magazine, whose major source of income is advertising; frequently, the profit from sales of copies is marginal. A successful magazine is expected to break even through advertising sales alone.

Magazine circulation departments attract enterprising people who are willing to start as circulation assistants and hope to go on to become managers of collection, assistant directors of circulation, and eventually circulation managers.

Magazine production involves the services of art directors, photoengravers, typesetters, press operators, and supervisory personnel such as production managers and layout coordinators.

The business or administrative structure of major magazines calls for other positions such as promotion director, business manager, director of administration, general manager, and publisher. Some magazines have a separate operations department.

Broadcast Journalism

Radio and television have become the main source of news for the majority of the population. Although entertainment continues to be the broadcast media's main function, they have been increasing their news output, especially through the introduction of the all-news format, which requires the services of journalists.

The growth of broadcast journalism in the United States has created a steady increase of jobs for journalists. The electronic media hire reporters, announcers, newscasters, newswriters, news directors, and producers of news programs and features.

Business Communications

Corporations, businesses, and institutions employ writers and journalists to work on newsletters or publications for internal and external audiences, press releases issued by PR departments, and maintenance and operations manuals. Writers and journalists also work with scientists, engineers, and executives in preparing scientific and trade journal articles.

SALARY INFORMATION

A number of magazines and associations conduct salary surveys and publish reports on trends in employment and working conditions. Although it is important to skim through salary data to gain an overall sense of fair compensation, it is equally important not to get hung up on the numbers. Below are selected numbers from several surveys to give you a snapshot and lead you to the sources.

The U.S. Department of Labor's Bureau of Labor Statistics provides a wealth of information about salaries and employment in journalism and other fields in its *Occupational Outlook Handbook, 2004–05 Edition.* According to the bureau, in 2002 the median annual earnings figure for salaried writers and authors was $42,790. The middle 50 percent earned between $29,150 and $58,930, and the highest 10 percent earned more than $85,140.

Salaries for news analysts, reporters, and correspondents vary widely. Median annual earnings of news analysts, reporters, and correspondents were $30,510 in 2002. The middle 50 percent earned between $22,350 and $47,170. The lowest 10 percent earned less than $17,620, and the highest 10 percent earned more than $69,450. Median annual earnings of news analysts, reporters, and correspondents were $33,320 in radio and TV broadcasting

TABLE 2.1 Television Station Average Salaries

Job	Salary
News Director	$73,800
Assistant News Director	62,300
Managing Editor	56,900
Assignment Editor	32,800
News Reporter	32,300
Newswriter	32,300

For more information on this salary survey, go to www.rtnda.org/research.
Also, refer to Chapter 6, "Television and Video."

and $29,090 for those working for newspaper, periodical, book, and directory publishers in 2002.

Median annual earnings for salaried editors were $41,170 in 2002. The middle 50 percent earned between $30,770 and $56,360. The lowest 10 percent earned less than $24,010, and the highest 10 percent earned more than $76,620. Median annual earnings at newspaper, periodical, book, and directory publishers were $40,280.

According to the Society for Technical Communication the salaries of technical writers and editors in the United States rose from $59,700 in 2002 to $61,730 in 2003—a gain of 3.4 percent. Salaries for Canadian technical writers and editors grew from $56,870 in 2002 to $58,190 in 2003 for a gain of 2.3 percent. The average salary for entry-level technical writers/editors in the U.S. was $43,260. For these professionals in Canada, it was $41,030. The mean annual salary for mid-level nonsupervisory technical writers was $54,510 and for senior-level nonsupervisory technical writers, $66,590.

According to the 2002 Radio-Television Salary Survey report issued by the Radio-Television News Directors Association, broadcast news salaries stayed flat in the tough economic downturn of 2001. At television stations, the average salaries were as shown in Table 2.1.

JOB DESCRIPTIONS: NEWSPAPERS

News Department

The news or reporting department consists of reporters, writers, and photographers. The entry-level job involves research, filing, rewriting press releases, and writing simple stories and announcements such as community events and obituaries. At some small-circulation papers, news assistants are also given the responsibility of reporting on meetings and community events. Beat reporters cover specific settings of community importance, such as police headquarters, city hall, and the school system. General assignment reporters and more experienced staff reporters cover major local events and events of national importance. Proven reporters receive investigative reporting assignments and coverage of special areas such as sports. Critics and columnists complete the news team.

Rewriters are writers who rewrite stories phoned in by staff reporters or filed by wire services. Rewrites are often done by copyeditors or reporters who are in the newsroom rather than out in the field. They are distinct from staff writers, who are in fact reporters at small-circulation newspapers.

Photographers are on the same salary scale as reporters and are considered an important part of the news-gathering team. Experienced photographers sometimes even direct the work of less-experienced reporters with whom they team up for assignments.

Editing Department

The editing department is headed by the managing editor, who supervises the city editor, the news editor, and the section editors, who handle sections such as sports, business, and lifestyle. Reporters and photographers work directly under the city editor, whereas copyeditors work under the news editor. The editorial page editor and editorial writers are an independent unit that works parallel to the managing editor.

Copyeditors prepare copy for publication by correcting factual, linguistic, and legal errors; they also write headlines. It is often easier to obtain a job as copyeditor than as a reporter or writer. The copy desk is the best training ground for future reporters and writers.

Advertising Department

The advertising department consists of account executives, advertising managers, and the advertising director. Most advertising beginners start in the classified department and move on to the display department. They assist the senior sales personnel who handle accounts. Large-circulation newspapers usually have specialized advertising managers for client categories such as automobiles, real estate, and retail sales. More experienced executives handle national accounts.

Production Department

Production departments offer job opportunities for creative, mechanical, and administrative talent. The composition of newspapers is a specialized job, even in these days of computerized typesetting and page makeup. Photoengravers prepare photographs for printing. Printers work on the printing machinery in the pressroom. At most medium-sized daily newspapers, the pressroom and composing room are separate operations.

Circulation Department

Circulation departments market the newspaper to the public. People with business skills can find employment in this branch without much difficulty. Personnel in this department are responsible for customer relations and for increasing circulation. They also supervise the delivery staff. The entry-level position is district manager. Senior positions demand considerable market research and labor management experience.

Education

Entry-level positions in a news department often call for a college degree. More than 300 U.S. universities and colleges offer journalism education. (A list of the departments and schools accredited by the Association for Education in Journalism and Mass Communication is provided at the end of this chapter). Word-processing is a requirement for reporting and editorial positions at all newspapers. Superior linguistic and writing abilities and being able to work under pressure and tight deadlines are desirable qualities for reporters. Photographers are trained at schools of journalism or fine arts or at other institutes of photography.

Advertising, circulation, and business departments of newspapers seek college graduates for entry-level positions. A degree in journalism or business-related areas is desirable. Good interpersonal communication skills and telephone etiquette are essential. Familiarity with advertising and retail business will be a great advantage for job seekers in these areas.

The production department is usually staffed by people who have acquired their skills through apprenticeships in composing, printing, or photoengraving. Also, trade schools and institutes offer training in these crafts. A basic knowledge of journalism, such as can be acquired in high school, is a great asset for these technical positions.

Experience

The best way to obtain an entry-level job in newspapers is by participating in an internship during your college career. Many companies hire their most promising interns. Experience on your college newspaper is another major resource if you wish to enter the profession. As a college graduate, you could be hired as a news assistant by a major newspaper or as a reporter or staff writer at a small newspaper. After two or three years, you could be promoted as a reporter of a medium-sized newspaper. Three to six years in that capacity will make you eligible for a position as a reporter at a major newspaper or as a section editor or city editor at a medium-sized newspaper. You could even become the editor of a small paper at that stage. At least ten to fifteen years of journalism experience are required for an editorial position at a major metropolitan newspaper.

Copyeditors with three to five years of experience may be promoted to positions as reporters or staff writers. Department editors are promoted from the ranks of writers and reporters. Editorial page editors are carefully chosen from among experienced staff members who are loyal to the philosophies and goals of the newspaper management.

In advertising, a college degree is required for an entry-level position at a small newspaper. One or two years at a small paper will give you the experience you need to obtain a similar position at a medium or large-sized metropolitan daily. Five to six years of experience could bring you the position of advertising manager at a small or medium-sized newspaper, while seven to ten years will be required for a comparable position at a large metropolitan daily.

The top job in the hierarchy, advertising director, calls for at least ten years' experience at a small or medium-sized paper and well over fifteen years at a major metropolitan daily.

Most jobs in the production department require hands-on experience, usually gained through apprenticeships at a newspaper or through experience in related industries such as printing and publishing. Promotion to supervisory positions is based on technical skills and experience within the organization.

If you are interested in working in the circulation department of a newspaper, a college degree could earn you the entry-level position of district manager. Branch managers and circulation directors require up to ten and fifteen years of experience respectively.

JOB DESCRIPTIONS: WIRE SERVICES AND SYNDICATES

The basic entry-level job at wire services is that of stringer. These part-time positions are popular with students who want to gain experience before seeking a reporting or editing job at a newspaper or magazine. The full-time position at the entry level is editorial assistant. That job often consists of rewriting routine stories from local newspapers and gathering information and verifying facts over the phone.

Reporters, copyeditors, rewriters, and photographers for wire services and syndicates perform almost the same functions as their counterparts in newspaper organizations and enjoy the same status. After several years as editors or reporters, some are promoted to bureau chief at small or medium-sized bureaus. Foreign correspondents are the stars of the wire service world.

Education

The qualifications for wire service employment are almost the same as for newspapers. Entry-level positions require a college degree. The nature of the job involves assignments all over the United States and abroad. However, twenty-four-hour-a-day deadline pressures are much greater on wire service personnel than on newspaper staff members, who may have only one major deadline a day. Wire service staff members must be aggressive, fast, accurate, concise, and able to make quick decisions under pressing circumstances. High-quality writing and editing skills are expected, and the ability to write extremely quickly is a major asset because this work often requires more editing and rewriting than reporting.

Experience

Personnel turnover is very high at wire services because many journalists use them as training grounds for newspaper or magazine jobs. The wire services are known for their willingness to hire recent college graduates and inexperienced people. Often, new employees find themselves in charge of late and overnight shifts, which gives them a chance to perform almost all the journalistic functions possible.

Five to ten years of experience are required for promotion to a small or medium-sized bureau. Foreign correspondents and bureau chiefs are required to work in the New York or Washington, D.C., bureaus before an overseas assignment. Opportunities for advancement slow with years in the agency, which seems to be one reason for the high turnover.

JOB DESCRIPTIONS: MAGAZINES

Editing

The entry-level magazine job is editorial assistant or researcher. The tasks assigned to the beginner are not very exciting or creative, and include routine duties such as answering the telephone, typing manuscripts and correspondence, contacting writers on the phone, and filing. At smaller magazines, novices may receive assignments to do some rewriting, copyediting, proofreading, and even writing minor items.

The level of assistant editor involves more writing and editing. Assistant editors are able to write in areas of their specialty and interest. They also discuss story ideas with writers and work with them. At small or medium-sized magazines, this position may involve some work with art directors and printers.

Associate editors and senior editors do less writing and more editing and rewriting. They work closely with the writers of major stories. Senior editors are in charge of the editing of specific sections of the magazine.

The top position, which may be called executive editor, managing editor, or editor-in-chief, involves the overall administration of the magazine. At small magazines, these positions are combined with that of the senior editor.

Business and trade magazines that are published by organizations for internal and external publicity are edited by comparatively small staffs. In many cases, these may be one-person operations with some clerical help. The editing of an organization's magazine or newsletter is only one of the many tasks assigned to a director of media relations or to PR personnel. In recent years, many "house organs" have become quite sophisticated in content and appearance, and more resources and staff have been assigned to them. People with all-around editing, writing, and production skills will find this kind of operation exciting and rewarding.

Advertising

Magazines hire sales assistants, or sales trainees, in their advertising departments. This position is mainly clerical and involves tasks such as answering the telephones, typing letters, and filing. Research on clients and their products and helping senior personnel prepare for meetings and accompanying them to presentations are creative tasks that are often available at this level only at small magazines.

Many sales representatives work with advertising agencies that represent individual advertisers. Direct contact with advertisers takes place only for classified ads and some local ads. Group sales managers deal almost exclusively with ad agencies. The director of advertising is responsible for developing long-term advertising clients.

Production

Most magazines do not have in-house printing facilities, so the work of the magazine production department is less technical and more administrative. The beginner in the profession is appointed as a production assistant or a traffic assistant. Production assistants do typing, filing, and the dummy file. Traffic assistants manage the flow of layout and proofs, and keep track of production schedules; they also do some work with the printer and suppliers. Layout coordinators are responsible for supervising the layout and printing process, while production managers arrange contracts, prepare the schedules, and negotiate the budgets. The entire operation is supervised by the production director.

Circulation

Circulation assistants perform duties similar to those of editorial or advertising assistants. They also handle subscriber complaints. The manager of collections and renewals has the responsibility for maintaining and increasing the current subscriber base, especially through creative and persuasive direct-mail marketing. The assistant director of circulation is also entrusted with the task of increasing circulation, but also focuses on newsstand sales. The circulation director oversees both of these operations.

Education

Most facets of magazine work involve writing and creative abilities. Formal training in magazine journalism, as offered by a number of colleges and universities, will be a major asset for beginners. Many institutions offer short programs in magazine writing, production, and publishing through their schools of continuing education and summer workshops. The most basic skills are writing, interviewing, and editing.

Entry-level positions in the editorial department of a magazine require good linguistic skills and creative ideas. A typing speed of at least forty words per minute is a must, and computer skills have become a basic prerequisite. Basic knowledge of the printing and production procedures is desirable.

Assistant editors and associate editors must have proven writing and copyediting abilities. They should be able to generate story ideas and be familiar with current trends and developments. Good proofreading skills are an additional asset.

Because senior editors must deal with literary agents and writers, they should have excellent negotiating skills. A sound knowledge of copyright laws and other legal issues related to publishing is also important for a senior editor.

The editor-in-chief or managing editor should have strong administrative skills in addition to editorial and creative talent.

People who work on professional journals such as medical or business periodicals need considerable knowledge about the journal's subject. Technical writing also requires the ability to write for the average casual reader.

Personnel at company or house journals should have a thorough knowledge of the organization's goals and loyalty to its policies. Their main function is image- and morale-building rather than investigative and objective reporting of information.

A degree in advertising or business management could be very useful for entry-level advertising department employees. Some business experience, basic secretarial skills, and good phone manners are basic requirements. The circulation and promotion departments call for identical skills, and magazines seem to prefer graduates in business administration or marketing for these operations. Basic computing skills are also useful.

The production department looks for people with good business skills and creative training. Many institutes offer programs in photography, layout and design, and magazine publishing and production. Also, apprenticeships in these trades are valuable training grounds for these jobs. Basic copyediting skills and excellent proofreading skills as well as some business experience are additional assets.

Experience

For entry-level positions in the editorial department, a magazine internship experience is the best qualification. Experience on college magazines and newsletters is also helpful. Two or three years as editorial assistant may lead to a promotion as assistant editor at a medium-sized magazine. At a large magazine, the wait will be longer.

Many small magazines, as well as trade and industry journals, employ recent college graduates as assistant editors and promote those who prove themselves to the position of associate editor in a year or two. Almost ten years of experience is required for promotion to senior editor at most medium-sized magazines. Higher editorial positions require a successful track record and several more years of experience.

A college degree and basic clerical skills will earn you an entry-level position in an advertising department. The move to sales representative may require three years' experience, and it will take another three years or so to attain the job of group sales manager. Advertising managers come from the ranks of people who have invested at least ten years in the business.

Recent college graduates who are hired as circulation assistants will have to prove themselves for three to five years before becoming collection or renewal managers. After that, another couple of years of experience can lead to the position of assistant director of circulation. The top job, that of the circulation manager or director, requires about ten years of experience in the field.

In the production department, the move from production or traffic assistant may be rather fast for a recent college graduate; in a year or two, you could become a layout coordinator. The next move, to the position of production manager, could be a good ten years away at a medium-sized or large magazine. The end-of-the-line job of production director involves a shorter wait for a good production manager.

An experienced and successful advertising director or editor can eventually be named publisher of the magazine. This move, like the promotions in most departments of magazines, depends mostly on the size of the publication.

JOB DESCRIPTIONS: BROADCAST JOURNALISM

Broadcast journalism is one of the most competitive career areas in mass media communication. Most jobs go to insiders, and the road to the top is long and narrow. The competition for on-air jobs is much more intense than it is for the behind-the-scene jobs.

Radio

In radio, most beginners start as desk assistants or news assistants at network stations. Their duties include answering the telephones, some amount of clerical work, basic research, filing, making phone calls to verify information, and even rewriting minor, routine stories.

Reporters gather news and record events on tape. Some technical skills and good reporting, writing, and speaking ability are required. Reporters work under tremendous deadline pressure. Most start as reporters for small independent or network stations and move on to become reporters in a major market. The highest rung on the reporting ladder is that of network reporter.

Large stations employ newswriters and editors who prepare copy for the announcers. Newscasters are on-air personalities who get maximum public exposure. Reporters also receive on-air time when their words are recorded as part of the "cuts." Newscasters at many stations are also required to write at least part of the newscast.

Reporters can also rise to the position of news director. The news director is responsible for the news operation of the station or network, and this position is the dream of many broadcast journalists.

Television

In television, desk assistants perform almost identical duties as desk assistants in radio. At major TV stations, they distribute leads and stories from the wire services to the appropriate newswriters as well as serve as internal messengers. They may be asked to check facts by telephone for reporters and writers. At small stations, they rewrite wire copy and review film clippings.

Newswriters are responsible for preparing newscasts, whereas correspondents or reporters go out into the field and gather news with the assistance of camera crews. The emphasis on live telecasts has increased the importance of this work—and the pressures. News editors also edit copy submitted by reporters.

The assistant news producers help the news producer to assign stories and organize them in the order of priority for the newscast. They also oversee routine production operations. Again, the position of news director is the ultimate career goal of most behind-the-scenes broadcast journalists.

The anchors and reporters for newscasts and news magazines such as *60 Minutes* are the stars of TV journalism because they are seen by the viewing public. The position of network anchor is one of the most coveted in the communications industry.

Education

Hundreds of colleges and universities offer curricula in broadcast journalism. Some radio and TV institutes also offer short-term courses. College radio and TV stations continue to be major training grounds for aspiring broadcast journalists.

A career in radio requires good voice quality. One must possess considerable self-confidence and voice control techniques to go on the air as a newscaster or reporter. Knowledge of basic production techniques is a must for reporters and newscasters.

Writers and reporters should have good writing skills and the ability to handle deadline pressures. On-the-spot reporting also requires a great degree of courage and a spirit of adventure because reporters must often literally physically push themselves close to events and people. Good interviewing skills are the lifeblood of a good broadcast journalist.

On-camera jobs in television require a pleasing appearance and personality. Confidence and an ability to improvise are expected of reporters and newscasters, especially when they are on camera live. Fluency of speech and a good command of the language are critical to success. A successful anchor will also be a good newswriter and interviewer.

Experience

Because of the strong competition for jobs in broadcasting, experience is a crucial factor. Most jobs are not advertised; rather, insiders who have been working their way up earn them.

In radio and in television, beginners often start at small stations outside metropolitan areas and move to metropolitan stations and network stations after gaining substantial experience. This pattern of job mobility is frequent both in radio and television.

College graduates who enter radio journalism as desk assistants at network stations or as reporters at small network stations serve in those capacities before becoming reporters at medium-sized stations. After several years as a reporter at a major station or as news director at a small station, a position as network reporter or news director may open up.

AWARDS AND SCHOLARSHIPS

The Dow Jones Newspaper Fund (DJNF) is the best source of information about scholarships, internships, fellowships and listings of journalism and mass communications programs at colleges and universities. The DJNF also provides internships and scholarships to college students, and fellowships for high school journalism teachers. Its website (http://djnewspaperfund .dowjones.com) describes organizations that offer information about other sources of fellowships and scholarships. Here is a sampling of awards and scholarship programs that show the range offered:

- The Nieman Fellowships, sponsored by The Nieman Foundation for Journalism at Harvard University, are awarded to mid-career reporters, editors, photographers, producers, editorial writers, and cartoonists, as well as Internet specialists with at least five years of full-time professional experience in the news media. Detailed information is available at www.nieman.harvard.edu.

- The Hearst Journalism Awards Program consists of school year competitions in which prizes are awarded in writing, photography, and TV and radio news to undergraduates at accredited schools of journalism. The program is under the auspices of the William Randolph Hearst Foundations. Details are posted at http://hearstfdn.org.

- The Newspaper Guild's Heywood Broun Award recognizes achievements by working journalists, particularly reporting that helps to right wrongs or correct injustices. First consideration is given to individuals or two-person teams. The guild's David S. Barr Award also recognizes one high school and one college student for their journalistic achievements. More information is available at www.newsguild.org.

- Pulliam Journalism Fellowships (PJF) are designed to enhance the newsroom experience of participants who are assigned to the *Indianapolis Star* or the *Arizona Republic* newspapers. Fellows work as reporters, editorial writers, or copyeditors, depending on their areas of interest and experience, and also participate in group and individual sessions conducted by a writing coach. Details and applications are at www.indystar.com/help/jobs/pjf/2004_application.pdf.

- The Scripps-Howard Foundation honors excellence in journalism with several awards as well as a comprehensive program to improve journalism and thereby make a positive difference in local communities. More information about programs and projects is available at www.scripps.com/foundation.

- The Society of Professional Journalists holds national competitions for working journalists as well as college and high school students. The Sigma Delta Chi Awards recognize achievements in all forms of journalism, including online reporting. SPJ's Mark of Excellence competition is open to anyone enrolled in a college or university and studying for an academic degree. The society's Freedom of the Press High School Essay Contest is intended to increase knowledge and understanding of the importance of the First Amendment to American life. Entry forms are available at www.spj.org.

Broadcast Journalism Scholarships

For scholarships in broadcast journalism, check the websites of the trade associations listed in Chapter 6 on Television and Video. Among the associations that serve broadcast news professionals are the National Association of Broadcasters (NAB) and the Radio–Television News Directors Association (RTNDA). Both associations serve entry-level and veteran broadcasters in career advancement and fulfillment. The RTNDA Foundation awards several scholarships for undergraduates, graduate students, and working professionals. For more information, go to "Awards and Scholarships" on the association's home page at www.rtnda.org. The NAB Education Foundation is at www.nabef.org.

The Broadcast Education Association, dedicated to the development of students and professionals involved in teaching and research related to radio, television, and other electronic media, awards several scholarships. Detailed information is available at www.beaweb.org.

The John Bayliss Broadcast Foundation awards radio scholarships to students pursuing careers in all areas of radio broadcasting, including broadcast journalism.

The application form is available at: www.baylissfoundation.org.

ACCREDITED JOURNALISM PROGRAMS

The journalism programs of the following colleges and universities have been accredited by the Association for Education in Journalism and Mass

Communication (AEJMC). By the time you are ready to make your selection, additional institutions may have received accreditation, so you should contact the AEJMC for the most recent list.

American University
Arizona State University
Arkansas State University
Ball State University
Bowling Green State University
Brigham Young University
California State University, Fresno
California State University, Fullerton
California State University, Long Beach
California State University, Northridge
Colorado State University
Columbia University
Drake University
Eastern Illinois University
Florida A&M University
Humboldt State University
Indiana University
Iowa State University
Jackson State University
Kansas State University
Kent State University
Louisiana State University
Marshall University
Memphis State University
Michigan State University
New York University
North Texas State University
Northern Illinois University
Ohio State University
Oklahoma State University
Pennsylvania State University
San Diego State University

San Francisco State University

San Jose State University

South Dakota State University

Southern Illinois University, Carbondale

Southern Illinois University, Edwardsville

St. Cloud State University

Syracuse University

Temple University

Texas A&M University

Texas Christian University

Texas Tech University

University of Alabama

University of Alaska, Fairbanks

University of Arizona

University of Arkansas, Fayetteville

University of Arkansas, Little Rock

University of California, Berkeley

University of Colorado

University of Florida

University of Georgia

University of Hawaii

University of Illinois, Urbana–Champaign

University of Iowa

University of Kansas

University of Kentucky

University of Maryland

University of Minnesota

University of Mississippi

University of Missouri

University of Montana

University of Nebraska, Lincoln

University of Nevada

University of New Mexico

University of North Carolina, Chapel Hill

University of North Dakota

University of Ohio

University of Oklahoma
University of Oregon
University of Rhode Island
University of South Carolina
University of South Florida
University of Southern California
University of Tennessee, Knoxville
University of Texas, Austin
University of Utah
University of Washington
University of West Virginia
University of Wisconsin, Eau Claire
University of Wisconsin, Madison
University of Wisconsin, Oshkosh
University of Wisconsin, River Falls
Virginia Commonwealth University
Washington and Lee University
Western Kentucky University

The AEJMC has also accredited the broadcast journalism programs of the following colleges and universities:

American University
Bowling Green State University
Brigham Young University
Colorado State University
Florida A&M University
Indiana University
Iowa State University
Jackson State University
Louisiana State University
Marshall University
Memphis State University
New York University
Ohio State University
San Jose State University

Syracuse University
University of Alaska, Fairbanks
University of California, Berkeley
University of Illinois, Urbana–Champaign
University of Minnesota
University of Missouri
University of Ohio
University of Oregon
University of Texas, Austin
University of Utah
University of Washington
University of West Virginia
University of Wisconsin, Madison
Virginia Commonwealth University

SOURCES OF INFORMATION

Associations and Societies

Many professional organizations have served the field of publishing over the years. Some focus on the interests of those involved in the newspaper industry, while others focus on the magazine publishing industry. Several associations focus on specific areas of news gathering and reporting, such as technical writing. The scope of some organizations is defined by geographical regions or ethnic concerns. For associations in support of journalists from minority communities, see Chapter 11 on Women and Minorities. If you are interested in broadcast news, check the lists in Chapter 5 on Radio and Chapter 6 on Television and Video. Here is a selected list of organizations that serve the print industry. More detailed contact information appears in the Appendix. For ease of reference, some of these listings appear in several chapters.

American Society of Newspaper Editors (ASNE): (www.asne.org)
Associated Press Managing Editors (APME): (www.apme.com)
Association for Education in Journalism and Mass Communication
　(AEJMC): (www.aejmc.org)

Canadian Association of Journalists (CAJ): (www.eagle.ca/caj)

Education Writers Association (EWA): (www.ewa.org)

Investigative Reporters and Editors (IRE): (www.ire.org)

Society of American Business Editors and Writers (SABEW):
(www.sabew.org)

Society of Professional Journalists (SPJ): (www.spj.org)

Periodicals

Here is a short list of recommended publications. Numerous newsletters and magazines focus on specific topics of interest to writers, journalists, and editors, while others address issues of interest to publishers. Some are available only to those currently working in the field. If you are unable to subscribe to a publication of interest, you may be able to read selected articles online, read it at a library, or borrow it from a professional in the field.

American Journalism Review (www.ajr.org)

Columbia Journalism Review (www.cjr.org)

Copy Editor (www.copyeditor.com)

Folio (www.foliomag.com)

Editor & Publisher (www.editorandpublisher.com)

Directories

Annual Agency Guide: Writers Network. New York: Fade In, 2003.

2004 Writer's Market Online: 10,000+ Book and Magazine Editors Who Buy What You Write. Cincinnati: Writer's Digest Books, 2003.

The American Directory of Writer's Guidelines: A Compilation of Information for Freelancers from More Than 1,400 Magazine Editors and Book Publishers. Edited by Brigitte M. Phillips, Susan D. Klassen, and Dorris Hall. Fresno, CA: Quill Driver Books, 2003.

Recommended Reading

Alterman, Eric. *What Liberal Media? The Truth About Bias and the News*. New York: Basic Books, 2004.

Attkisson, Sharyl, and Don R. Vaughan. *Writing Right for Broadcast and Internet News*. New York: Pearson Allyn & Bacon, 2002.

Brooks, Brian S., and Jack Z. Sissors. *The Art of Editing*. 7th ed. New York: Pearson Allyn & Bacon, 2000.

Calishain, Tara, and Rael Dornfest. *Google Hacks: 100 Industrial-Strength Tips & Tools*. New York: O'Reilly & Associates, 2003.

Dotson, Bob, Matt Lauer, and Mervin Block. *Make It Memorable: Writing and Packaging TV News with Style*. Chicago: Bonus Books, 2000.

Freedman, Wayne. *It Takes More Than Good Looks to Succeed at TV News Reporting*. Chicago: Bonus Books, 2003.

Goldstein, Norm. *AP Stylebook and Briefing on Media Law*. New York: Basic Books, 2004.

Houston, Brant et al. *The Investigative Reporter's Handbook: A Guide to Documents, Databases and Techniques*. 4th ed. Bedford, MA: St. Martin's Press, 2002.

Rosenstiel, Tom, and Bill Kovach. *The Elements of Journalism: What Newspeople Should Know and the Public Should Expect*. New York: Three Rivers Press, 2001.

CHAPTER 3

PHOTOGRAPHY

A career in photography is one of the most satisfying that a person can have. But don't be misled—if you are interested in photography only for the money, for the glamour, or purely as an art form, be careful and cautious in your planning.

- Money: Many professions and crafts pay a great deal more and require less work than photography. Although many professional photographers do well enough financially to live comfortably, own their own homes, and send their children to college, few are extremely wealthy.
- Glamour: It is true that the general public views photography as a glamorous field. And it can be. Once in a while, you hear about photographers who are members of the jet set or who associate with sports and entertainment celebrities, but very few photographers get to photograph the "beautiful people" or travel to exotic places in the line of duty. Even the professionals who shoot big sports and entertainment events work very hard and under conditions that are often less than ideal.
- Art: Photography as an art form has gained worldwide recognition and acceptance—not bad for a technology that has been around for a little more than 150 years. However, very few photographers make a living at selling their photographs as art or as collectibles.

The good news is this: If you sincerely want to be a professional photographer, whether to satisfy clients' needs or to improve communications, you have a good chance of success, provided you have the ability, the business acumen, and the strong desire that this highly competitive field requires.

Actually, getting into photography is easy. All you really need is a telephone, business cards, some equipment, and credit at a photo lab. But getting into photography is one thing; staying in it is quite another.

According to the U.S. Bureau of Labor Statistics, in 2002 more than half of the 130,000 professional photographers in the country were self-employed. Many operate their own photo studios and event photo/video businesses, while others work as freelance or contract photographers for various media outlets. According to the bureau, most salaried photographers work in portrait or commercial photography studios, while newspapers, magazines, TV stations, and advertising agencies employ most of the others. In 2002, only the top 10 percent of salaried photographers earned more than $49,910, with most earning between $17,000 and $35,000. On the average, independent and self-employed photo pros earn less than staffers, but elite commercial photographers charge thousands of dollars for a single photo session.

Photography is one of the few remaining art/crafts in which entrepreneurs can develop at their own pace. A formal education isn't necessary, although a person who has professional training will probably have a better shot at succeeding than one who does not. A large number of colleges, universities, and art institutes offer courses in photography, and thousands of students are taking these courses. Many of these students aspire to get into professional photography. Because of this fierce competition, only the most talented and most aggressive will reach and keep the top spots. Not only are new graduates trying to enter the marketplace, but so are people of all ages from other fields. In addition, because the United States is the "focal point" of the world for this art and craft, students and photographers from many other countries come here hoping to build their careers.

CURRENT CHALLENGES

Professional photographers continually face the challenge of keeping up with emerging technologies such as digital photography and digital image manipulation. Although the quality of electronic photography has yet to equal the very best film camera images, digital imaging has made major inroads in every aspect of the field. This has resulted in increased competition as digital image-makers compete for business that used to belong to traditional photographers in advertising, corporate communications, and other areas. But these new technologies have also opened up a world of opportunities for photographers who are able to embrace them. In some fields, most notably photojournalism, high-resolution digital single-lens reflex cameras (SLRs) have become more popular than film cameras—for use in news and event photography. Even when images are still captured on film, they are frequently modified with image manipulation programs like Adobe Photoshop before reaching their final audience.

THE TECHNOLOGY ADVANTAGE

Electronic photo-imaging, once a scientific toy, has become the basis for whole new industries. This change has come about as a result of the rapid development of five technologies: personal computers (PC), multimegapixel solid-state image sensors such as charge-coupled devices (CCDs), powerful photo-imaging software such as Photoshop, the proliferation of inexpensive data storage in the form of flash memory cards and recordable CD-ROMs, and high-speed Internet connections that enables the rapid transmission of high-resolution photo files.

Image manipulation software such as Adobe Photoshop, Corel Photo-Paint, and Jasc's Paint Shop Pro have freed photographers from the darkroom and allowed them to create virtually any image that can be imagined. Such techniques as pixel-by-pixel retouching, photomontage, and matting, which once had an aura of magic, are now everyday tools. A photo-imager who cannot use these tools is like a carpenter who can't handle a power saw and plywood.

An in-depth knowledge of Photoshop and related applications not only provides an imager with wonderful creative tools but also virtually guarantees instant employability anywhere in the country. Photo-manipulation and illustration have become basic to such diverse industries as advertising, videogame production, and space exploration.

CCDs and other solid-state imaging sensors have made it possible to bring real-world images into the digital domain through scanners and digital cameras. Expertise in electronic image capture has become the bread and butter of industrial and technical photographers as well as many photojournalists. From photomicrography for scientific research to shots of homes for real estate websites, silver is out and CCDs are in. Scanners that cost less than $300 are routinely used to digitize photos for publication, and electronic cameras costing less than $1,000 from Canon, Nikon, and others meet the resolution and quality requirements of most magazines.

Conventional photo technology continues to advance as well. Ever-faster film that produces super-fine-grained images is loaded into cameras with automatic settings that would, perhaps, even be acceptable to master photographer Alfred Stieglitz; and pictures are shot through lighter, faster lenses designed on supercomputers. Many professionals now use the same fine, and expensive, lenses from their favorite manufacturer with both film and digital camera bodies.

Powerful, low-cost PCs and Macs have made sophisticated digital photo-imaging techniques accessible to artists, journalists, and visual communicators of every stripe and budget. The computer revolution encompasses not only the processing of images but also their archiving, access, and distribution. In a few seconds, professional photographers can access photo databases and search archives containing tens of thousands of shots in response to a customer request and can deliver the required high-resolution file minutes later via high-speed Internet connections. Cataloging and work-flow software such as Canto's Cumulus and Extensis Portfolio make it easier to manage the large numbers of images generated by working photographers.

The market for electronic images has grown rapidly with the expansion of the World Wide Web and the booming sales of CD-ROMs and DVDs.

Inkjet printers now offer the quality of conventional photgraphic prints. Beyond the proliferation of high-quality, low-cost consumer photo printers, professional-level inkjet printers from Epson, Canon, Olympus, and HP are routinely used for business graphics, and even for gallery and museum-quality photo reproductions.

High-speed networks, image compression, and optical storage have resulted in a host of other cost-effective tools for the efficient archiving, cataloging, and retrieval of myriad images.

The explosive growth of digital photo-imaging has created many opportunities for the professional and creative advancement of photographers, especially those who can make the most of the new tools of the trade.

ONLINE RESOURCES

The World Wide Web is making it easier for aspiring photographers to learn more about the science and art of imaging. Practicing professionals also use the Internet to network with other photographers, to learn more about the art and business, and to market their work. Here is a selection of stock agency, electronic magazines, and other websites to check out.

Photography Stock Agencies

The websites of these agencies display thousands of images. Some display and sell both traditional rights-controlled stock photography and royalty-free images. These websites also carry information on the purchase and use of images, and some provide advice on selling photos to stock agencies.

Comstock Stock Photography (www.comstock.com)
Getty Images (www.gettyimages.com)
Pickerell Services (www.pickphoto.com)
Stock Photo (www.stockphoto.net)

E-Zines and Photo Magazine Websites

Electronic magazines on the Web that focus on photography include:

- *Apogee Photo* (www.apogeephoto.com). This website includes well-illustrated articles accompanied by a gallery of the author's or photographer's work; an extensive, searchable, worldwide directory of photo schools, tours, and workshops; a forum for exchanging messages with other photographers; and a separate area where anyone can add a link to their own Web pages. Bimonthly photo contests are open to all.

- *The Digital Journalist* (http://digitaljournalist.org). This fine website, published and edited by Dirck Halstead, offers product reviews, industry news, interviews with top photo-journalists, and firsthand reports from photographers in the field.
- *Photonet* (www.photo.net). This website is an in-depth resource for photographers that includes essays, equipment analyses, suggestions, discussion groups, a huge library of photographs extensively cross-referenced, as well as many good basic and intermediate online tutorials, with links, on the creative and technical aspects of photography.
- *Popular Photography* (www.popphoto.com). This very useful website from the leading photo magazine in print offers extensive advice on technique and technology, reliable reviews, and forums with hundreds of thousands of postings.
- *Shutterbug* (www.shutterbug.net). This widely read photo magazine's website is extensive and useful.
- *Studio Photography and Design* (www.imaging-info.com/ spdonline). The website continues this magazine's coverage of high-end studio photography.
- *Rangefinder* (www.rangefindermag.com/magazine). The website for this useful magazine for working photographers includes profiles, business advice, product reviews, industry news, and a message board.

Associations

A number of the associations listed at the end of this chapter under "Sources of Information" offers excellent information as well as additional resources on their websites.

WHERE THE JOBS ARE

Professional photography, truly a service industry, is thought of in four categories: portraiture and event photography, commercial-illustration photography, photojournalism, and industrial photography. Nearly everyone who earns a living as a photographer will probably fit into one of these general classifications. There is crossover among the four disciplines, and within each are subdivisions and levels of activities.

Portraiture and Event Photography

Portraiture—making pictures of people—is the most difficult area of photography to gain recognition in. There are as many different styles of portraiture as there are portrait photographers and studios. This area also includes photographers who specialize in weddings and other special events.

Record Photography

This simple, structured, straightforward record-type of portraiture, usually of children and family groups, can be found in shopping centers and in department stores such as Sears, J. C. Penney's, and K-Mart. The poses are straightforward, the lighting is standard and preset, and the number of poses is limited. Unquestionably, this type of photography offers consumers the best value for their money. The photography is "clean," the resulting prints are of good quality and good color, and the photos provide adequate records of the people pictured.

Working in one of these studios is a good entry-level job that offers good experience in dealing with the public in a studio atmosphere and an opportunity to make photographs in the real world.

Portrait studios are the next level up. Most of these businesses depend upon photographing weddings for a substantial part of their income. They also usually specialize in the portraiture of babies, children, family groups, and adults of all ages. The photographer offers a variety of "documentary" poses and arrangements, perhaps including props and accessories. Sometimes makeup is applied to hide skin blemishes. Lighting is carefully placed to complement the subject. Some studios offer garden or outdoor settings. This kind of studio offers a wide choice of poses and generally provides larger prints than the record-type businesses, although small sizes are also available. The large prints are delivered in moderate to expensive frames for placement in the home or office. The prices charged are relative to the quality of the work produced.

These studios may range in size from small to large. They are usually family owned and operated, although some belong to large photography companies. Some of these studios add to their bottom line by specializing in the portraiture of high school seniors, sports teams, and other groups.

Working in a portrait studio usually requires some experience. A job as an assistant cameraperson, a finisher (matting and framing), or a salesperson, for example, would require previous experience. However, some photographers will train an entry-level person who shows promise. An apprenticeship in which a good beginner works under an experienced photographer can benefit both the studio and the beginner.

The personal attributes necessary for portraiture and special-occasion work include the ability to deal well with coworkers, skill in working with the public, and a pleasant personality. A willingness to follow the suggested dress code and to take direction is necessary, as is adaptability in learning the studio's particular style of portraiture. A knowledge of photography, particularly lighting and posing, is essential.

Special Events

Thousands of professional photographers make a living documenting weddings, bar mitzvahs, confirmations, and other milestones in the lives of their clients. Many find this work particularly rewarding because their pictures become treasured reminders of these happy occasions.

Wedding and event photographers must have a thorough knowledge of these types of occasions and the best ways to shoot each traditional "scene"—at a wedding, for example, photos of the veiling, the first dance, and family groupings are essential. The many religious and cultural traditions linked to these events, all have their own emotionally charged expectations, and these offer photographers different opportunities and challenges.

An entire industry exists to support the work of wedding and event photographers. At a recent Wedding and Portrait Photographers International (WPPI) conference in Las Vegas, more than 200 exhibitors ranging from album, camera, software, and lighting manufacturers to custom photo labs and specialized online service providers vied for this multibillion-dollar business.

The business of photographing weddings and other special events has several un ique aspects. Many wedding photographers have branched out into videotaping events or have added these services to their repertoire and subcontracted the additional work. This makes sense from a business perspective, because many clients want both of these related services, and from an artistic and production perspective, because the production elements work better when shooting activities are coordinated. Another element is the logistics that have to be worked out in conjunction with other service providers such as catering. There are many approaches to wedding and special occasion photography ranging from elaborate formality to high-end creativity to the more spontaneous approach of the members of the Wedding Photojournalists Association (WPA). For more information on these and other aspects of this rewarding business, check out the WPPI website (www.wppinow.com).

The Custom Portrait Studio

The custom portrait studio is at the top of the "people photography business" when it comes to quality and price. The studios in this relatively select group are usually small enterprises, as businesses go, and may be run by one, two, or three people—often only a photographer and her or his spouse, with the spouse acting as business manager, salesperson, and even retoucher. The photographs produced by this type of studio are true works of art, and the matting and framing are of the best quality as well. A few studios offer dye-transfer photographic prints, the ultimate in quality. Print sizes vary, the largest being 40 by 60 inches. Interpretive portraits made by custom studios are the potential heirlooms of tomorrow.

Custom studios also make the fine executive portraits that find their way into corporate annual reports as well as to the spot above the fireplace at home. When photographer James R. Israel was head of the portrait studio at General Motors Corp., his photograph of the chairman of the board was the first nonpainting to hang in the boardroom.

One of America's leading portraitists is Christopher DerManuelian, who also specializes in architecture and sophisticated wedding photography. He owns a one-person business in San Mateo, California. He learns as much as he can about his subject and even visits the room where the photograph will be displayed so he can complement the environment with the portrait. DerManuelian studied civil engineering in Beirut, Lebanon, and completed his studies in the United States. He entered his new profession with little preparation. He says, "When you do your best, sooner or later people will come to recognize and appreciate your work."

At most studios that do these three types of portraiture, the processing and printing are finished by outside professional laboratories. However, with the advent of one-hour "mini-labs," some studios have begun doing their own photofinishing, sometimes in cooperation with other local studios. Matting, framing, and packaging are usually done by the individual studios.

Commercial-Illustration Photography

Commercial-illustration photography includes a wide variety of creative modalities and specialties. A commercial studio may offer photography for many different purposes, or it may specialize in only a few types. For the most part, these studios produce photographs for advertising, annual reports, brochures, catalogs, editorial use, packaging, and promotion and public relations. Although most commercial-illustration photographic work is published in some form, prints and transparencies are also used for convention exhibit displays, point-of-purchase (POP) displays, sales meetings, sales presentations, wall decor, and window displays.

Commercial photography is used to document manufacturing processes and illustrate products ranging from computer chips and glassware to aircraft. Architectural photography is a specialty, as is aerial photography. Illustration photography appears in magazines and newspapers, depicting people, places, and products.

Commercial-illustration studios can be small rooms designed for product shots with a staff of one or two people. A medium-sized operation might have a drive-in bay, one or two additional smaller studios, and six or eight employees. The largest photographic companies, such as Kranzten in Chicago, occupy multistory buildings in several locations where dozens of people fill a variety of jobs including stylists and home economists, photographers and assistant photographers, laboratory technicians, salespeople, and office staff.

Few commercial studios are located in small towns; most are located in light industrial areas in or around major cities. A good place to seek employment is in any city that has a major league baseball team, because these cities tend to have not only manufacturing and service industries but also advertising and PR agencies that use photography on a regular basis. Although New

York is the biggest center of such activity, successful photo-illustrators also work in Hillsboro, Oregon; Nashville; Baltimore; Mannheim, Pennsylvania; Birmingham, Alabama; and Los Angeles.

The 35mm transparency is a popular delivery medium in commercial photography, particularly for multi-image presentations. Producing slide/sound programs for presentation to the business-industrial community and the public is akin to producing a film or TV show, except that the medium encompasses slides, visual effects, and recorded sound. Special skills are needed in the photography, scripting, programming, and projection of a multi-image show.

Increasingly, these multimedia presentations incorporate digital tech nologies that range from digital photography and image manipulation to the use of presentation software such as Macromedia Director and Wet Electric Production Designer.

The national association for commercial illustrators is the Advertising Photographers of America, which has affiliated groups in New York City, Chicago, Los Angeles, Atlanta, San Diego, and other cities. Photo District News sponsors conferences and seminars for professional photographers, including the big PhotoPlus Expo in New York City each October.

Personal attributes essential to a commercial photographer are self-motivation, dependability, business acumen, good verbal and visual communication skills, and the ability to work well with others in high-pressure situations. Most assignments have rigid deadlines, so the ability to provide speedy and dependable service is crucial.

PHOTOJOURNALISM

The field of photojournalism is occupied primarily by independent freelance entrepreneurs who are in the business of taking pictures for publication. Photojournalists also make photographs for publicity and for multi-image presentations. They usually specialize in two or three fields such as sports, entertainment, agriculture, annual reports, business and industry, personalities, or travel.

Stock photography is a prime source of income for many freelance photojournalists, who turn over transparencies and digital photo files by the thousands to picture agencies or "stock houses." The images on file are of every conceivable subject or situation and are used in textbooks, encyclopedias, annual reports, magazines, and other products. The agency has exclusive rights to the images in its files and pays photographers a percentage of the fee paid each time a picture is used. This way it is possible for one slide image, which is replicated as needed, to earn thousands of dollars for a photographer.

Although the field of photojournalism is relatively small, some major newpapers, magazines, TV stations, and news services such as Associated Press have staff positions for photographers. These settings also offer opportunities for photo editors, librarians, and picture researchers. Two organizations devoted to this aspect of photography are the American Society of Picture Professionals and the National Press Photographers Association.

Life in the Field

The lives of photojournalists are interesting and varied. Award-winning newspaper photographer Bill Strode once said, "I tackle my routine assignments as if they were of national importance." Arthur Rothstein, photographer of the famous "Oklahoma Dust Storm" and many other images of that era, observed, "Photojournalists are the observers of people and events who report what's happening in photographs, interpreters of facts who write with a camera." Rothstein went on to become chief photographer for *Look* magazine and later to a new career with *Parade*. Annie Liebovitz, of *Rolling Stone* fame, is a well-known photographer of people and events who is carrying on a tradition of women in photography that began with Julia Margaret Cameron in the nineteenth century. George Kalinsky, the official photographer for Madison Square Garden for more than three decades, has taken some of the most memorable sports and entertainment photographs of all time, including classic shots of Muhammad Ali, Frank Sinatra, and Pope John Paul II. Kalinsky, who seems to have an almost magical ability to reveal the entire story of a personality or event in a single picture says, "I always look to capture the moment of emotion."

Digital Photojournalism

Kalinsky and other photojournalists have pushed the technology envelope by bringing digital photography into the realm of mass media communications.

The value of digital photography's immediacy in news and sports photography is obvious. Beating the deadline with a picture of a championship-winning shot is a lot easier if you need not stop off at a photo lab first. The digital photos "smuggled" by modem out of China during the Tiananmen Square crisis of June 1989 helped to arouse and focus world opinion, and the image of a lone brave protestor confronting a row of tanks and heavily armed troops became the defining image of the student movement.

But digital imaging technology is a double-edged sword that can distort as well as reveal the truth. According to Associated Press photojournalist Bebeto Matthews: "In the digital age, deadlines are on the 'minute,' sometimes driving quantitative concerns over qualitative. Some editors assume that everything can be covered and delivered in an almost real-time state. Then there is the credibility issue—it's easy to manipulate images, reshaping original content for a desired outcome other than the truth. The reporter can control these issues by safeguarding the integrity of the reporting process to ensure qualitative and creditable results." Matthews concludes, "The need to cover all angles and deliver many pictures from a story should be tempered by professionalism."

In addition, the technology itself presents operational advantages and drawbacks for the photojournalist, particularly in hazardous environments. According to Matthews: "For a photojournalist concerned with documentary feature work, digital equipment can be a burden. Unlike the days when I was film-based with lighter equipment, digital gear can quickly become back-breaking, heavy, and high-maintenance. When the gear is too much, it affects my mobility and increases concerns about security, especially when I have to put some gear aside to focus on getting the picture. Keeping equipment fully charged also means always having access to electricity, a convenience not present in the field."

Ultimately, however, the ability to integrate and apply knowledge of digital technologies helps the photojournalist to excel in a very competitive field. Matthews reports: "Recently, I coordinated five photojournalists during the coverage of the final day of jury deliberations in the Martha Stewart trial. Each of us was equipped with a computer to file our digital pictures like all the other competing media there. To stay ahead of the competition, I used a personal digital assistant (PDA) customized to process work at AP standards. While our competition stood around waiting for the next moment, afraid to leave their shooting locations to file with their laptops, I stood in place and removed the digital film card from my camera, and used my handheld device to process and file. I helped to introduce this method of digital filing with a PDA to improve the effective delivery of early pictures from newsbreaks, as well as to economize on weight and size of gear. This sort of initiative is impossible without grasp of digital knowledge."

Strength in Numbers

Many photojournalists and TV news camerapeople belong to the National Press Photographers Association (NPPA). They subscribe to *News Photographer* magazine and attend the NPPA's annual conference and NPPA-sponsored short courses.

The book *A Day in the Life of America*, an excellent example of the best in today's photo-reportage, shows how photojournalists from around the world can work together to compile an important record of a nation. Working as an employee or on retainer for a magazine, newspaper, or wire service can be an exciting and rewarding career of taking pictures of events as they occur as well as their aftermath or follow-up events. Competition with other photographers is a constant, and one can expect a bit of "jostling" at important news events.

To be a news photojournalist, the photographer must be strong enough physically to carry heavy equipment (photojournalists are the "pack horses" of the industry), and also ready and willing to go anywhere at a moment's notice. The photographer must always be alert and have the stamina for rigorous, and even dangerous, assignments.

A degree in liberal arts, with courses in journalism, anthropology, and human relations would be beneficial background for this work, but a "good eye," determination, and the ability to exhibit grace under pressure are the primary requirements for success in this exciting field.

INDUSTRIAL PHOTOGRAPHY

Industrial photography has traditionally meant photography (whether still, motion picture, or television) produced by the photographic departments of corporations, institutions, and government facilities.

The concept of industrial photography is changing and has been broadened by in-house departments and by commercial and freelance photographers as well. It has been estimated that there are a few thousand photographic departments in business and industry in the United States. That number is not likely to increase because photography is only one of the media used by business and industry.

Photography is often included in audiovisual (AV) or communications departments and, like television, is only one of the disciplines in the department. Some organizations are now reevaluating the function of staff photographers and because of corporate downsizing mandates are reducing the size of these departments.

Still, ongoing turnover and the creation of a few new jobs mean that there will always be career opportunities in in-house photography on company premises because many companies must, of necessity, keep their technical achievements and manufacturing processes proprietary. The benefits of working for a company can include medical insurance, paid vacation time, holidays, and even company-sponsored retirement programs. Although most companies and institutions have 40-hour work weeks, the work of a photographer, like that of many other professionals, can demand longer working days.

Fringe benefits for in-house photographers sometimes include paid attendance at seminars, workshops, and conventions. Sometimes travel is part of the job and is regarded as an attractive perk. But a heavy travel schedule, working in unfamiliar environments, and the responsibility for expensive equipment can add to the high stress level of this exciting job.

In general, the pay rates for industrial photographers are among the highest in the photographic industry. The trade-off, however, can be slower advancement than might be found in a commercial photographic business. Also, this career path is unlikely to lead to great advancements within the company.

In preparing for a job as an in-house photographer, a related college degree is helpful, as is experience in technical photography and photo lab technology.

"Experience in any kind of photography is also a plus," says Robert E. Mayer, former chief photographer for Bell & Howell. Mayer studied photography at Ohio State University. The personal attributes of good industrial photographers include competence, versatility, and imagination; they must also be self-starters and possess a willingness to perform any kind of photography.

SCIENTIFIC AND TECHNICAL PHOTOGRAPHY

It has been said that there are two directions you can take in photographic sciences. You can work in the application of photography to the needs of industry, medicine, and government, or you can carry out pure research aimed at the discovery and control of the basic elements of photography.

William G. Hyzer, an internationally recognized authority on technical photography, scientific instrumentation, and photogrammetry, says, "Photography today has completely overrun its natural boundaries as a photochemical recording process and is penetrating deeply into the adjoining photoelectronic and photophysical disciplines."

The picture-making aspects of scientific and technical photography include high-speed photography and videography, photomacrography, photo micrography, holography, and color printing. According to the Rochester Institute of Technology (RIT), in Rochester, New York, there are more than 250 job titles in technical photography. Non-picture-making jobs in this field include chemist, physicist, mathematician, and photographic scientist, technical writer, laboratory supervisor, and even a technical representative for a manufacturer of photographic materials and/or equipment. RIT offers both two-year AAS and four-year BS degrees in technical photography.

Photogrammetry

Photogrammetry and remote sensing are imaging processes that are used for geospatial information gathering. It is an important part of scientific and technical photography, and courses on the subject are offered at a number of colleges and universities. People who desire to become career photogrammetrists should acquire a fundamental background in physical mathematics as well as scientific and technical subjects. A professional photogrammetrist is usually a college graduate, while technicians will have completed high school and attended a technical college. For information on careers in photogrammetry and remote sensing, visit the American Society of Photogrammetry and Remote Sensing at www.asprs.org.

Biomedical Photography

A career in biomedical photography can be challenging and rewarding. Job opportunities can be found in medical schools, hospitals, and veterinary facilities. A visit to a local facility will let you see firsthand what the job is all about.

Several schools offer programs that lead to either associate or bachelor's degrees in biomedical photography, and some colleges and universities offer master's-level courses in biomedical communications. The BioCommunications Association is a source of information (www.bca.org) for education, networking, and technical expertise in biological and medical imaging. Personal attributes include an interest in science, especially medicine or biology, and an interest in research, which takes perseverance and an analytical mind.

Law Enforcement, Civil Evidence, Forensic, and Firefighting Photography

Forensic photography—the documentation of evidence performed by photographers and technicians in police and sheriffs' departments, as well as in offices and laboratories of state highway patrols—is as great a challenge as the crime it helps to solve. Helping to solve a crime or investigate an accident or fire can give photographers a feeling of pride and real accomplishment.

The Evidence Photographers International Council has developed the widely consulted "Standard for Crime Scene Photography." A specialty within this field is that of examiner of questioned documents. New developments in detection methods continue to help solve mysteries that these examiners face. Information on the field of forensic photography is available at the council's website (www.epic-photo.org). The International Fire Photographers Association provides educational resources for those interested in this important aspect of forensic photography. For more information, go to the association's website (www.ifpaonline.com).

Photographers in this field need an inquiring mind, perseverance, patience, technical ability, and an interest in research and in police work.

Benjamin J. Cantor, who has specialized in civil evidence photography for five decades, has an engineering degree from Northeastern University and a JD degree from Boston College Law School. Cantor's experience as an expert witness in evidence photography led him to write *Courtroom Guide for Non-Lawyers,* an important reference for anyone interested in court procedures or in becoming a skilled or expert witness for trials.

TEACHING

Teaching photography as a career takes two different forms. The first, continuing education for professional photographers, includes lectures and courses taught by instructors who are also active practitioners in the subjects they teach.

For example, Veronica Cass runs a school in Hudson, Florida, as well as short courses around the world through the Veronica Cass Academy of Photographic Arts (www.veronicacass.com). Because she began her career as a retoucher and colorist, her classes focus on retouching for negative and print enhancement.

The second option is found in the many colleges and universities that employ professional teachers to teach courses. Vocational and technical schools hire both professional photographers and professional teachers. In addition to being an accomplished photographer and having a solid background in photography, a teacher of photographic courses must be a good communicator and have the necessary skills and personal qualifications to teach effectively.

Different school systems have their own academic requirements. If you want a career in teaching photography, investigate the school system that interests you to determine the requirements that a teacher must complete to be eligible for employment. You also must be an accomplished photographer in the area you wish to teach before you start teaching.

The Society for Photographic Education is an organization of 1,500 teachers of photography at the secondary and college levels that provides a forum for the development of photographic practice, teaching, scholarship, and criticism.

The U.S. federal government employs many photographers, most of them in Cabinet-level and other major departments such as Agriculture, Defense, Justice, and the Veterans Administration. Information on qualifications and application forms for federal government jobs are available in all U.S post offices. Each branch of the armed forces has top-notch training programs in a number of photographic disciplines. Many prominent civilian photographers and technicians learned their craft in one of the armed forces. State, county, and local governments also employ photographers. Information about these jobs is usually available from civil service commissions, employment offices, or from the website of the appropriate agency.

PHOTO PROCESSING, RETAIL, AND OTHER OPPORTUNITIES

There are many positions in photography other than being behind a camera. Two support services to consider are photo processing and finishing, and photo retailing. Many famous photographers who processed their own film and made their own prints, spent many hours mastering darkroom techniques. That's what put the stamp of individuality on their work. Most professional photographers send their film to commercial photo labs for photo processing and finishing.

A job at a photo lab is a great way to gain expertise in developing and printing. In making enlargements, for example, every aspect of the image—composition, exposure, special effects, the processing—each with many degrees of control is in your hands. A skilled photographer/printer is a rare individual, indeed. Printing your own work is good training for becoming a commercial photographer. You should gain experience in all phases of the photographic process, both chemical and digital. Such experience will enhance your understanding of the craft.

Custom Printing
Today, few professional photographers process their own film or make their own prints. These steps are handled by professional processing laboratories

or, in some cases, by custom printers. Custom printers are accomplished artists and technicians who "finish" a photographer's work. They must be good communicators who can interact with the photographer to interpret how the photographer envisions the final print.

Pay for custom printers can be higher than that for photographers. Patience, perseverance, artistic ability, and stamina are important characteristics for a custom printer. Custom printers must spend hours standing at the enlarger or processing tray in the darkroom while still concentrating on getting the best results possible. Be sure you are not allergic to the processing chemicals. In these days of predominantly color photography, the capability to make good black-and-white prints is rare indeed, and premiums are paid for such work.

Photofinishing

Professional photo processing laboratories offer film processing and printing to studios and corporate departments. There are employment opportunities at these labs for qualified technicians and managers.

Photofinishing of a different sort is available for the general public. These laboratories range in size from large-scale, high-volume factories to mini-labs, now estimated to number almost ten thousand nationwide, that provide one-hour service from film to prints.

A third class of photofinishing facility fills the gap between high-end custom labs and common mini-labs. These storefront imaging centers serve the photographic and digital image processing needs of both local businesses and quality-concious amateurs.

A career in photofinishing is a good choice for a person who is interested in working with images and equipment. In large labs the processing equipment is automated and little technical skill is needed to operate the systems, but there is a need for people trained in the operation and maintenance of the equipment. In smaller "boutique" labs and imaging centers, there is much more hands-on work, such as color correction and the retouching of old or damaged photos.

The digital photo revolution has changed the photofinishing business and the prerequisites for many jobs in the industry. "Knowledge of computers is now becoming as important as good attitude, personal habits, and the willingness to help people with their imaging needs. Almost every person who applies for a job says they are computer literate, but training in Adobe Photoshop or a similar program is very important," says Paul Schneiderman, who owns and runs MotoPhoto stores in White Plains, New York, and Stamford, Connecticut.

Schneiderman, who studied photography and marketing at the Fashion Institue of Technology (FIT) in New York City, adds, "A basic understanding of photography is important but can also be taught. We hire for attitude, and then we train for the job. Anyone who works in this environment also needs to be able to multitask."

Professional organizations can be an important source of information and assistance, as Schneiderman reports: "PMA [Photo Marketing Association International] provides me with informational brochures for my customers on all aspects of picture taking as well as market surveys about consumer buying habits and needs. PMA also runs the largest trade show and convention in our industry and, on a local level, offers round table discussions and other useful meetings four or five times a year." PMA offers literature on careers in photofinishing.

Training is helpful, and some technical schools have courses in photofinishing. Some programs lead to a two-year diploma or certificate; others, to a four-year degree. In a typical photofinishing career path, you would start as a technician and work up to a management position or possible ownership of a processing laboratory. Part- or full-time experience in a lab will help you to decide whether you wish to pursue a career in this segment of the photographic industry.

In addition to labs and photo processing facilities, entry-level job opportunities exist in studios, photographic departments, and in the companies that manufacture and sell such equipment.

Photo Retailing

Photo retailing is a multibillion-dollar business. Discount outlets and online merchants sell equipment with no real after-sale support or follow-up. Specialty camera stores and the camera departments of some major retailers, on the other hand, hire salespeople who consult with customers and help them to decide what equipment to buy. A successful salesperson is knowledgeable about photography and can intelligently discuss the full range of available equipment and software and their capabilities.

Salespeople at camera stores have to be thoroughly familiar with photographic equipment—much of it complex and most of it expensive. Customers, whether advanced amateurs or professional photographers, expect salespeople at professional photo dealerships to have detailed knowledge about equipment, accessories, film, and other supplies. In this environment, the salesperson is truly a consultant to the photographer.

A career in photo retailing can provide a good life. It requires not only an interest in photography but also technical training. To succeed in photo retailing, you should be at ease with the public and have a sales-oriented personality. The Photo Marketing Association also conducts courses in retailing.

Photo Equipment Technology

It's possible to devote an entire career to knowing what makes cameras and flashes work and keeping them in working order. The manufacturers, distributors, and dealers of photographic and AV equipment depend on technicians and service companies for the maintenance and repair of that equipment. Independent repair shops and factory service departments employ full- and part-time equipment technicians.

Look through the pages of *Popular Photography* magazine, and you will see test reports that actually take cameras apart and analyze their parts. Reading a few of these reports will give you an idea of the complexity of these instruments, which combine mechanics and electronics to determine exposure, control the flash, trip the shutter, advance the film, and rewind it back into the cassette.

If you have an interest in what makes things work and are agile at handling small parts, a knowledge of electronic controls, and a knack for fixing things, then a career in photo equipment technology may be for you. Facility in quickly diagnosing problems and making repairs will be to your advantage, as will the ability to be innovative in modifying existing equipment for special purposes.

Training is necessary to enter this field. Several schools, located primarily in the western United States, offer courses in camera repair. C&C Associates (www.cchomestudy.com) offers a home-study course in camera repair. Occasionally, a repair facility will hire and train an apprentice. For information on courses and job opportunities, contact the Society of Photo-Technologists (www.spt.info) or the International Communications Industries Association (www.infocomm.org).

Some of the job titles in photo equipment and AV technology include camera service specialist, inspector, modification designer, photoinstrumentation specialist, quality control technician, repair technician, test operator, and service manager.

EDUCATION AND EXPERIENCE

You can learn the basics of photography in a relatively short time, but the most important aspect of preparing for a career in photography is preparing for the life of a photographer. Because most photographers deal with a great variety of subjects and are in contact with a wide range of people, someone with a well-rounded academic education, plus life experience in the real world, stands a better chance of success than someone with narrower training. Courses in the liberal arts and social sciences, and especially business, should be high on your list.

Show me two people of equal artistic talent and ability who are about to go into business as photographers, and I'll place my bet on the one who has more business acumen and is the more aggressive of the two. This is a fact of life. Getting into photography is easy, but staying there and advancing is quite a different matter.

The most common route to photography as a profession begins with informal portraits. Picking up a camera and aiming it at a family member, neighbor, or friend is an easy thing to do. And everyone, it seems, likes pictures and wants to look at them.

The next step is to respond to requests for prints. As the demand for your work increases (by now you will have photographed a wedding or other social event and possibly a store window), your interest in learning more about photography will increase.

Reading photography magazines and books, visiting with professional photographers, and joining photography organizations such as a camera club or the local chapter of a professional organization will lead you to a decision as to whether you want to go into business for yourself full time or to seek employment as a photographer. At this point, seek further counsel. Talk with everyone you can find who is in the industry—photographers, studio owners, photo or AV department heads, photo lab managers, technicians. Listen to them.

There will come a time when you have asked too many people for opinions and advice, and you must make your decision. If another profession or business would give you more career enjoyment, choose that one instead and let photography become your hobby.

The important thing is to give serious and adequate thought and research to the subject. Ask yourself whether you have the necessary skills, training, and perseverance to meet your goals. Should you decide to study photography formally, choose your school carefully. Some schools specialize in photography, while several technical and art schools offer basic programs, and many colleges and universities offer very good courses in photography.

Once you decide to pursue a photography career, choose the locale in which you would like to work. As mentioned earlier, start with a major league baseball city as your center of activity, and research the names of photography studios and firms with photographic or AV departments in the area.

When you know something about the community, consult the local business telephone directory and other information available from the chamber of commerce or department of development. Get names and addresses of likely contacts. Get copies of all the local or regional newspapers, check out the classified ads, read the business and financial pages (the Sunday paper should have a job marketplace section), and find out about business and advertising activity in the area.

Talk with studio owners and corporate AV department managers. Ask about opportunities for employment or the prospects for a possible business in the area. Should you wish to pursue commercial-illustration photography, seek out art directors at advertising agencies. Ask about their views of the current advertising scene and even about the future as they see it for this type of photography in the area.

If you are interested in possible employment as an industrial or newspaper photographer, do your homework: Know where the jobs are likely to be found. Set up appointments with department heads and/or with personnel departments of the enterprises where you you would like to work. If you or a friend or relative know someone in a company that interests you, ask for help in getting in touch with that person to see if he or she can be of assistance.

By this time, you will have surely prepared your résumé. Write individual letters to people you wish to contact, and send them a copy of your résumé. In your letter, offer to send or bring in samples of your work. It is not advisable to send photographs and clippings of your work unless there is a prior agreement for you to do so. Then follow up with at least one telephone call to all your contacts—first, to see if they have received your letter and résumé and then to let them know that you are really interested in working for them.

YOUR PORTFOLIO

Your portfolio, or "book," must be an honest record of your own capabilities, not "typical student work," although class exercises will show what you are capable of doing. In any event, the person who interviews you will recognize work that was done under an instructor. Be honest and straightforward when presenting samples of your photography. Published pieces such as tearsheets and clippings are always useful. Familiarize yourself with the company to which you are applying, and tailor your portfolio to that studio, photo department, or agency.

Your portfolio shouldn't be elaborate. A zippered artist's portfolio with a handle and at least one inside pocket for items too small to mount is appropriate. You can slip extra sleeves of transparencies and clippings into the pocket. Put most of your transparencies in pocketed plastic sheets, but mount your favorite or best transparencies, regardless of size, individually on standard masked black cardboard mounts. Place prints between clear plastic spiral-bound sheets. Organize your work into series or themes. Tailor your portfolio specifically for each interview, and edit your samples by rearranging, eliminating, or adding pieces according to what you think each interviewer may want to see. In many situations, a digital portfolio is acceptable. A well-organized selection of photos and other material stored on a CD-ROM either as a PowerPoint slide show or in another simple form, makes it easy for a prospective employer to evaluate your work.

If you have the capabilities, an online portfolio is a great way to let the world know what you can do.

Advertise your availability—sell yourself—through classified ads in the local newspapers and through professional and trade periodicals. You will need at least two months' time to get responses to magazine ads. You might also consider registering with a personnel agency.

When you are selecting a locale, you would be well advised to stay away from major metropolitan areas such as New York, Chicago, or Los Angeles unless you know that you have unusual talent, plus the ability to compete for a job in such an area and the ability to support yourself for quite a while while you are looking for a job.

Ask the members and officers of your photographic society for guidance. Consult your school's career counselor, and work through your school's placement service as well in pursuing employment. Be aware, however, that photography is not like other disciplines such as business, engineering, or science. The recruiters aren't looking for you. You must take the initiative.

CONTINUING EDUCATION

It is an accepted fact of life in photography that photographers must continue their vocational education throughout their career. Techniques in photography are forever changing, and equipment is always undergoing improvements.

The marketing of photography, particularly if you are an independent freelancer or a studio owner, is becoming increasingly important, and sophisticated marketing strategies are offered at workshops run by the 105-year-old Professional Photographers of America (PPA) and other trade organizations.

This continuing education is available at reasonable cost, and sessions are held at convenient locations for a minimum of time. There are also privately run workshops and industry-sponsored short courses. This kind of continuing education helps photographers to keep up with current developments in business and technology. It furthers personal and professional growth and provides practical, proven ideas for improving both technique and business.

The student seeking a career in photography should get involved in a professional group as early as possible. Membership is useful in making contacts and in becoming part of a network, which could be the beginning of a lifelong association. Belonging to a professional group is a two-way street: You gain by learning from others, and you also gain by sharing with others as you grow.

Workshops That Grant Academic Credit

The following workshops and institutes offer programs that grant academic credit:

Brooks Institute of Photography
801 Alston Road
Santa Barbara, CA 93108
(805) 966-3888 ext. 217 or 218
www.brooks.edu

The institute offers one five-day summer workshop for photo educators at the high school and junior college level for three graduate credit units; topics range from black-and-white to digital imaging.

Golden Gate School of Professional Photography
P.O. Box 187
Fairfield, CA 94533
(707) 422-0319
www.goldengateschool.com

The school is a nonprofit committee of the Professional Photographers of the Greater Bay Area (affiliated with PPA). It awards PPA merits to members who successfully complete the course. The five-day summer school includes entry-level courses in basic portrait and wedding photography, while advanced courses cover studio portraiture, photographic art, and commercial photography. Tuition costs about $350.

The Maine Photographic Workshops
Rockport, Maine 04856
(207) 236-8581
www.theworkshops.com

More than 100 intensive one- and two-week workshops are held each year in Rockport from February through December. The classes are designed for the serious study of photography as an art and career. The format includes lectures, critiques, and field and studio assignments.

Winona/PPA Affiliated Schools
57 Forsyth Street, N.W., Suite 1500
Atlanta, GA 30303
(800) 742-7468; (404) 522-3030
www.ppa.com

Winona is a not-for-profit subsidiary of the PPA. The PPA and affiliated schools offer hundreds of workshops and classes around the country.

SOURCES OF INFORMATION

More detailed contact information appears in the Appendix. For ease of reference, some of these listings appear here.

Associations and Societies

Advertising Photographers of America (APA) (www.apanational.com)
American Society of Media Photographers (ASMP) (www.asmp.org)
The Center for Photography at Woodstock (CPW) (www.cpw.org)
Evidence Photographers International Council (EPIC)
   (www.epic-photo.org)

International Center of Photography (ICP) (www.icp.org)

International Fire Photographers Association (IFPA)
(www.ifpaonline.com)

National Association of Photoshop Professionals (NAPP)
(www.photoshopuser.com)

National Press Photographers Association (NPPA) (www.nppa.org)

National Stereoscopic Association (NSA) (www.stereoview.org)

North American Nature Photography Association (NANPA)
(www.nanpa.org)

Photo Marketing Association (PMA) (www.pmai.org)

Photographic Society of America (PSA) (www.psa-photo.org)

Professional Photographers of America (PPA) (www.ppa.com)

Society for Photographic Education (SPE) (www.spenational.org)

University Photographers Association of America (UPAA)
(www.upaa.org)

Wedding and Portrait Photographers International (WPPI)
(www.wppinow.com)

White House News Photographers' Association (WHNPA)
(www.whnpa.org)

Periodicals

Many magazines and newsletters have served this industry over the years. But the publishing industry is constantly changing, with new owners, new magazines, and often new subscription rates. Most magazines for amateur photographers also can be purchased at newsstands. Trade publications like *Advanced Imaging* are sent to professionals at no charge. If you are interested in a trade magazine, you may be able to read it at a media library or borrow it from a professional photographer. Publications from associations are usually available as a membership benefit. Here is a list of recommended publications.

Advanced Imaging (www.advancedimagingmag.com)
Aperture magazine (www.aperture.org/magazines)
Photo Techniques (www.phototechmag.com)

Popular Photography (www.popphoto.com)

Shutterbug (www.shutterbug.net)

Studio Photography and Design (www.imaging-info.com/spdonline)

Rangefinder Magazine (www.rangefindermag.com/magazine)

Useful Magazines for Working Photographers

Journal of Evidence Photography (www.epic-photo.org)

News Photographer (www.nppa.org/news_and_events/magazine)

Photo District News (www.pdnonline.com)

Photo-Electronic Imaging (www.peimag.com)

PSA Journal (www.psa-photo.org/psajindx.htm)

Professional Photographer (www.ppmag.com)

Directories

Photographer's Market, 2004. Central Islip, NY: Writer's Digest Books, 2003.

Recommended Reading

On Photography

Edgerton, Harold E. *Exploring the Art and Science of Stopping Time: A CD-ROM Based on the Life and Work of Harold E. Edgerton.* Cambridge, MA: MIT Press, 2000.

London, Barbara, et al. *Photography. 7th ed.* Englewood Cliffs, NJ: Prentice Hall, 2001.

Peterson, Bryan F. *Learning to See Creatively: Design, Color & Composition in Photography.* New York: Watson-Guptill Publications, 2003.

On Special Areas

Cantrell, Bambi, et al. *The Art of Wedding Photography: Professional Techniques with Style.* New York: Watson-Guptill Publications, 2000.

Kobre, Kenneth. *Photojournalism: The Professionals' Approach. 4th ed.* Woburn, MA: Focal Press, 2000.

McDonald, Tom. *The Business of Portrait Photography.* New York: Amphoto, 2002.

Schaub, George and Kenneth Sklute. *Professional Techniques for the Wedding Photographer: A Complete Guide to Lighting, Posing and Taking Photographs That Sell.* New York: Watson-Guptill Publications, 2003.

Suess, Bernhard J. *Creative Black and White Photography: Advance Camera and Darkroom Techniques.* New York: Allworth Press, 2003.

Wilson, David, et al. *Photographing People: Portraits Fashion Glamour.* East Sussex, England, Rotovision, 2001.

On Business

ASMP *Professional Business Practices in Photography.* New York: Allworth Press, 2001.

Krages, Bert P. *Legal Handbook for Photographers: The Rights and Liabilities of Making Images.* Buffalo, NY: Amherst Media, 2000.

Piscopo, Maria. *The Photographer's Guide to Marketing and Self-Promotion.* New York: Allworth Press, 2001.

CHAPTER

4

FILM

The cinema is still the great entertainer and has the power to evoke in most people the deepest sentiments and emotions. Working in the film medium provides the broadest and most varied creative opportunities of all today's mass media. Film has developed into a universal art form that transcends cultural differences and geographic boundaries. Because the language of film developed first as a silent visual medium, movies became the most accessible and thus the most international medium of communication. The advent of sound expanded the film language and made it a more complete communication and entertainment medium. Businesspeople have turned it into a multibillion-dollar industry, while purists who value its creative potential continue to experiment with it as an art form.

Films can be broadly classified as features, documentaries, commercials, made-for-TV movies, music videos, industrials, and governmental or educational films. The U.S. film industry went through tremendous changes with the advent of television, and, much more recently, with developments in digital production and distribution technologies. For years, Hollywood was synonymous with the movies, and the major studios dominated the production and distribution of feature films, which had a large domestic and overseas market. Today, the major studios are less involved in production and more engaged in financing and distribution. There are also growing numbers of medium-sized studios and independent production companies.

Until a few years ago, independents were associated with low-budget films. Today, some independent productions are major, big-budget ventures. Developments in technology, especially the miniaturization of equipment, have also made location shooting easier for independent filmmakers by enabling them to shoot in natural locations instead of on expensive sets and sound stages. However, despite the increase in the number of independent films, the feature film industry is still dominated by large studio conglomerates that, traditionally, have limited true creative freedom.

Television, although viewed at its inception as a threat to the film industry, has actually given viewers a greater appreciation for film and has, over the years, fueled further developments in film technology. Many producers prefer to use film as a medium for recording television programs. Today, more than half of prime-time TV programming is produced on film.

The introduction of home videocassette recorders (VCRs) in the early 1980s created a new distribution outlet, and the film industry underwent a resurgence. The recent successful rollout of DVD technology has caused sales of videocassettes to nose-dive but has also provided a replacement technology for the VCR. Despite revenues lost to piracy, the film industry has been able to reap substantial gains from the home video market. According to Adams Media Research, consumers spent $10.3 billion on more than 700 titles distributed on DVD in 2002.

In addition, the more than 35,000 movie screens across the United States continue to provide a strong base for the film industry. New releases during 2002 numbered 449, and U.S. box office revenues totaled $9.5 billion, according to the Motion Picture Association of America (MPAA).

CURRENT CHALLENGES

Three major challenges are currently facing the film industry: "runaway" productions to Canada and other countries; the consolidation of ownership by mega-media companies; and a lack of diversity in hiring. All three factors are making an already competitive job market even more difficult to break into. The good news is that the Directors Guild of America (DGA) and a broadly based alliance have been active at the federal, multistate, and local levels to introduce tax incentives to keep film and TV production in the

United States. If and when the U.S. Senate Bill "Independent Film and Television Production Incentive Act of 2003" is passed, low-budget independent productions filmed in the United States would receive wage tax credits aimed at stemming the flight of production to foreign countries.

During the past couple of years, many large media companies have bought smaller companies. This has resulted not only in a decrease in the number of media companies, but also more competition for jobs because the megacompanies have layed off media professionals during the consolidation process. With regard to the diversity issue, several associations and organizations have taken up the cause and started diversity initiatives. Read more about it in Chapter 11 on "Women and Minorities."

Piracy of U.S. films continues, and member companies of the MPAA, along with DreamWorks and New Line, have launched initiatives to combat digital thievery and to save movie jobs in the future.

On the creative side, the industry is facing the challenge of integrating new digital technologies into the medium while preserving its unique characteristics. According to Dan Curry, the visual effects producer for all ten years of the *Star Trek* TV series, "The blending of film and digital technologies enable us to tell any story, but it's the integrity of the people and their ability to collaborate in realizing a shared vision that really matters."

Almost every feature film now uses digital effects. The results can either be astoundingly obvious, like the liquid metal "cop" in *Terminator 2*, or so subtle, as in *Titanic*, that the audience is unaware of the extent of the illusion.

Many TV series and commercials are shot on film but edited on tape. These productions also rely heavily on computers for animation and special effects. Anyone seeking to succeed in the production or business end of filmmaking must be familiar with the capabilities and limitations of a wide range of digital tools such as 3-D animation, digital compositing, and the use of virtual sets and actors.

THE TECHNOLOGY ADVANTAGE

Modern films make it virtually impossible to tell the difference between what is real and what has been created or computer enhanced. A vast array of tools, including computers from SGI and Apple, software from Alias and

Pixar, and editing systems from Lightworks and Avid, to name only a few, go into creating these illusions. Developments in hardware and software have expanded the scope and job opportunities for animators. The use of animation has expanded from the traditional cartoon films to the creation of virtual worlds in which people can interact with cartoon characters and scenery in game arcades and amusement parks.

Motion control systems allow filmmakers to synchronize the apparent movement of life-sized, miniature, and virtual sets, and to create an array of mystifying visuals. Digital compositing systems combine the images from a variety of sources—film, miniatures, computer graphics, and animation—to create a seamless realization of the director's vision.

Over the past few years, the cost of these tools has continued to plummet, and the skills and techniques developed by creative filmmakers have expanded at warp speed. As a result of falling prices, many small production companies can now afford high-end equipment. Because the special effects and animation work for many commercials and rock videos, and even some features, are done in these "boutiques," they are good places to learn the latest tricks of the trade.

Despite all the advances in technology, success in the film business still demands great creativity and a solid foundation in writing/scripting, cinematography, lighting, visual composition, and, most importantly, creative teamwork.

WHERE THE JOBS ARE

Although the movie industry employs thousands of people in the areas of marketing, advertising, and public relations, most people who want to pursue a career in film are interested in the production area, which involves the actual making of movies. Although feature film production is the most sought-after area of filmmaking, commercials, documentaries, music videos, and educational films also offer a wealth of creative opportunities. These areas often provide valuable experience and can serve as stepping-stones to feature film production. Because more than half of the jobs in all branches of the film industry are done on a freelance, part-time, or contractual basis, career paths are often not as clear-cut as in other media professions. For this reason, up-to-date advice and assistance from teachers, friends, associations, and publications in the business is particularly important.

The Feature Film Market

The entertainment feature film industry is concentrated in Los Angeles and New York City, so those who wish to pursue careers in this field must generally relocate to these metropolitan areas. Other cities, such as Dallas, Miami, San Francisco, and Seattle, also attract independent film producers by offering tax incentives and better production facilities. In Los Angeles and New York, however, extensive communities of independent production companies and specialized service providers have grown up around the major studios and distribution companies, and these provide many entry-level opportunities. The big studios produce an average of ten to fifteen feature films a year. They have impressive facilities that house numerous departments including music, makeup, and props. Landing even a minor job working on a production at a studio "lot" can provide many opportunities for learning and advancement.

The Documentary Film Market

Recent technological advances are fueling impressive growth in the documentary film industry. Public television, commercial TV stations, and cable stations have expanded the market for these programs.

The introduction of the 16mm and super-8mm formats made the task of the documentary filmmaker easier. Miniaturized equipment in the 35mm format and low-cost digital video gear have also streamlined the production process. The affordability of equipment rentals has prompted many individuals to undertake documentary production, and pubic television, commercial TV stations, and cable TV stations provide markets for their programs.

Several well-known feature filmmakers started their careers as documentary producers, and production companies that specialize in the documentary format are good hunting grounds for beginners.

TV Stations

Opportunities for those with training and experience in filmmaking are available at broadcast TV stations. This area is discussed in depth in Chapter 6, "Television and Video."

The Educational Film Market

In recent years, the educational film market has shifted from extensive use of the 16 mm format to Betacam videotape. Although the educational and training fields continue to use VHS tape for program distribution, the increased use of CD-ROM for interactive programming has led to a greater need for interactive program designers and producers.

Industrial Films

The AV/video/multimedia departments of organizations in the corporate and nonprofit sectors are frequently involved in in-house production. However, the corporate use of film has rapidly declined, and many film-based projects are contracted to outside production companies. These films are most often intended as PR vehicles—information sources for employees, stockholders, and consumers, and as training for employees and customers.

Government Films

Each year, agencies of federal and state governments produce many films to disseminate information and training. Some are made using in-house production facilities, while others are assigned to independent filmmakers. Employment at a government agency provides an ideal training ground.

Commercials

Commercials are usually made for the clients of advertising agencies and shown on television and in movie theaters. Major advertising agencies have extensive production facilities. Others contract with independent production companies to produce commercials, although some midsized and smaller agencies do have in-house production capabilities. Commercials are as challenging as any other kind of film and demand strong creativity and technical skills.

JOB DESCRIPTIONS

One way to learn about the many varied job titles in the film industry is to lean back in your theater seat after a film ends and read the almost never-ending list of credits at the end as hundreds of jobs, big and small, scroll down the screen. These, plus the credits at the beginning of the movie, provide an almost complete list of the jobs and on-screen roles involved in the making of that film. Although a major feature film will include literally hundreds of credits, short films or documentaries will not list as many.

In addition to acting, main creative jobs in filmmaking include writing, cinematography, lighting, sound recording, editing, directing, and production.

Scriptwriting

Movies begin with a concept or an idea that the writer then develops into a script. The concept may be a construct of a writer's or filmmaker's imagination, or may be based on real-life incidents or events. Sometimes the original idea may come from the director and the writer is asked to develop it, or a writer may also adapt an existing literary work into a screenplay.

Writers may also develop original ideas and submit them to filmmakers in the form of treatments. Once the treatment is approved, the screenplay is written. The last stage is the shooting script, which the director often develops and which contains technical details and guidelines for shots, camera angles, and lighting. In many films, the scriptwriter's work ends with the screenplay.

Scriptwriters work through agents who work on commission to find them writing assignments or film projects and then negotiate and handle their contracts. Scriptwriters work closely with directors, who are responsible for translating the words into pictures. Often, directors may request or demand alterations to scripts.

Production

Producer The producer is responsible for the financial aspects of a film. When a major studio is providing the financing, a producer is hired to head the production company set up to produce that film. Although producers are mainly responsible for the business side of the movie, they work closely with directors, particularly on the choice of the script and casting the leading actors. These decisions have a major impact on a film's ultimate financial prospects and success.

Production Manager The production manager works in conjunction with the producer and director and prepares a detailed budget and production schedule. Production managers are in charge of the actual production and oversee the entire production process from the planning stage to the editing stage. They are involved in major decisions such as locations, budgets, and scheduling, transporting, and housing the cast and crew. They also have to keep track of each day's production by making sure that the project is moving on schedule and preparing daily reports on its progress.

Direction

Direction is the essence of filmmaking, and that is why the director is often called the "filmmaker." In full-length feature films, the task of direction cannot be handled by one person alone, so assistant directors are hired. Their numbers will vary according to the size and complexity of the shoot.

Director The director's task is to translate the written word to visual images accompanied by an appropriate soundtrack. The director works with actors and other creative talent such as the lighting director to create the overall look and feel of the movie. Directors are in charge of the artistic and technical aspects of films, and the responsibility for the final product rests on them.

Directors make most of the major decisions regarding the movie. They approve the selection of the cast as well as the technical crew and have final say on costumes, sets, and locations. Directors closely supervise photography and editing and decide how each scene should be shot. They are in charge of rehearsals and guiding the actors. As mentioned above, many directors prefer to write the shooting script based on the scriptwriter's screenplay. Some directors also edit their films. In short, the director oversees the work of the entire cast and crew throughout shooting.

Unit Production Manager Unit production managers are in charge of production units on location. They are entrusted with the task of searching for and surveying potential locations and of working out the specific requirements of shooting. They are usually helped by assistant directors.

First Assistant Director Directors often delegate many directorial tasks to the first assistant director, who is charged with organizing the production process. The shooting schedule is usually the first assistant director's responsibility. It involves making sure that the cast and crew receive call sheets in advance. During the shooting, first assistant directors assist the director and keep a close watch over the cast and crew.

Directors often leave many production details to their first assistant director and his or her helpers. Crowd control can be a major task, and first assistant directors may occasionally be charged with directing some routine scenes or background action.

Second Assistant Director Second assistant directors assist the first assistant director. Their main responsibilities include distributing call sheets, handling extras, overseeing the transportation of equipment and crew to locations, and arranging food and accommodations for the cast and crew, as well as coordinating the production staff.

Continuity Person (Script Supervisor) In the past, the person who performed this task was called the "script girl." The continuity person acts as the director's eyes and ears by keeping track of details related to the sequence of events in the film. Script supervisors assure continuity of the film's time breakdown by taking careful notes about the span of days, months, or years between scenes and sequences. They also record details of all the props, costuming, makeup, and other details in every scene of the film to assure continuity. Accuracy of details is important because films are seldom shot in the sequence of events as they appear in the final cut, chronological order, and discrepancies in continuity can damage the film's credibility.

Art Direction

The art direction department handles the physical environment of the film, which determines its mood and atmosphere. The preparation of sets and props, the designing of wardrobe, hairstyling, makeup, and the creation of certain special effects come under this department.

Art Director The art director supervises the above-mentioned operations and is responsible for the physical look of the film. Art directors oversee the production of sketches of the set designs and miniatures, and also select locations in consultation with the director.

Art directors are in charge of the construction of sets and supervise a small army of carpenters, painters, laborers, electricians, and technicians. Art directors are assisted by the chargeman scenic artist and journeyman scenic artists.

Scenic Artists The chargeman scenic artist prepares the miniature models and the journeyman scenic artists assist. They also take care plastering and painting the sets and doing other decorative work on the set walls.

Shop Person The shop person, who is in charge of all the tools and materials required by the scenic artists, supplies materials and supervises cleanup operations after the work is done.

Cinematography

The task of capturing movie scenes on film is called cinematography. Cinematographers, often referred to as cameramen or film photographers, and their assistants use film cameras to capture whatever the director wants on celluloid. Many scenes require several "takes," and directors with big budgets behind them may ask for a dozen or more takes.

Cinematographer The cinematographer, also called the director of photography, works closely with the director to determine the photographic style of the film. Cinematographers are responsible for the overall visual look and thereby the mood that the movie seeks to create. In short, they compose the shots that make up the movie. Cinematographers do not operate the camera, although they check the framing of scenes through the viewfinder. They also make decisions on lighting and camera positions. The selection of different types of shots and the lenses required for them is one of the cinematographer's major tasks.

Cinematographers also work in conjunction with the lab to assure the quality of processing and printing.

Camera Operator The cinematographer is assisted in the composition of shots by the camera operator, who works with the first assistant camera operator, also known as the focus puller. The camera operator handles all camera movements and is responsible for the focus of the shots. Smooth camera movements are important for good photography.

First Assistant Camera Operator The first assistant camera operator's main responsibility is to maintain the camera. First assistant camera operators check the equipment during preproduction and prepare and load the camera for shooting. They are also responsible for changing lenses and filters during shooting, and they must make sure that the camera is running at the right film speed and is in focus. They also help with the crew call sheets.

Second Assistant Camera Operator The second assistant helps the first assistant in the above tasks, also operates the clapper board before each take. This job involves considerable paperwork because the second assistant is in charge of the equipment inventory and must keep records of camera rentals and repairs. The second assistant also handles the shipping of the film shot each day (the "dailies") to the lab and keeps the lab reports on the dailies.

Key Grip The key grip determines the placement of cameras and their movements as required by the camera operator. The key grip also places orders for equipment and works with assistants who take care of a variety of tasks such as placing reflective materials and hanging gels.

Gaffer Gaffers are responsible for lighting. The gaffer offers the cinematographer creative suggestions about lighting and sets up different lighting arrangements as required during the filming.

Sound Recording

The members of the sound recording department record dialogue and sounds during the filming. The sound recording engineer, or mixer, supervises this operation.

Sound Engineer (Mixer) The sound engineer or mixer supervises all live sound generated and recorded during the production. The actors' dialogue and other sounds are recorded during the shooting. The sound engineer is responsible for selecting microphones and overseeing sound levels during the recording to assure the quality of the reproduction.

Recordist The recordist runs individual tape recorders and assists the sound engineer in setting up equipment.

Boom Operator The boom operator sets up the microphones and operates the microphone boom. Boom operators must make sure that microphones never appear in film frames during shooting.

Editing

Editing, although one of the least visible aspects of filmmaking, is perhaps the most crucial stage in filmmaking. Many poorly crafted movies have been saved on the editing table by creative and talented editors who have given new meanings and dynamism to the strips of film submitted to them. Conversely, unimaginative editing can ruin the best-shot film. For these reasons, many of the world's most renowned directors insist on editing their own films—they believe that good films are made on the editing table.

Editor After the dailies are processed in the lab, they are sent to the editor for a "rough cut." The editor studies the footage, selects the best shots, and assembles them in the most effective sequence. The director and cinematographer view the rough cut daily while shooting continues. In the postproduction stage, the sound and the film images are synchronized, and an answer print is made.

Editors create a film's dramatic continuity and determine its pace and tempo. They determine the final combination of image and sound that will appear on the screen and assure the organic unity and aesthetic beauty of the film as a whole. Until editing is complete, the film remains a mass of disconnected bits and pieces.

Dubbing Editor The dubbing editor is the editor's main assistant in the postproduction or rerecording stage. Dubbing editors select the sound and music tracks for mixing and add special sound effects to the dialogue and tracks of natural sound.

Assistant Editor The assistant editor reserves and prepares the editing rooms and works on logging the dailies (each day's film that has been processed by the lab) scene-by-scene.

Editing Room Assistant The editing room assistant is charged with the most boring routines of editing, including splicing, patching, rewinding, coding, and storing film. However, these are also basic skills that any beginner who wants to learn the art of editing must learn.

Makeup Artists Makeup artists and their assistants prepare and apply the actors' makeup. This can be a monotonous routine, but some unusual roles call for originality and creativity.

Acting and Talent Jobs

Actors Those interested in onscreen jobs must take courses in acting. Graduates majoring in theater learn about acting as well as staging and other theater crafts. There are several excellent schools for actors that can be located through an Internet search and books on the subject. Aspiring actors and filmmakers should watch the televised program *Inside the Actors Studio* for firsthand accounts from celebrities, on working in the film industry.

Musicians Musicians in the film industry belong to two categories: music directors and composers, who are responsible for composing film scores, and the musicians, who perform the score as it is recorded. Some scores are original creations, while others are adaptations of existing material.

EDUCATION AND EXPERIENCE

The film industry is one of the most demanding communications settings in which to establish a career. Breaking in is hard for most newcomers, who must start at the very bottom and prove themselves before getting a major assignment. This career path requires a tremendous amount of patience and perseverance. In addition to artistic and technical skills, aspirants should possess considerable organizational ability because the industry requires rigorous planning, scheduling, and budgeting.

The ability to work under deadline pressures is a must for the members of this industry. Being able to work with others and a willingness to take direction—in fact, to take orders—are essential, as is flexibility in making adjustments and accommodations.

Scriptwriters, in addition to writing skills and creativity, must also master the elements of the film language and the basics of filmmaking if they expect to succeed in writing for the visual medium of film.

Producers and production staff need business and organizational skills because they handle both money and people. Skills in diplomacy, negotiation, and problem solving are important when dealing with agents, cast, and crew.

Directors should be versatile people with a sound and complete knowledge of every aspect of filmmaking from scriptwriting to editing. They should also have the patience to work with the many varied kinds of people who collaborate in the making of a movie.

Cinematographers must have formal training in their craft, gained either at a college or institute or through an industry apprenticeship. They must have the ability to work with and take orders from directors, even when they may disagree with their ideas.

Editors too need formal education or extensive apprenticeship experience to be eligible for their trade. They must be able to understand the mind of the director and to collaborate in bringing the film's vision to life.

Actors need discipline as well as talent. Perseverance is the name of the game. Most actors struggle for years and survive by working odd jobs before they get a major role. Even a first important role, however, is no guarantee of success or continued steady employment. Raw talent alone is not sufficient, and formal training from a university or acting institute is required. Basic skills in dancing and singing are also very useful.

The main prerequisite for a job in filmmaking is an earlier job. Students at colleges and universities should build up their portfolios with scripts and student films. An internship with a film production company during college is an invaluable experience.

Film festivals are important stepping-stones for aspiring filmmakers. A number of U.S. competitions and festivals are held nationally each year to locate budding talent, and student films are well received at these events. Awards from these competitions can open the door to future work.

In almost every area of filmmaking, newcomers must start at the bottom. Before becoming scriptwriters, aspiring writers usually acquire credits through their published writing in other media. They should also write sample original scripts to submit at interviews. Many writers attempt to write teleplays for episodes of TV series or stage plays to accumulate credits.

Producers usually gain their jobs after years of waiting and experience, first as production assistants and then as production managers.

The path to the director's chair is also long and arduous. Aspiring directors often start out working as script supervisors and then move on to the position of second assistant director. The next move is to the position of first assistant director, and then to unit production manager. But there is no automatic promotion to the director's chair after that. Directors come from all areas of filmmaking.

Cinematographers go through similar stages of progress. The best entry-level position available to most newcomers is second assistant camera operator, with next step being first assistant camera operator.

Many sound recordists start their careers as boom operators and gradually work their way up into recording and end up as sound engineers.

Similarly, the boring routine of an editing room assistant has been the beginning of many brilliant careers in editing.

Career Development Programs

The major universities with film and television departments offer undergraduate and graduate programs. Notable among them are the UCLA School of Theater, Film & Television (www.tft.ucla.edu), and, on the East Coast, the Kanbar Institute of Film & Television at New York University's Tisch School (http://filmtv.tisch.nyu.edu).

A number of independent institutions also offer hands-on training in filmmaking. In addition, the associations that serve the needs of the filmmaking community offer workshops and courses. Many Internet resources for the film industry feature links to workshops, seminars, and training programs. The following short list will give you an overview of the range of topics and programs available.

- Action/Cut Filmmaking Seminars. These live two-day events, conducted in several cities, feature top-notch film industry veterans including casting directors, writer-directors, director-producers, and documentary filmmakers, among other specialty areas. Details are at www.actioncut.
- The American Film Institute (AFI). The AFI conducts several workshops including its "Directing Workshop for Women," an eight-month program with three weeks of full-time attendance at the AFI campus in Los Angeles. The AFI Conservatory offers a five-semester MFA program. Details are at www.afi.com/education.
- Craig Worsham. This award-winning director of commercials conducts two-day seminars on topics such as how to create an effective "spec" reel, how to find a production company, and how to win jobs. The schedule and seminar locations are posted at http://directingcommercials.com.
- The Foundation of the National Academy of Television Arts and Sciences (NATAS). NATAS offers internships for college students, programs for visiting professionals, and faculty seminars. For more information, visit www.emmys.com/foundation/education.php. The "Events" link on the home page lists upcoming workshops, lectures, and panel discussions on topics such as "The Reel You: How to Sell Yourself with a Great Reel."
- The New York Film Academy. The academy offers courses at its New York headquarters, at Universal Studios in the Los Angeles area, and at King's College in London, England. Summer workshops are held at Harvard University, Princeton University, and in Paris, France, and Florence, Italy. Programs vary in length from four weeks to one year and include topics such as screenwriting, 3-D animation, and acting for film. Details are at www.nyfa.com.

- Rockport College in Maine. Rockport offers a unique environment and excellent courses taught by masters of the medium. Programs are of varying duration, and participants can earn academic credit. Summer jobs and other employment opportunities are posted at www.rockportcollege.edu. You can even test your current level of film knowledge by taking an online quiz.

UNIONS AND GUILDS

Unions, an integral part of the motion picture industry, control the destinies not only of their established members but also of aspirants to the film world. To a great extent, they determine most newcomers' employment prospects.

Writers, actors, producers, and directors call their unions guilds, while other industry labor organizations are called unions.

Two unions dominate the film industry: the International Alliance of Theatrical and Stage Employees (IATSE) and the National Association of Broadcasting Employees and Technicians (NABET).

Theoretically, a newcomer need not be a union member to work in the film industry. However, without work experience a newcomer cannot join a union. It is a vicious circle. Most film production companies and TV networks sign shop contracts with the local unions. Nonunion members can be hired for thirty working days, but after that they must pay the union initiation fee and membership dues to continue working. They need not become formal members, but they must meet the terms of the union shop contract. If they do not, the union can demand their dismissal. Although the unions might seem like big hurdles to some newcomers, they serve their members' interests by defining job titles, job descriptions, duties, remuneration, and benefits.

The Directors Guild of America (DGA) represents film and TV directors, unit production managers, assistant directors, second assistant directors, technical coordinators and tape associate directors, and stage managers and production associates. It currently has a membership of almost 13,000. The guild maintains a qualification list of people who have appropriate experience in each category and makes it available to prospective employers, but does not directly find employment for its members.

The Writers Guild of America (WGA) is a labor union, so writers can become members only if their employer is a signatory to the guild agreement. Among other services, the WGA allows members and nonmembers alike to register scripts so that evidence of the author's copyright can be provided if necessary. Like the DGA, it does not provide employment services.

SOURCES OF INFORMATION

Associations

A number of associations, societies, unions, and guilds have served the film industry over the years. Many also serve the professional audio and video industries. Check Chapter 5, "Radio and Audio in Media and the Recording Industry," and Chapter 6, "Television and Video"; several of the organizations listed there also have special-interest groups that focus on specific areas of filmmaking. Also check the websites of the following organizations. More detailed contact information appears in the Appendix. For ease of reference, some of these listings appear here.

Academy of Canadian Cinema and Television (ACCT) (www.academy.ca)

Academy of Motion Picture Arts and Science (AMPAS) (www.oscars.org)

American Film Institute (AFI) (www.afi.com)

American Society of Authors, Composers, and Publishers (ASCAP) (www.ascap.com)

Association of Independent Video and Filmmakers (AIVF) (www.aivf.org)

Audio Engineering Society (AES) (www.aes.org)

Directors Guild of America (DGA) (www.dga.org)

Motion Picture Association of America (MPAA) (www.mpaa.org)

National Association of Latino Independent Producers (NALIP) (www.nalip.org)

Screen Actors Guild (SAG) (www.sag.org)

SigGRAPH (Computer Graphics SIG of ACM) (www.siggraph.org)

Society of Motion Picture and Television Engineers (SMPTE) (www.smpte.org)

Sundance Institute (http://institute.sundance.org)

Periodicals and Online Resources

Dozens of publications focus on filmmaking. Although some specialize in production aspects, others include information on the casting, acting, and performance sides of the business. Many of these publications cover marketing and other business topics as well. Because film production is interdisciplinary, it would prove useful to check the periodicals listed in other chapters, especially Chapter 6 on "Television and Video." Also check the newsletters, magazines, and journals published by associations. If you are unable to subscribe to a publication of interest, you may be able to read it at a library or borrow it from a production company or a professional in the field. Here is a selected list of recommended trade publications.

Animation World Network (www.awn.com)
Backstage (www.backstage.com/backstage/index.jsp)
DirectorsNet (www.directorsnet.com)
Film & Video (www.filmandvideomagazine.com)
HighDef (www.highdef.org)
The Hollywood Reporter (www.hollywoodreporter.com)
Millimeter (http://millimeter.com)
United Entertainment Media Web Communities
    (www.uemedia.com/cpc/cinematographer)
Variety (www.variety.com)

Directories

Film Canada Yearbook. Toronto, Ontario: Moving Pictures Media. Annual.
Hollywood Creative Directory—Distributors. Hollywood, CA: iFilm
    Publishing, 2004.
Hollywood Creative Directory—Producers. Hollywood, CA: iFilm
    Publishing. Updated three times a year.
Motion Picture, TV, and Theatre Directory. New York: MPE
    Publications, Inc.

Recommended Reading

On Directing

Jarecki, Nicholas. *Breaking In: How 20 Movie Directors Got Their First Start.* New York: Broadway Books/Random House, 2001.

Katz, Steven D. *Cinematic Motion: A Staging and Camera Workshop for Directors, Includes Interactive Online 3-D Storyboards.* Studio City, CA: Michael Wiese Film Productions, 2004.

Patz, Deborah S. *Film Production Management 101.* Studio City, CA: Michael Wiese Productions, 2002.

Rabiger, Michael. *Directing: Film Techniques and Aesthetics.* Woburn, MA: Focal Press, 2003.

Weston, Judith. *The Film Director's Intuition: Script Analysis and Rehearsal Techniques.* Studio City, CA: Michael Wiese Film Productions, 2003.

On Digital Films

Billups, Scott. *Digital Moviemaking: All the Skills, Techniques, and Moxie You'll Need to Turn Your Passion into a Career.* Studio City, CA: Michael Wiese Productions, 2003.

Ohanian T., and M. E. Philips. *Digital Filmmaking: The Changing Art and Craft of Making Motion Pictures.* Woburn, MA: Focal Press, 2000.

On Independent Filmmaking

Donaldson, Michael C. *Clearance & Copyright: Everything the Independent Filmmaker Needs to Know.* Los Angeles, CA: Silman-James Press, 2003.

Simens, Dov. *From Reel to Deal: Everything You Need to Create a Successful Independent Film.* New York: Warner Books, 2003.

On Scriptwriting and Screenplays

Straczynski, J. Michael. *Complete Book of Scriptwriting.* Cincinnati: Writer's Digest Books, 2002.

Vorhaus, John. *Creativity Rules: A Writer's Workbook.* Los Angeles, CA: Silman-James Press, 2000.

On Animation

Kerlow, Isaac Victor. *The Art of 3-D Computer Animation and Effects*. New York: John Wiley & Sons, 2003.

Whitaker, Harold, and John Halas. *Timing for Animation*. Woburn, MA: Focal Press, 2002.

Williams, Richard. *The Animator's Survival Kit: A Manual of Methods, Principles, and Formulas for Classical, Computer, Games, Stop Motion, and Internet Animators*. London: Faber & Faber, 2002.

On Career

Rozwarski, Mickael L. *Life or Movie: Which Comes First?* Parkland, FL: Universal Publishers, 2002.

CHAPTER

5

RADIO AND AUDIO IN MEDIA AND THE RECORDING INDUSTRY

Radio and other audio-related media continue to be the way that most people around the world receive information and entertainment, particularly news and music. The radio "landscape" has changed dramatically over the past decade. Corporate consolidation and automated musical "formats" have reduced the number of jobs available in over-the-air commercial radio, but satellite and Internet radio have created many new opportunities for creative expression and employment.

THE BIRTH OF BROADCASTING

On December 24, 1906, shipboard wireless operators off the New England coast heard the heavenly strains of "Silent Night" and the distant voice of radio pioneer Reginald Fessenden wishing them a Merry Christmas from their radio receivers. After this first extended broadcast of the human voice, Fessenden and others worked on making voice radio practical. Fourteen years later, Westinghouse, in a bid to increase the sales of its radios, founded KDKA in Pittsburgh, Pennsylvania—the first commercial radio station in the United States. Over the next four years, growing numbers of people tuned in, the cost of receivers plummeted, radio advertising fueled the growth of regular programming, and the number of commercial stations in the U.S. rapidly grew to more than six hundred.

The period from the 1920s to the mid-1950s is regarded as the Golden Age of Radio, when, for example, New York mayor Fiorello La Guardia took to the radio air waves during the 1937 newspaper strike to read children the comic strips that appeared in the city's papers. This era is also remembered for on-air personalities such as comedians George Burns and Gracie Allen who softened the hard times of the Depression with their wit; and singer Frank Sinatra on the popular CBS program, "Your Hit Parade." These decades witnessed a flowering of creative expression through radio broadcasts. Most shows were broadcast live, which demanded ingenuity, creativity, and innovation from producers, on-air hosts, and performers.

RADIO TODAY

Radio broadcasts still keep people informed and entertained with their late-breaking news, music, and talk shows. However, communicating through the medium of sound alone is a real challenge because radio as a mass medium leaves communicators with little control over their audience. Still, many on-air personalities manage to keep their audiences tuning in regularly. Technological developments ranging from FM radio to digital recording and Internet radio continue to increase the reach, improve the programming, and fuel the growth of radio broadcasting.

Today, more than 13,000 radio stations in the United States and 30,000 worldwide reportedly broadcast to more than 95 percent of the world's population. According to the Radio Advertising Bureau, total revenues for the U.S. broadcast radio industry in 2002 exceeded $19.4 billion. In addition to traditional radio broadcasts, more than two thousand five hundred Internet radio streams from both conventional and Internet-only radio stations from around the world are available through computers. Hundreds of subscription-based satellite radio channels also give U.S. listeners an unprecedented choice of programming. In addition, many commercial and some college stations have adopted terrestrial (land-based) digital broadcasting systems developed by companies such as iBiquity, that promise better audio quality and additional services for local and regional listeners.

Because of radio's immediacy, local appeal, low cost, and widespread reach, it remains a vital medium. Amateur and ham radio clubs and associations continue to encourage young talent to learn and operate shortwave radio devices and thereby develop new listeners who appreciate the immediacy of communicating over the airwaves.

Localism is over-the-air AM and FM radio's main appeal, while Internet and satellite radio can target "vertical" audiences around the world based on musical taste or other special interests. Many AM and FM stations are focusing more of their programming on local and community matters because content that centers on local interests, from traffic and weather to cultural events and political issues, results in larger audiences. Internet radio includes both broadcasts of live or archived existing radio programming and content prepared solely for Webcasting by Internet-only stations.

Radio programming provides jobs for broadcast journalists, disc jockeys (DJs), on-air hosts, production and technical staff, and sales and marketing professionals. Many TV broadcasters started their careers working in radio before moving on to television. This has been especially true for those in on-air and production positions. Likewise, many professionals now in commercial radio started out in noncommercial radio, and Internet radio sometimes functions as a "farm system" for satellite broadcasters.

AUDIO IN MEDIA

The 1980s and 1990s will go down in history as the Golden Age of Digital Audio. Digital recording, the compact disc, MP3, music video, and stereo television have been more than technological breakthroughs—they have revitalized and transformed the audio industry. These new media have changed the program preferences of audiences all over the world, generated millions of new listeners, and made it easy for the industry to create, present, and distribute high-quality audio content.

Music videos, digital recording, and new modes of distribution are opening up opportunities for recording artists, audio engineers, and entrepreneurs. Developments in sound and video recording techniques and technologies have also expanded employment opportunities in recording studios, live venues, soundstages, and postproduction facilities for film, video, and multimedia.

THE RECORDING INDUSTRY

According to the Recording Industry Association of America (RIAA), U.S. record companies generated $12 billion in net domestic sales in 2002. This represented a 6.7 percent decline, the second year in a row during which revenues dropped after many years of growth. Although consumer demand for American music, ranging from rock to gospel, remains strong, competition from alternative means of access to music has had a major impact. These alternatives range from the distribution of music over the Internet and file sharing of questionable legality to the proliferation of pirated CDs and DVDs. As a trade commodity, U.S. sound recordings are a precious asset and a powerful contributor to the country's balance of trade—U.S. record sales in 2003 totaled more than $12 billion, almost a third of the world total.

The recording industry primarily attracts people with an interest in music. Some have their sights set on cutting albums, others are interested in the recording process and technical achievement, and some are drawn to the glamour, money, and power associated with popular music. The recording industry also employs large numbers of people in sales, marketing, and business management.

THE DIGITAL CHALLENGE

Advances in digital technologies have created challenges for radio, television, and the audio recording industries. The ease with which audio and video content can be copied and shared has forced all these industries to develop new ways to generate revenue and to protect their ownership of their intellectual property. In some areas, revenue losses due to reduced sales has limited job growth. In other areas, though, these same technical and economic trends have created new opportunities and challenges. For example, the increasing automation and regulation of radio advertising and content has resulted in more work for traffic directors, who were traditionally responsible for ad scheduling and billing, because they may now find themselves involved in other aspects of daily radio station operations, sometimes even organizing, logging, and generating reports on the "content" of multiple stations if they work for a large network.

According to the Traffic Directors Guild of America, average salaries for traffic directors in commercial radio in 2003 increased by more than 15 percent, but the number of people in each station's traffic departments and the number of actual broadcast logs being prepared by many multistation operations rose by 27.6 percent. So the salary increase has been offset by the additional workload caused by the increase in logs. In the music business, large recording companies have found it necessary to reduce staff as a result of corporate consolidations, losses caused by digital piracy, and rapid changes in musical tastes and distribution methods. These same trends have also created many opportunities for independent record companies, innovative artists, and pioneers of new music distribution methods and business models. Today, anyone with a PC equipped with a sound card, CD-R drive and software, an Internet connection, a little initiative, and—ideally—some musical talent or taste can start a record company.

A DEMANDING CAREER

Whatever your career interest in radio or professional audio—whether you want to be a DJ, a news reporter or anchor, a sportscaster, a recording engineer, or a producer—you must have an appreciation for the uniqueness of this medium.

Many newcomers to the radio and professional audio field concentrate on mastering the technology. Although good technical skills are required, being able to create good content and understanding the commercial underpinnings of the business are equally important. A solid understanding of the principles, aesthetics, and techniques of producing content for radio transmission, live performance, or distribution through other media such as cassettes or CD-ROMs will serve you well. Likewise, a realistic, down-to-earth grasp of the economic realities of the industry will make it much easier for you to achieve your goals.

It is becoming more difficult to forge a financially rewarding career in the audio and radio fields. Although top talent and upper management can command compensation in the high six figures, most entry-level and lower-echelon jobs provide only subsistence-level salaries. This is particularly true in the smaller markets outside major cities.

Several recent trends have made it even more difficult to land good first jobs in these fields. Widespread consolidations of station ownership and record companies, the increasing use of "canned" formats, and automation are narrowing employment opportunities in some industry segments. Reduced government support for National Public Radio (NPR) has forced budget cuts and adversely affected employment prospects in this area. The recording industry is also suffering from lower profits, which limits the creation of new staff jobs.

Despite these trends, radio and audio are alive, well, and offer plenty of opportunities for those with ambition and the right skills.

THE TECHNOLOGY ADVANTAGE

The use of digital systems in radio and audio has increased rapidly since the 1980s. Digital tape recorders, CD players, digital consoles, digital mixing and editing systems, and hard-disc recorders are in common use at many facilities. So are computer-based automation systems for both content and station management. In recent years, digital transmission systems have come to play an increasingly important role in the radio business.

The use of digital technologies such as iBiquity's HD Radio, which enables AM and FM stations to broadcast their programs digitally for CD-quality reception and the ability to provide new data services, is growing at a rapid pace. Market research firm In-Stat/MDR predicts that almost 40 million digital radio receivers will be in use in the United States by the end of 2006. Familiarity with these powerful tools and their capabilities is important to anyone seeking a job in this field.

Digital technologies have also created new career and business opportunities in audio and radio because the proliferation of narrowcast radio "channels" has resulted in an increased demand for content.

"Low-budget audio production" used to mean "low quality" as well, but inexpensive tapeless "personal studios" and portable digital recorders can now create sophisticated productions on shoestring budgets. "Garage" producers can even master and duplicate CDs and DVDs on their desktop PCs and Macs. Established producers and musicians have also taken advantage of the portability, low cost, and flexibility inherent in Pro Tools and similar computer-based recording systems to enhance their recording processes.

The Internet is also changing the business of music distribution. Independent and "personal" record labels can gain access to worldwide audiences simply by creating websites with audio clips of their latest creations. Even well-known recording artists such as Ryan Adams, Neil Young, and Steve Winwood have sometimes chosen to sidestep the music "industry" and to launch or test-market recordings through their websites. Publicity and promotion costs can also be reduced by creating links to informal networks of websites that share common interests.

Internet radio and other new technologies are also creating opportunities that could not have been imagined just a few years ago. For example, recent NPR job postings included the category of "Online Team." Radio commands a significant presence on the Internet. In addition to the 2,500 radio stations that make much of their programming available on the Web, thousands more have websites that offer a broad range of programming, news, and other information. You can search for stations by type, location, and other parameters at www.radio-locator.com.

By adding Webcasting capabilities, stations can expand their audience well beyond the reach of their transmitters or broadcast networks. For example, NPR is heard around the world via a growing "network" that includes radio stations, cable systems, satellite, and the Internet. At www.npr.org/worldwide, listeners can determine the easiest way to "tune in" to their favorite NPR programs from virtually anywhere on the planet.

Some "radio stations" exist only on the Internet. One of the better known of these is www.bnetradio.com. Others, like www.apnaradio.com, which serves the large Indian-Punjabi, and Pakistani-American populations as well as devotees of Bangra and other music from the subcontinent, target special-interest audiences. Stations that engage exclusively in such "bitcasting" can reach potentially enormous audiences for relatively little cost and may therefore represent the wave of the future. Unlike conventional radio stations, they can often broadcast without the need to obtain governmental licensing that may not be readily available for political or economic reasons. An interesting study of this topic is at: http://iml.jou .ufl.edu/projects/students/derechin/document2.htm.

EXPLORE THE INDUSTRY

The Internet is a good starting point for learning more about radio and the professional audio industry. The following websites will give you an overview of the breadth of information available, including career information such as salary surveys and links to other useful websites.

- Audio Engineering Society (AES) (www.aes.org). AES is the primary organization for audio engineers in both the broadcast and nonbroadcast areas.
- American Society of Composers Authors, and Publishers (ASCAP) (www.ascap.com). ASCAP, the foremost organization for songwriters and composers, is a great resource for information about any aspect of the creative side of the music business.
- Intercollegiate Broadcasting System (IBS) (www.ibsradio.org). IBS is a nonprofit association of mostly student-staffed radio stations based at colleges across the country. More than 800 IBS member stations operate all sizes and types of facilities including Internet Webcasting, closed-circuit, AM carrier-current, cable radio, and FM and AM stations. The association sponsors numerous events across the country, with a total of 160 seminars planned in 2004.
- Mix (www.mixonline.com). This is the Web edition of the leading print magazine for the professional audio and recording trade.
- The National Association of Broadcasters (NAB) (www.nab.org/radio). This website includes information about both radio and television and provides a wealth of data on topics including legal and regulatory issues, science and technology, and research and planning. The "Career Center" page offers career guidance as well as information on employment opportunities within NAB.
- National Federation of Community Broadcasters (NFCB) (www.nfcb.org). The NFCB, an alliance of stations, producers, and others committed to community radio, is a leading advocate for localism, diversity, and public service in radio. The NFCB publishes useful guides and newsletters and sponsors a number of educational programs including the National Youth in Radio Training Project, a

program to empower young people with the skills necessary to start their own radio stations or work at existing stations.

- National Public Radio (NPR) (www.npr.org). At this website, you can select from a list of countries to listen to your favorite NPR programs abroad. The "Inside NPR" page has an area with job postings and internship opportunities. Read the job descriptions to get an idea of what radio employees are expected to do.

- The Radio-Television News Directors Association (RTNDA) (www.rtnda.org). The RTNDA has packed its website with useful information for anyone who wants to learn about the industry as well as for the practicing electronic journalists. It provides a list with links to resources for electronic journalists. You can also find information on a wide range of scholarships, internships, and fellowships offered through or in conjunction with the RTNDA.

- The Recording Industry Association of America (RIAA) (www.riaa.com). This website offers good information, including statistics on the recording industry and a discussion of copyright issues and other concerns facing the industry.

- The Society of Professional Audio Recording Services (SPARS) (www.spars.com). The SPARS community includes audio recording and mastering facilities, manufacturers, engineers, schools, and multimedia specialists—everyone from single-operator studios to large multiroom facilities. Although the society does not have a student membership category, it does work with educational institutions and offers a small student assistance program.

- World Radio Network (WRN) (www.wrn.org/stations.html). This robust website provides a global perspective on news and current affairs as well as links to the websites of international radio broadcasting organizations in several countries worldwide.

WHERE THE JOBS ARE

Radio stations provide a great variety of jobs for creative and competitive communicators in the areas of announcing, programming, traffic, sales, engineering, and management. Radio and audio professionals may also qualify for a variety of jobs at TV stations. Jobs for audio professionals such as music directors, recording artists, sound mixers, and engineers are available at recording studios, video postproduction facilities, rental and staging companies, and live performance venues. In addition, an increasing number of jobs for audio professionals are opening up at production companies and corporate media departments that produce audio for video and other media.

Manufacturers, consultants, and dealers involved with broadcast, professional, and consumer audio equipment are also a source of jobs for those trained in this field.

The Audio Engineering Society (AES) has a membership of more than 10,000 audio engineers, managers, technicians, professors, and students. AES members represent radio and TV stations, audio recording studios, video and film production and postproduction companies, manufacturers of sound equipment, design consultants, dealers, and colleges and universities. The association has an active student initiative and an online job board where AES members can find listings of a wide range of available jobs.

Radio Stations

Radio has long been the most effective medium of mass communications used to rapidly disseminate information over long as well as short distances. Radio relays news faster and to a greater number of people than any other medium. People listen to the radio for news and entertainment in their homes, offices, cars, and even on the beach.

The majority of the more than twelve thousand radio stations on the air in the United States devote most of their airtime to playing some particular type of music, with scheduled updates for news, traffic, and weather. Other stations focus primarily on news, talk shows, and special-interest programming.

Specialized programming formats help give each radio station, or type of station, a distinctive personality. National Public Radio (NPR), for example, is a major supplier of programming for educational and other noncommercial radio stations. If you are interested in working in educational radio, a state-by-state listing of jobs currently available at public radio stations around the country is available at www.npr.org/about/jobs/jobopps. For jobs available at NPR, you can go to www.npr.org/about/jobs/index.html. Information on internships at NPR is available at www.npr.org/about/jobs/intern/index.html.

Working at a radio station can be both exciting and challenging. Your best source for identifying radio stations that have specialized programming formats in particular geographic regions of the U.S. and Canada is the *Broadcasting & Cable Yearbook* published by R.R. Bowker, and available in the reference section of many public libraries.

TV Stations

Job opportunities for broadcasters and audio professionals are available at TV stations. Many TV stations hire people with radio experience to fill positions as newscasters and audio engineers. You can also find a listing of TV stations in the *Broadcasting & Cable Yearbook*. For more information about jobs in broadcasting and a listing of available jobs, go to the NAB Career Center at www.nab.org/bcc.

Production Studios

Recording studios and production companies that record, enhance or "sweeten," master, and duplicate audiotape for the recording, broadcast, film, and video industries have job openings for audio pros. The Society of Professional Audio Recording Studios (SPARS) estimates that there are almost three thousand production studios in the country. The major recording centers in the United States are in New York, California, Nashville, and Chicago. You can identify major facilities in the geographic region of your interest by using *The International Recording Equipment and Studio Directory* (New York: Billboard Publications, Inc.), available in the reference section of most local public libraries. The AES Job Board at www.aes.org/jobs is a good source of current audio-related job offerings.

Corporations

Corporate media departments use audio for video and other media such as AV presentations. The number of jobs for audio-only specialists in this market segment is limited, but corporations with large media departments do hire audio engineers and technicians. Universities and colleges that have broadcasting facilities and live performance venues offer jobs to both programming and technically trained audio specialists. Some speech and foreign language training organizations use the services of audio people to produce foreign language learning tapes.

JOB DESCRIPTIONS

The responsibilities and job functions of radio and audio professionals vary considerably depending on the nature of programming at the radio station or production studio.

Radio Stations

Job titles in the area of programming include program manager, music director, traffic manager, music librarian, announcer or DJ, production manager, public service director, news writer/editor, and scriptwriter.

Programming tasks at all-music radio stations can be quite simple. Typically, broadcasts consist of hour after hour of prerecorded music interspersed with newscasts and public service announcements (PSAs). At some stations, the bulk of this music and other programming is provided by national syndicators or networks. At others, the station management or the station group's management predetermines playlists based on demographic and other considerations. The increased record keeping resulting from regulatory and other requirements has led to a substantial increase in the hiring of traffic managers and directors at music stations over the last decade.

At all-news and talk-radio stations, programming can be quite challenging. These stations require program staff to constantly screen audio news sources such as the wire services and to edit items of interest for the station's primary audience group. Talk-show producers likewise must be on their toes at all times and must possess superior research and people skills. These jobs call for speed, spontaneity, and flexibility.

Many radio stations have contractual affiliations with national radio networks to air certain programs. Network affiliation is advantageous to radio stations with limited staff because they receive hourly newscasts and on-the-spot coverage of major events as well as complete program blocks of preformatted material.

Program Director The program director heads the programming team and is responsible for a staff of writers, producers, and on-air personalities. Program directors schedule broadcasts on a day-to-day basis and handle staff, schedules, budgets, and license renewal applications.

Music Director The music director is responsible for selecting and arranging prerecorded music to fit the station's programming format. An effective music director must appreciate music, share the listening preferences of the station's audience and the station's management, and spend many hours auditioning new records. Music directors often double as announcers and must also be able to interview recording artists.

Music Librarian There are a limited number of jobs for music librarians. Typically, this job calls for cataloging and indexing skills as well as an understanding of relevant music genres and history.

Announcers and DJs Announcers and DJs occupy perhaps the most visible positions at radio stations. According to the U.S. Bureau of Labor Statistics, in 2000 there were about seventy-one thousand jobs for announcers and disc jockeys in the U.S., with intense competition for every job. The number of these jobs in commercial broadcasting is expected to decline slightly over the next few years due to industry consolidation and the increasing automation of broadcast operations. On a brighter note, there should be increased opportunities related to the growth of Internet and satellite radio and the growing popularity of DJs in live performance venues.

Most radio listeners identify programs by referring to the announcer. Good announcers become well-known personalities by building a rapport with their audiences. The job includes reading the news and commercials, interviewing guests, and introducing new recordings. Stations with formats that mix talk and music require on-air personalities who can talk at length, in an entertaining manner, on virtually any topic. Traffic reporting, weather reporting, and news reading are often stepping-stones to more prominent roles in front of the mike. A demo reel that documents an aspiring DJ's or announcer's verbal talent is as important as a résumé or recommendation in landing an on-air position.

DJs Off the Air

Many successful DJs work in clubs, at dance parties, and at other live venues before getting on the air. For aspiring radio personalities, live DJ work can be a source of substantial income and valuable experience. Indeed, live performance and audio mixing is the primary means of income and creative outlet for many DJs. Disco, dub, house, electronica, hip-hop, and other emerging forms of popular music have made the DJ a central figure in the presentation and the creation of musical entertainment. Many DJs have become famous for their mixes, their record production, and their live performances. For example, Tiësto, Sasha, Paul Oakenfeld, DJ Grandmaster Flash, Brazil's DJ Marky, Deep Dish, and other DJs are international superstars. They are role models for the thousands of club and band DJs who make their living spinning, scratching, and mixing discs.

One distinct element of the DJ business is the "record pool," organizations that distribute advance copies of new recordings on vinyl or CD to DJs in particular cities or who spin a particular genre of music. DJs may pay a monthly membership fee to receive large numbers of discs, and they are expected to provide feedback through the pool to record companies and to play charts at clubs. Labels hope that the pool will generate "buzz" for new songs and jump-start record sales. The most popular and influential record pools include the International Music Center Record Pool, Ricketts Record Pool, Direct Hit, and the Latino Unidos Record Pool. *DJ* magazine's website at www.djmag.com and www.allhiphop.com are two good starting points for more information about the rapidly evolving live DJ field.

Other Radio Jobs

Production Manager At larger stations, the production manager has the distinct function of ensuring that programs are aired on schedule. At smaller stations, the functions of program manager and production manager are often combined.

Public Service Director The public service director, also known as a community affairs director, is responsible for ensuring that the station airs PSAs to meet FCC requirements. The public service director must determine community needs and decide which ones call for broadcast exposure.

Not all stations hire a separate person for this function, and public service responsibilities are frequently assigned to programmer-news directors.

News Department The news department of a radio station is an exciting place to work. The jobs of news director, writer/editor, and reporter all call for keeping on top of major breaking news events such as political meetings, disasters, and social issues. This department also covers weather and traffic-related news.

You can learn more about radio journalism through the Radio–Television News Directors Association's website (www.rtnda.org), which includes a job bulletin and other career-related resources.

Scriptwriter Although radio scriptwriting jobs per se are scarce, a number of stations that air radio dramas and talk shows use the talents of good scriptwriters. Scriptwriters who are hired on staff at radio stations are responsible for preparing continuity copy between programs as well as commercial announcements and PSAs.

Radio Sales Radio stations hire sales staff in the positions of general sales manager, national and local sales managers, and radio sales reps. The sales department's primary responsibility is to generate revenue for the radio station by selling advertising time. In any of these positions, you will be required to represent the station and to present demographics on its audience to potential advertisers.

Radio Traffic The traffic department is responsible for the preparation of minute-by-minute schedules and logs at one or more radio stations. Daily schedules contain specific information on all programming and advertising to be aired and the precise time of broadcast. Logs record precisely what was broadcast and when. A radio traffic director or supervisor's job calls for handling schedule changes and maintaining a close watch on all departments to ensure that schedules are met. Larger stations may employ traffic assistants to handle such tasks as traffic flow, record keeping, and billing reports. An increasing number of radio stations are automating traffic functions, and familiarity or experience with traffic management systems such as Marketron and RCS is a plus. At some stations, especially those with limited programming staff, traffic personnel are also responsible for maintaining programming logs to ensure compliance with regulatory, financial, royalties, and other programming-related obligations.

Radio Engineering All radio stations employ broadcast engineers and technicians. Radio stations must meet government regulations, and the engineering department is responsible for this function. The chief engineer is responsible for heading the technical operations team, which installs, repairs, and maintains studio and transmitter equipment. The spread of digital technology into every aspect of radio production and broadcasting has made it necessary for radio engineers to possess a practical understanding of computers, networking, the Internet, and digital audio.

Management and Administration The station manager is responsible for formulating policy and for the overall supervision of the station. The administration department of a larger station may include jobs such as personnel director, purchasing manager, and security officer.

Production Studios and Companies

Jobs in this segment of the industry call for a good understanding of audio production and the ability to use a wide range of audio equipment. Audio professionals who can record, mix special effects (SFX) into sound tracks, edit, and handle multitrack recording and signal routing can apply for jobs at numerous production studios across the country.

Some job titles in the creative area include the following: recording engineer, recording supervisor, rerecording mixer, SFX rerecording mixer, music rerecording mixer, supervisor sound mixer, and production sound mixer. The audio teams who work on sound tracks for the recording and motion picture industries include these jobs, which all involve selecting and mixing music and special effects as specified by the producer. They also entail eliminating noise or other extraneous elements from audio tracks.

On-location recording jobs require expertise in selecting and using microphones, portable mixers, and recorders, and the ability to use noise-reduction and sound reinforcement equipment. Similar skills are required for those involved with audio for live entertainment venues. Companies that rent equipment and those that manage the staging of large events such as concerts also hire professionals with audio expertise.

Postproduction recording facilities require audio professionals to be adept at the audio "sweetening process," which involves enhancing the quality of the soundtrack with music, sound effects, and background "presence." Technically speaking, an audio track is enhanced or sweetened by eliminating noise and disturbance.

Sweetening the audiotrack allows the producer to perfect aspects of the audio that may have been neglected at earlier stages of the production process. Hollywood-scale productions and many large-budget commercial radio "jingles" not only mix various sound sources but often rebuild and replace every audio element. The proliferation of computer-based recording systems with advanced software such as Pro Tools has raised the bar in all areas of audio production, particularly in the sweetening process. These tools make it possible to replace or correct even single syllables or notes, to eliminate unwanted noises, or to add desired sounds and effects such as applause, in seconds.

"Audio-for-video" is the process of mixing and synchronizing audio elements with video images. Talented recording technicians and artists who work on the creative aspects of audio can aspire to such recognition as the 3M Lyra Awards given to Academy Oscar major film sound nominees each year on the Saturday before the Academy Awards, or the the C.A.S. Awards sponsored by the Cinema Audio Society (CAS) for outstanding achievement in sound mixing for motion prictures and television.

Production companies and rental/staging companies also employ audio engineers and technicians whose primary responsibility is to set up and maintain studio and on-location equipment at its optimum performance level.

Audio engineers are often responsible for selecting state-of-the-art equipment and are often called upon to participate in the design and construction of sound rooms, studios, and live performance venues.

Corporations

The only positions in corporate media departments that are dedicated solely to audio are those of audio engineers and technicians. The responsibilities that go with these titles in a corporation are similar to those in a production studio. If you are interested in the creative aspects of audio in a corporate media department, you must also acquire AV production skills.

EDUCATION AND EXPERIENCE

Every year, almost twenty thousand students graduate from radio, television, and communications schools. Most of them go on to seek jobs at radio and TV stations, but the broadcast industry can absorb only a limited number of these graduates—so entry into the profession is competitive and tough.

In the long run, it pays to develop skills in more than one area, such as video, computer networking, and website technologies, that radio stations or studios can use. More than three hundred schools in the country have telecommunications departments that offer courses in broadcasting. A number of these departments offer a structured program of courses in theory and skills development that move students into what is frequently referred to as a "broadcast track."

Many colleges operate their own radio stations and concert venues, thus providing students with the opportunity to gain practical experience. Some junior colleges and community colleges also offer broadcasting courses.

For more information on universities and colleges that offer broadcast courses, check the catalog of the Association of Education in Journalism and Mass Communications (AEJMC); it lists the programs that have gained association accreditation.

Skills for Programming

Programming departments at radio stations require strong writing and oral skills. You must be able to write effectively for the sound medium. Radio journalists must be adept at gathering news and at interviewing. As part of the programming team, you will need to develop technical proficiency in handling microphones, turntables, tape recorders, and media servers.

As a radio announcer, you will be required to have excellent audio presentation skills. You might want to join a debating society or drama group to train in voice projection and control. You should also develop the ability to speak extemporaneously and to ad-lib. DJs and talk-show announcers are top-notch speakers who have the ability to capture and hold audiences with their words and voices.

If you are interested in a radio programming career, you should develop strong research skills and also have a broad knowledge of community, national, and international affairs. Your college training should be a good balance between the liberal arts and specific radio-related skills. Managerial jobs in radio programming departments call for hiring and training newscasters and announcers, scheduling studio and staff, and managing the budget. Those who aspire to the position of program director would do well to get a master's degree in communications or business as well as broad experience in broadcasting.

The Broadcasters Training Network (www.learn-by-doing.com) offers an apprenticeship-based training program through arrangements with mentor/instructors at hundreds of local radio stations. Over the past twenty years, the program has reportedly placed 90 percent of its graduates in broadcasting jobs.

Skills for Radio Sales

A job in the radio sales area of broadcast requires at least a high school diploma, a pleasant personality, and selling abilities because you will be calling on potential advertisers and advertising agencies to sell "spots." You must be able to do research on audiences and to understand ratings so you can present your station's audience demographics to potential advertisers. Basic sales training or some business-to-business sales experience is helpful.

Skills for Radio Traffic

Traffic is one of the fastest growing areas of employment in the radio field. Because many traffic functions are now being automated, traffic supervisors and assistants must have computer skills. A high school education is necessary for these jobs, and junior college or business school training will undoubtedly increase your employment opportunities. Familiarity with traffic management systems from companies such as Marketron (www.marketron.com) and RCS (www.rcsworks.com) is also very useful.

Skills for Radio Engineering

To start a career as a radio engineer or technician, you must have a keen interest in electronics and gadgetry. A high school diploma and technical or trade school courses are necessary for an entry-level job as a radio technician. You must be able to perform a full range of maintenance and repair services.

Many stations prefer to hire technicians with first-class FCC operator's licenses. A chief engineer should have a first-class operator's license and be completely familiar with FCC rules and procedures. To be successful as a radio engineer, you should get a college degree in engineering or two years of technical school training, followed by at least five years of experience as a broadcast technician.

Increasingly, technical jobs in radio and audio require a high degree of computer expertise. For this reason, the appropriate Microsoft or Cisco certification is a significant advantage for those seeking to enter this field. Certification by the Society of Broadcast Engineers (SBE) is also a big plus for those looking to land better jobs in the technical end of radio. Recent surveys have shown that SBE certified engineers earn significantly more than those without such certification.

Skills for Studio and Production Work

Audio professionals should have a good knowledge of production, post-production editing, recording, rerecording, mixing, monitoring, and sound reinforcement techniques. When recording in a studio or in the field, you must be able to recognize the limitations of the room design and acoustics and use appropriate techniques to get the best possible recording. You must also know how to use a mixing console or board as well as multi-channel recorders. In a nutshell, you must know how to use every kind of audio equipment to produce the desired results. A number of trade schools and colleges offer courses in audio recording, mixing, and signal routing.

SALARIES IN RADIO AND AUDIO

Because of the intense competition for jobs in radio and audio, salaries vary considerably depending on experience, skills, and market conditions.

In 2000, for example, half of the DJs at radio stations earned between $6.84 and $14.28 an hour, according to the U.S. Bureau of Labor Statistics. Only the top 10 percent made more than $24.35 an hour. As with most jobs in communications, salaries were higher in larger cities and markets than in small ones. Also in keeping with the competitive "show business" aspects of broadcast communication, star DJs, announcers, and radio hosts often receive star-level salaries, reportedly in the high six-figure range.

This star-power equation is also applicable to other "creative" jobs in radio and audio, with top recording engineers, producers, newspeople, and others receiving large salaries. The same can be said for those in sales and marketing positions, where compensation is usually linked directly to commercial success. For the majority of radio and audio professionals, however, salary prospects remain good but continue to be limited by economic conditions and by the large numbers of people seeking entry into the field.

The 2002 Radio and Television Salary Survey from the Radio-Television News Directors Association/Foundation (RTNDA/F) Research found that radio news salaries were down half a percent in 2001 from 2000; real wages after accounting for a 1.6 percent inflation, actually fell 2.1 percent.

Median Radio News Salaries by Market Size

The survey reflected in Table 5.1 was conducted in Q4 2001 among a random sample of 1,505 radio stations. Valid responses were gathered from 249 news directors and general managers representing 622 stations.

Major markets are defined as those with one million or more listeners. Large markets are from 250,000 to one million listeners. Medium markets run from 50,000 to 250,000 listeners, and small markets have fewer than 50,000 listeners. Since 2000, the only significant growth in news director salaries were in the small markets, and news reporter salaries were down across all markets.

The audio production and recording industries have suffered from revenue losses due to Internet audio file sharing and other factors. Despite this, Monster.com predicts that overall employment in some very competitive specialties, such as broadcast and sound technicians, is expected to grow by about 9 percent through 2008. Salaries for audio engineers and technicians currently average from $15 to $50 per hour.

TABLE 5.1 Median Radio News Salaries by Market Size

	Major	Large	Medium	Small
News Director	$46,000	$33,000	$28,500	$23,000
News Anchor	38,500	29,000	24,000	22,000
News Reporter	34,900	22,000	21,000	18,500
News Producer	37,000	*	26,500	23,000
Sports Anchor	35,000	29,500	21,500	*

*Insufficient data.

Source: RTNDA/Ball State University Annual Survey. Reprinted with permission from the RTNDA/F.

Entry-level jobs in the business areas of the audio recording industry are often at the subsistence level, but successful producers, marketers, and management are among the best paid personnel in any medium.

Since 2000, salaries in most areas of radio and audio have remained flat, due in part to the post-9/11 economic downturn.

SOURCES OF INFORMATION

Associations and Societies

Some of the organizations listed here do not have a student membership category, but you will benefit from learning more about industry issues and careers by accessing their websites. Also check the list of associations in Chapter 6 for organizations that cover both radio and TV broadcasting, and Chapter 7 for those that serve the audio segments of the media community. More detailed contact information for the following organizations appears in the Appendix. For ease of reference, some of these listings appear in several chapters.

American Society of Composers, Authors, and Publishers (ASCAP)
  (www.ascap.com)
American Women in Radio and Television (AWRT)
  (www.awrt.org)
Audio Engineering Society (AES) (www.aes.org)

Cinema Audio Society (CAS) (www.cinemaaudiosociety.org)
Institute of Electrical and Electronics Engineers (IEEE)
(www.ieee.org)
National Association of Broadcasters (NAB) (www.nab.org)
Radio-Television News Directors Association (RTNDA)
(www.rtnda.org)

115
Radio and Audio in Media
and the
Recording Industry

Periodicals

Here is a short list of recommended publications that have served this industry for years. Some are available only to those currently working in the field, but many radio and audio hobbyist periodicals, such as *Stereo Review*, are available at bookstores and newsstands. If you are unable to subscribe to a publication of interest, you may be able to read it at a library or borrow it from your local radio station, a recording studio, a production facility, or a professional in the field.

AES Journal (www.aes.org/journal)
All HipHop (www.allhiphop.com)
ASCAP Playback (www.ascap.com/playback)
BE Radio (www.beradio.com)
DJ (www.djmag.com)
Djzone (www.djzone.net)
Mix (http://mixonline.com)
PlayBack (Canada) (www.playbackmag.com)
Pro Sound News (www.prosoundnews.com)
Professional Sound (www.professional-sound.com)
Rental and Staging (www.rentalandstaging.com)
Sound and Communications (www.soundandcommunications.com)

Directories

ASCAP's Guide to Resources in the Music Business. New York: American Society of Composers, Authors and Publishers. (www.ascap.com/resource).

Broadcasting & Cable Yearbook. Washington, DC: Broadcasting & Cable
   Publications. Annual. (www.bowker.com/bowkerweb/catalog/
   prod00100.htm).

Directory of Religious Media. (on CD-ROM). Manassas, VA:
   National Religious Broadcasters. Annual. (www.nrb.org).

Recommended Reading

On Radio

The Associated Press Broadcast News Handbook. New York: McGraw-
   Hill/Contemporary Books, 2000.

Edwards, Bob. *Edward R. Murrow and the Birth of Broadcast Journalism.*
   New York: John Wiley & Sons, 2004.

Geller, Valerie, and Turi Ryder. *The Powerful Radio Workbook.* New
   York: M Street Corporation, 2000.

Hausman, Carl. *Announcing.* Belmont, CA: Wadsworth Publishing, 2003.

Laster, Clay. *The Beginner's Handbook of Amateur Radio.* 4th ed. New
   York: McGraw-Hill, 2000.

Maltin, Leonard. *The Great American Broadcast: A Celebration of Radio's
   Golden Age.* New York: New American Library, 2000.

Priestman, Chris. *Web Radio: Radio Production for Internet Streaming.*
   Woburn, MA: Focal Press, 2001.

Schultz, Bradley. *Sports Broadcasting.* Woburn, MA: Focal Press, 2001.

Utterback, Ann S. *Broadcast Voice Handbook.* 3rd ed. Chicago: Bonus
   Books, 2000.

Weigant, Chris. *Careers As a Disc Jockey.* New York: Rosen Publishing
   Group, 1999.

Zemon, Stacy. *The Mobile DJ Handbook: How to Start & Run a
   Profitable Mobile Disc Jockey Service,* 2nd ed. Woburn, MA:
   Focal Press, 2002.

Audio and Recording

Alten, Stanley. *Audio in Media: The Recording Studio.* 6th ed. Belmont,
   CA: Wadsworth Publishing, 2001.

Avalon, Moses. *Confessions of a Record Producer: How to Survive the Scams and Shams of the Music Business.* 2nd ed. San Francisco: Backbeat Books, 2002.

Baskerville, David. *Music Business Handbook & Career Guide.* 7th ed. Newbury Park, CA: Sage Publications, 2000.

Brice, Richard. *Music Engineering.* Boston, MA: Newnes, 2001.

Nisbett, Alec. *The Sound Studio: Audio Techniques for Radio, Television, Film, and Recording.* 7th ed. Woburn, MA: Focal Press, 2003.

Passman, Donald S. *All You Need to Know About the Music Business.* 5th ed. New York: Free Press, 2003.

Schultz, Barbara. Editor. *Music Producers: Conversations with Today's Top Hitmakers.* Auburn Hills, MI: Intertec Publishing Corp., 2000.

Whitaker, Jerry C. Editor. *Master Handbook of Audio Production.* New York: McGraw-Hill/TAB Electronics, 2002.

Zemon, Stacy. *The Mobile DJ Handbook: How to Start & Run a Profitable Mobile Disc Jockey Service.* Woburn, MA: Focal Press, 2002.

TELEVISION AND VIDEO

Television's ability to grab viewers emotionally and intellectually has made it the dominant news and entertainment medium for more than half a century. Recently, the Internet has begun to compete with broadcast television for the top spot in the media food chain. In the near future, we can expect to see Internet TV, a combination of the two, delivering information to us and changing the ways that we work, learn, and play.

Television continues to be the instant informer, the effective teacher, the primary persuader, and the great entertainer. Over the past decade, advancements in TV technology have dramatically changed the nature of news. We can now deliver, and see, news as it happens—instantly, accurately, and vividly. Television as a teacher has revolutionized education by making learning more interactive and interesting while increasing access to learning through distance learning programs. The persuasive power of television commands billions of advertising dollars annually. Television encourages consumers to buy, helps politicians and social activists to mold public opinion, and enables preachers to spread their message. As an entertainment medium, television brings both the amazing and the banal right into the living room. In short, the influence of television on our society has been and remains incalculable.

Rapid technological advances have expanded the uses of television and video in all sectors of society, including business, for applications such as employee communications, training, and marketing.

The cable TV industry has also seen significant growth. Originally developed to bring network broadcasts to remote communities, cable TV now delivers a wide range of programming. It has created many opportunities for producers of specialized programming to find their audiences. The growth of cable TV and its sibling technology, direct broadcast satellite, has created a rapidly expanding market for programming on every subject from cooking to religion.

The widespread use of all forms of video and television has led to a multibillion-dollar industry and generated employment opportunities in the programming, production, technical, marketing, and administrative areas.

CURRENT CHALLENGES

In the broadcast market, the consolidation of TV stations and network ownership, coupled with the increasing automation of some technical operations, has made an already very competitive job market difficult to crack. Many entry-level opportunities still exist in all areas, but stronger skills and more experience are required to compete for these jobs.

In the corporate arena, the dual trends of downsizing and outsourcing have reduced in-house opportunities, especially those at the nonmanagement level.

Because many organizations are increasing their use of video communications while at the same time reducing staff, the best career opportunities are often found in independent production companies that are taking up the slack.

The rapid convergence of video, Internet, computer, and telecommunications technologies has created new challenges for employers and job seekers alike.

Many companies have found it difficult and expensive to keep up with the "state of the art" in TV and video systems. Digital TV production, management, and transmission systems offer real competitive advantages, but they also carry a large price tag and a steep learning curve. Job seekers may find it difficult to get valid hands-on experience with the latest tools and technologies.

Digital technologies of all kinds have invaded the traditional analog world of television and video. Digital video recorders, digital nonlinear editing and special effects systems, studio automation with robotic camera operators, and digital transmission via satellite and fiber optics are just a few of the new tools that are making this versatile medium even more efficient and powerful.

On the high end, they allow producers and broadcasters to deliver spectacular images to bigger audiences—at the cost of investing millions in the necessary hardware, software, and distribution infrastructure. On a more modest scale, industrial and independent producers can now create and distribute broadcast-quality programs at a fraction of what they would have cost just a few years ago. Many schools can now afford basic digital video compact (DVC) camcorders and nonlinear editing systems that allow teachers to train students in basic skills that they will need to succeed in the real world.

Digital (nonlinear) editing has had perhaps the greatest impact on the way that television is produced and delivered. Nonlinear systems range from simple PC- or Mac-based systems that cost less than $2,000 to multi-megabuck supercomputer studios. These systems all allow video, audio, computer graphics, and special effects to be edited on computer in a random-access or nonlinear fashion, thereby saving time and money while multiplying the creative possibilities. The differences between entry-level units and big budget systems are primarily in their speed, the quality of the finished product, and their ability to create seamless blendings of real-world and computer-generated images.

Those who have the skills and knowledge to blend television, multimedia, and the Internet will find a wealth of opportunities in TV and video production, operations, sales, technical areas, and management.

INSIGHTS OF WORKING PROS

New York and Los Angeles are the headquarters for most companies that specialize in the production of commercials for advertising agencies. New

York, Hollywood, Chicago, Dallas, Nashville, and Miami all have a large number of companies that focus on producing music video and entertainment programs. Every major city has hundreds of small and large production companies that offer job opportunities to video professionals. But to work in a production company, large or small, you must have both creative and technical skills.

Norry Niven, a partner in Dallas-based Stone Core Films, has received five Emmy Awards for his network promotions and dozens of awards for his varied film works. He has directed hundreds of national commercials for such varied companies as Sears, Chrysler, Perrier, Sea World, and The Movie Channel. In discussing the career of a director/producer, he says, "Directing a commercial requires many different skills. The first and most important is the ability to understand the intent of the creative. What is the purpose of the communication in a given commercial? Without an understanding of that, a director is lost. The second skill is the ability to place a 'style' upon the commercial—to decide the direction of the spot. This may sounds simple, but the director will be required to hold up that style and see it through the completion of the commercial. The third skill is to manage people.

"There are many different people and personalities involved in the production of a commercial. So it isn't enough to be able to simply manage a crew or to direct talent. In fact, a director of commercials spends the least amount of time directing talent. People skills are called into play from the first conference call with the advertising agency and continue all the way through to the postproduction facility."

Niven, who has been directing commercials and music videos for fifteen years, says that whether you are directing a commercial or a music video, your goal should be to inspire your team to a higher creative aesthetic: "I think that a director should inspire and excite those people involved in the creative process to make the most incredible commercial possible. The director's goal should be the creation of pure art, and, to achieve that, it is necessary to rally the production team around that effort. That is the number one skill a director should possess. Forget the limitations of budget, at least in the initial part of the process, and allow the spot or the music video to become what it has the potential of becoming. In film, as in any art form, making the viewer feel emotion is paramount to the artist. Selling products or entertaining viewers will naturally follow after this emotional goal is reached."

Corporate or nonbroadcast TV production calls for most of the creative skills involved in producing TV programs and many of those used in feature film production. According to James Tusty, president of Mountain View Group, headquartered in Schenectady, New York: "All creative work requires a curiosity to learn about new things, but corporate work tests one's ability to learn the subject matter of a wide range of topics. Also, most clients do not have film production experience and often don't know exactly what they want. It can take some patience to guide them through the process. So those who simply want to 'get the job done' will likely fail."

Nearly fifty percent of Mountain View Group's seventeen employees are media professionals. When hiring, Tusty looks for attributes such as a strong willingness to "do whatever it takes." He concedes: "I value a liberal arts education more than a background in film production because we are doing films on a variety of topics. It always helps when you have some base knowledge related to the client's business. A little math, a little music, a little history—all help at different times. The technical part of making films is the easy part. Truly becoming an effective communicator takes a lifetime of experience."

WHERE THE JOBS ARE

Commercial Broadcasting Companies

Because almost two-thirds of U.S. TV channels are allocated to commercial stations, most jobs in the broadcast industry are available at those stations.

Networks The largest and best-known commercial TV enterprises are the three major networks: Columbia Broadcasting Services Corp. (CBS), National Broadcasting Corp. (NBC), and American Broadcasting Corp. (ABC). Commercial TV stations that are associated with the networks and receive network feeds via microwave, satellite, or fiber-optic transmissions are known as network affiliates. But, in recent years, the monopoly of the big three has been broken by networks such as Fox, UPN, and Warner Bros. (WB), which have gained momentum and are competing for first-run original programming.

Independent Stations Commercial TV stations that are not affiliated with a network are referred to as independent stations. Within this group are stations owned by companies like Cox, Jones Intercable, and Time Warner, which air entertainment and educational programs. Independents use a variety of sources, including syndicated shows, for programming. Although it is not uncommon for an independent station to rely heavily on the use of movie classics and reruns of programs previously shown on the networks, many also generate local news and other original programming. A number of nationally known broadcasters began their careers at independent stations.

Cable TV The fastest growth in the industry over the past few years has been in cable TV. This tremendous growth has led to keen competition among stations for original programming, which in turn has led to the birth of new production companies and resulted in more jobs. Some cable operators offer consumers "premium" monthly services such as HBO, Showtime, and the Disney Channel, or pay-per-view (PPV) services. The increase in programming resulting from the demand for made-for-cable movies, "specials," and PPV coverage of sporting events and concerts has also led to an increase in production and technical jobs.

Some cable TV operators also create their own local news and special-interest programming, provide access channels for public and institutional uses, and lease access channels to providers of such services as electronic shopping. All these activities create opportunities for entry-level jobs.

Regional cable networks such as SportsChannel, NY1, and Cable News that focus on news and sports programming are gaining increased viewership. A number of local cable TV channels also maintain their own websites that include information about related job and internship opportunities.

Cable stations all across the country are hungry for original programming. Because of cable's focus on individual communities, it can air programming that the networks might consider too narrow in appeal—hence, the explosion of growth in special-interest programming.

The Cable Advertising Bureau's (CAB) website (www.cabletvadbureau .com) is a good source for statistics and related information on the state of cable TV and ad-supported cable TV.

Noncommercial Broadcast Companies

The FCC assigns channels to communities for noncommercial educational TV stations. Public broadcasting stations are operated by nonprofit institutions such as local community groups, universities and colleges, and religious institutions. These not-for-profit stations do not sell time for commercials, so they depend on funding from foundations, corporations and local businesses, and individual viewer contributions. Public broadcasting stations are expected to provide programming on topics that usually would not be supported by commercial stations.

CPB In 1967, Congress passed the Public Broadcasting Act, under which federal funds were allocated to public broadcasting. The Corporation for Public Broadcasting (CPB) was set up as a nonprofit organization responsible for receiving, distributing, and administering federal funds for the entire system. Congress appropriates federal tax dollars for the public broadcasting system. The appropriation for fiscal year 2004 is $377.8 million.

CPB also receives grants from foundations and corporations for specific projects.

These grants allow CPB to fund a variety of public service and telecommunications projects, including helping communities and creating inventive and effective new uses of technology for education. CPB is the largest single source of funding for public TV programming. To search for available positions in public broadcasting, go to www.cpb.org/jobline.

PBS In 1969, CPB established the Public Broadcasting Service (PBS) to manage the production and distribution of programs and connections among local stations within the system. Most PBS employment opportunities are at its headquarters in Alexandria, Virginia, but you should also check with your local PBS station for jobs in your area. PBS hires professionals with experience in communications, creative services, program development, program acquisition and scheduling, educational services, engineering, broadcast and technical operations, video marketing, interactive services, and a variety of other areas. To check out available positions at PBS, go to www.pbs.org/aboutpbs/aboutpbs_jobs.

PBS is the largest noncommercial network in the United States and has for years been referred to as the "fourth network." Through its 349 noncommercial TV stations, PBS reportedly serves almost a hundred million viewers each week. The major package of programs distributed to member stations includes children's, cultural, educational, news and public affairs, science and nature, fund-raising, and skills programs.

PBS's Adult Learning Service, a partnership between public TV stations and more than two thousand colleges and universities, provides college-credit TV courses to more than four hundred thousand students each academic year. In the area of education, the Teacher Resource Service provides instructional programs and related materials for classroom use in grades K–12. PBS also provides national advocacy and leadership for the use of learning technologies in elementary and secondary schools.

ITVS The Independent Television Service (ITVS) is concerned with keeping public television public. It was founded when a group of independent film and video producers noticed that most independent programs funded by PBS were produced by local PBS affiliate stations. The group took its demands that the funding be spread more widely to the CPB and to Congress. As a result, ITVS was created, with CPB funding, to fund, distribute, and promote independent film and video productions by independent producers on a range of subjects and viewpoints that might not have received funding from PBS and CPB. Visit www.itvs.org/producers for resources designed to help producers.

Public Access Cable TV Local cable TV franchise agreements obligate operators to provide "public access" to the community. Check with your local system to find out about the resources available, which may include the use of professional equipment and facilities, sometimes at very low cost, in addition to air time for your program.

According to the Alliance for Community Media (ACM), a nonprofit, national advocacy group that represents community media centers and provides them with critical support: "Public, Educational, and Governmental (PEG) access television channels on cable TV serve a wide range of community organizations, including churches, synagogues, Lions and Rotary Clubs, local political party organizations, high schools, and colleges. Through PEG access centers, thousands of community groups and over one million individuals produce more than 20,000 hours of new local programming each week."

ACM's membership consists of more than a thousand organizations that provide PEG access services. These channels can be good ways to get "real world" TV experience while also having a positive impact on your community. To learn more about community media, visit www.alliancecm.org.

Teleproduction and Postproduction Facilities

The increased demand for original programming has led to rapid growth in the number of production companies nationwide. Many postproduction facilities that had invested in high-end editing suites with sophisticated 3-D paint and animation technology are now in the business of producing commercials, infomercials, and half-hour situation comedies (sitcoms). Large production companies such as Lorimar and MCA produce programs for syndication or cable television. These programs include game shows, made-for-TV movies, sitcoms, and "specials."

Every major city has hundreds of small and large production companies that offer job opportunities to video professionals. Most companies maintain a small full-time staff but flesh out their crews with freelance help on a project-to-project basis. Producers of programs for the consumer, corporate, or broadcast markets use the high-end editing suites and production studios of companies referred to as postproduction facilities. Large companies such as the Post House in Hollywood and Unitel in New York City known as full-service companies, offer a complete range of production and postproduction equipment and services.

Some companies specialize in DVD authoring (i.e., specialized programming to enable user interactivity) and premastering (i.e., processes to prepare a master disc from which copies are made), while others specialize in tape duplication and disc replication, including packaging and distribution for the home entertainment and corporate/institutional markets. The hiring emphasis in these firms is on engineers, technically skilled personnel, and marketing/account executives.

Corporations and Nonprofit Institutions

Corporations and nonprofit institutions use television and video extensively for training, sales and marketing, employee communications and other nonbroadcast uses. This segment of the industry is frequently referred to as organizational TV, corporate TV, corporate media, business TV, or professional video. It embraces all organizations—business and industry, educational institutions, government agencies, and other not-for-profit institutions such as hospitals and museums. These organizations are not media companies in that their primary business is not the making and distribution of television and video. Rather, they use media technologies to communicate more effectively with their specific audiences, such as employees, customers, and stockholders, or, in the case of nonprofit institutions, donors, supporters, corporate sponsors, and the public.

Although most programs produced by these organizations are not broadcast, some larger corporate media departments transmit their programs to other geographic areas using broadcasting technologies. Many companies also use videoconferencing and satellite technologies to reach audiences at multiple locations.

Media Communications Association-International is the foremost industry association in the organizational TV area. Its members represent corporations; health, medical, and educational institutions; video production and postproduction facilities; manufacturers, dealers, and distributors of equipment; and service companies. Many of these companies have full-fledged video departments staffed by managers, producers, directors, writers, designers, technicians, and engineers. However, in-house corporate media departments are among the first to be hit by corporate downsizing, reengineering, or other cost-cutting and employee-reduction measures. Fortunately, during such times a corporation's need for video and other media continues and often increases, so corporations then outsource by hiring independent producers to make their programs. And with outsourcing comes the birth of new production companies.

Government Organizations

The largest government-operated broadcast enterprise is the U.S. Armed Forces Radio and Television Services (AFRTS). It operates more than a thousand radio and TV outlets in more than 175 countries and U.S. territories as well as on board U.S. Navy ships. In some cities, AFRTS operates out of conventional broadcast stations; in others, it operates closed-circuit television (CCTV) operations. AFRTS employs both military and civilian personnel to operate its TV facilities and to create programming.

Other government agencies at the local city or county, state, and federal levels also use television extensively. Although few broadcast programs, most operate and maintain AV equipment. Some departments generate their own programming, while others contract with independent production companies to develop programs, and still others rent or purchase prerecorded programs.

At the federal level, the U.S. Bureau of Land Management (BLM) uses video to communicate internally within the bureau, with other government agencies, and with the public regarding the approximately 262 million acres of public land that it manages. The BLM produces courses that are broadcast through its satellite network to more than 130 locations nationally. Local BLM offices have their own videographers who produce programs at the local level.

Other government agencies that use video include public health, postal services, transportation, agriculture, and law enforcement. County, city, and state agencies are finding that, with cutbacks in workforce and tight budgets, video is an effective medium for disseminating information to employees and citizens. Some counties are using local cable TV channels to transmit their programming.

The foremost organization that serves professional communicators in this area is the National Association of Government Communicators (NAGC).

SALARY INFORMATION

A number of organizations report on employment figures, salaries, and fringe benefits of TV and video employees based on surveys of their members or of specific segments within the industry. These surveys, usually conducted on an annual basis, allow those working in the industry to compare their income with national norms. Survey results will give you a good indication of the opportunities available by various job titles as well as current salary ranges for those jobs.

Because salaries reflect the general health of the industry to some extent, survey results should give you some insight into how those working in the industry are faring financially. You'll be able to judge which segments of the industry are doing well or facing hard times. In addition, a number of survey reports will point out trends in salary increases or decreases.

However, you should take salary and employment statistics with a grain of salt because the methods for gathering and analyzing data vary quite a bit from study to study.

To further complicate matters, finding the truth in this welter of data sometimes requires more complete analysis than is provided in summaries and published accounts.

A good source of useful information that can be accessed on the Web is the *Occupational Outlook Handbook*, published annually by the U.S. Bureau of Labor Statistics and available at www.bls.gov.

Compensation in Broadcast Organizations

The *RTNDF/Ball State University Survey* reports on salaries for both radio and television by job title and market size.

The NAB is another source for information about salaries at broadcast companies. The following tables are from the *2001 NAB/BCFM Television Employee Compensation and Fringe Benefits Report*.

Questionnaires requesting information about salaries and fringe benefits were mailed to all 1,095 U.S. commercial (nonsatellite) TV stations in May 2001. Of these, 441 stations returned useable questionnaires for a response rate of 40.3 percent.

From the information collected, 31 tables were prepared based on revenue categories, station type (affiliated or independent), and other criteria. Fox affiliate stations were included with ABC, CBS, and NBC affiliates, and UPN, PAX, and WB were separated from the other affiliates.

Table 6.1 summarizes average and median base salary figures for fifteen different department heads as well as average and median annual bonus figures. Also included are average annual and average starting salaries of twenty support staff positions.

The table also includes salary and compensation averages for sales staff as well as average, high, and low total compensation for account executives. A few TV stations included "regional sales manager" in either the national sales manager or local sales manager salary and compensation, so care should be taken when using the reported values for these positions.

Compensation in Nonbroadcast Organizations

TV and video professionals who work in the field of corporate or organizational TV will tell you that, although it may not be a road to fame or fortune, it does offer far more in terms of career choices than broadcast companies can. Although an on-air job at a broadcast station may offer a great deal of glamour, most people in the business agree that there is very

TABLE 6.1 Average and Median Base Salaries for Television Employee Compensation and Fringe Benefits

Department Heads	Average Base Salary	Average Bonus	Median Base Salaries	Median Bonus
General Manager	$163,172	$56,049	$150,000	$36,596
Assistant General Manager/				
Station Manager	104,156	24,555	95,500	15,500
Operations Manager	57,573	6,127	51,500	4,210
Program Director	53,320	8,796	45,000	4,250
Director of Engineering/				
Chief Engineer	66,412	8,136	61,781	4,625
News Director	83,986	9,230	75,000	5,950
Marketing Director	59,764	8,966	53,000	6,000
Promotion/Publicity Director	52,281	5,663	46,000	3,885
Production Manager	45,615	3,879	41,493	2,000
Business Manager/Controller	62,383	8,493	57,569	5,000
Traffic Manager/Supervisor	37,917	3,589	36,000	1,500
Community/Public Affairs				
Director	47,464	4,571	41,835	2,150
Art Director	47,568	3,325	45,000	1,100
Research Director	49,353	4,390	44,610	1,881
Human Resources Director	44,260	4,735	41,500	1,810

Support Staff	Full-Time Employees	Years Employed at Station	Average Annual	Starting Annual
Operator Technician	8	8	$28,551	$21,473
Maintenance Technician	4	12	38,369	28,730
Technical Director	4	8	30,577	24,603
Floor Director	3	9	27,760	22,028
Film/Tape Editor	3	7	27,190	22,254
Film Director	1	12	32,474	26,565
Weekday News Anchor	4	7	80,592	49,658
Weekend News Anchor	2	4	44,762	34,568
News Producer	6	3	30,287	25,035
News Reporter	7	5	34,647	26,885
News Photographer	9	6	28,996	23,364
Weekday Sportscaster	1	8	65,779	42,843
Weekend Sportscaster	1	4	37,405	29,358
Weekday Weathercaster	2	6	70,561	43,759
Weekend Weathercaster	1	3	36,655	30,703
Assignment Editor	2	5	34,925	27,325
Production Assistant	4	5	22,233	18,687
Producer/Director	4	8	34,818	26,072
Staff Artist	2	6	31,740	25,961
Traffic/Assistant	2	6	23,326	20,313

**TABLE 6.1 Average and Median Base Salaries for
Television Employee Compensation and Fringe Benefits,** *continued*

Sales Management	Salary Average	Other Compensation Average	Sales Personnel		
General Sales Manager	105,719	38,664	# of Account Executives: 8		
Local Sales Manager	77,839	30,246	Total Compensation		
National Sales Manager	77,437	30,126	Average	High	Low
Co-op Coordinator	45,118	30,908	66,542	103,581	37,343

Source: Reprinted with permission from the 2001 NAB/BCFM Television Employee Compensation and
Fringe Benefits Report. Copyright 2001, National Association of Broadcasters, 1771 N Street N.W.,
Washington, DC 20036. All rights reserved.

little, if any, job security. It is often said that in broadcast television you are
only as good as your most recent ratings. Those who work in corporate
video, however, seem to experience more job security.

Major cities like New York, Los Angeles, and Chicago offer many attractive opportunities for employment in television and video. But because
they also attract a glut of talent, the job market in these cities is very competitive. A better place to look for entry-level positions is in "secondary"
markets—midsized cities that are large enough to support a thriving production community.

The pay for the same job may vary quite a bit depending on the industry. A producer in a hospital media department may not earn a salary comparable to a producer at an aerospace company. Similarly, writing a
freelance script for a local corporate training tape will pay considerably less
than a comparable writing job for a glitzy product introduction video.

A 2004 compensation and financial survey by the International Communications Industries Association (ICIA) includes data gathered from its North
American membership. Anyone who works in or is seeking a job in management, sales and marketing, administration, or the technical side of the AV
industry should read this report. It offers detailed statistics on salaries for
more than thirty positions sorted by type of company, revenue, number of
employees, geographic region, and population of nearest city. In addition, the
report includes detailed financial data on revenues, profits, and end markets.
Copies of the report are available from ICIA at www.infocomm.org or by calling (800) 659-7469.

In addition, publications such as *AV Video/Multimedia Producer* conduct annual salary surveys and report on the data.

JOB DESCRIPTIONS

Broadcast Companies

In the broadcast industry, job titles and responsibilities are classified into five areas: program/production, news, sales, engineering, and administration. At a small station, one person may be called upon to handle a wide variety of assignments. At a large station, job functions are more specialized. A small station environment is the best way to develop versatility. The more jobs you can do well, the better and faster your chances of career advancement.

Program Production Among the job titles at a TV station are program manager, operations manager, TV producer, TV director, TV production assistant, scriptwriter, floor manager, set and props manager, art director, TV tape-film manager, TV staff announcer, and research director. Each of these jobs has distinct functions and responsibilities. For example, program managers need a thorough knowledge of how the entire station operates. In particular, they must have the skills and experience necessary to supervise the production staff as well as the ability to create, select, and purchase programs. The operations manager coordinates and supervises the efforts of both the commercial and noncommercial program departments scheduled for telecast on a day-to-day basis. A TV producer may often double as a TV director; job functions with both titles include planning and directing all the creative aspects of putting together a live or taped production. Responsibilities include overseeing the progress of the script, as well as the set, props, lighting, sound and budget, and, of course, "calling the shots" during production.

TV News The networks employ broadcast journalists and TV production professionals such as video editors, among others. The emphasis on news at any station can scarcely be overstated. This is due, in large part, to the increase in local TV news coverage. The growth of cable TV has resulted in more "narrowcasting" aimed at audiences with specific or special information needs. Although sports, weather forecasts, and traffic reports are regularly covered as specific news items, new special-interest topics such as farm reports, consumer economics, health, and science are receiving more and more local news coverage.

Job opportunities in TV news grew dramatically in the 1990s, but increasing automation in the newsroom is now restricting growth. Job titles in TV news departments include TV news director, TV managing editor, TV news producer/director, TV news production assistant, TV news reporter, and TV newscaster. TV news gathering and reporting are both exciting and demanding, and you must be a trained broadcast journalist for a job in this sector of the industry.

A TV news director has overall responsibility for a news team of reporters, writers, editors, and newscasters as well as the studio and mobile unit production crew. The job requires the ability to make quick decisions, especially in situations when news is breaking fast.

TV news reporting is both glamorous and challenging. For an on-camera news reporter's job, you must have good investigative and presentation skills.

TV Sales Job titles in the sales divisions of TV stations include TV general sales manager, national sales manager, sales service coordinator, TV traffic supervisor, and media coordinator. Jobs in this area deal with the sale of on-air TV time because the networks and independent stations derive their revenues from the sale of time for commercial announcements and from program sponsorships.

Sales reps or managers need dynamic selling skills and must be able to use research and audience demographics effectively in making sales presentations to potential media buyers. As an entry-level job in TV, sales requires only a high school diploma, so many people use it to "get a foot in the door" before moving on to the creative departments of TV news and program production.

Engineering The quality of video and audio signals transmitted by a TV station depends on its engineering and technical staff. Job titles in this department include TV chief engineer, assistant chief engineer, TV technical director, and audio engineer. These jobs require technical training and considerable experience.

The work involves regular checks and maintenance of studio cameras, video and audio tape recorders, remote relay equipment, mobile units, transmitters, and other equipment. A job as chief engineer or assistant chief engineer requires a first-class FCC operator's license and several years of experience in TV engineering.

If you are electronically inclined and want to start your career as a broadcast technician, you should first get some technical training. You can, however, start your career with minimal technical training and an apprenticeship. The best way to get an entry-level position is to be willing to work as an apprentice technician. It is also an excellent way to learn the job so you can take on greater responsibility as your skills increase.

Administration Job titles in the area of administration include general manager, TV station manager, TV business manager, and manager of office services. These managerial positions involve establishing policy and setting guidelines for the staff.

Managers must have a knowledge of strategic planning and a good business sense. General managers make decisions regarding the purchase of syndicated programs and prepare the station's application for FCC renewal, among other responsibilities.

Administrative jobs require a familiarity with broadcast law and experience in negotiating with unions. In addition, you must have excellent leadership qualities and a good public presence. Top-level administrative jobs are achieved by those who have demonstrated outstanding managerial abilities and who have years of experience in various sectors of the TV industry.

Nonbroadcast Organizations

Job titles, functions, and responsibilities in the media department of a corporation, institution, or government agency can be classified into production, management, and technical areas.

Production All the creative activities of TV production fall in this area. Job functions include scriptwriting, lighting, graphics and titles preparation, set design, camera operation, videotape editing, special effects generation, audio sweetening, and the duplication and distribution of videotapes.

In a corporate media department, a single job title may include several functions. For example, it is unlikely that you would be hired as an on-staff scriptwriter without other responsibilities. If you are a scriptwriter with TV production abilities, a company might hire you as a writer/producer. Because most corporate TV programs are used for training, writers and producers must be familiar with the principles of instructional design. As a scriptwriter for a proposed program, for example, you would be involved in conducting a needs analysis, researching the content, determining the objectives, and selecting the appropriate script format.

A producer/director is responsible for the design, production, distribution, and evaluation of the videotaped programs and any live TV programs, such as teleconferences, that a corporation might conduct. Job functions include controlling and directing the talent and crew during video productions. A corporate TV producer must have up-to-date knowledge of production techniques and hands-on experience in the use of state-of-the-art video equipment.

Management A media director is responsible for the overall planning, production, and distribution of AV, video, and TV programs. This job entails reviewing company reports, policies, and procedures, and recommending the use of television, video, and other media when they can serve as effective communications vehicles. This job also includes staffing and budgeting responsibilities.

Technical The TV engineering and technical staff is responsible for the purchase, maintenance, and replacement of capital equipment. Responsibilities include maintaining the technical standards of color TV equipment and ongoing troubleshooting and repairs.

EDUCATION AND EXPERIENCE

A high school diploma is the minimum qualification for an entry-level job in any sector of the TV industry. Because this is a highly competitive industry, college education is becoming increasingly important. Advanced education or training will increase your chances of obtaining employment and future promotions.

Traditionally, television courses at undergraduate schools have focused on subjects that give students an understanding of how the broadcast industry operates. In addition to basic TV production skills, students are taught to consider ratings, markets, advertising strategies, and broadcast laws and regulations. More than three hundred four-year colleges offer broadcast courses.

In recent years, more forward-thinking educational institutions have incorporated nonbroadcast corporate or organizational TV courses into their TV and video production programs. Some junior colleges, like the Borough of Manhattan Community College in New York City, have designed comprehensive programs to prepare students for jobs in corporations or in the cable TV industry. Nonbroadcast TV courses emphasize planning, scheduling, and budgeting procedures as well as video production skills. Because most corporate TV programs are used for training, these courses also focus on instructional design and program evaluation.

Although most universities have been slow to respond to the need for special training caused by the rapid growth in the cable TV industry, some colleges offer one or two courses in that area. The cable TV industry needs people who understand franchising and financing. In addition, you must know how cable TV audiences are targeted and measured, and how programs are rated.

The TV industry at large is experiencing a real shortage of technical people. With rapid developments in technology, trained and experienced technicians are hard to find. Although not all TV engineering or technical maintenance and repair jobs require a formal degree in engineering, most call for technical school training and on-the-job experience. Technical training can be acquired at engineering schools, technical colleges, community colleges, and various manufacturer-sponsored workshops as well as through in-service training.

PROFESSIONAL TRAINING

All major cities and many smaller ones offer an abundance of opportunities to train for video and TV jobs. The popular fascination people have for video, the rapid growth of employment opportunities, and the increased availability of affordable TV equipment have all led to a proliferation of short courses and workshops.

Nondegree programs can offer you several advantages. Many are conducted on days and at times that meet the scheduling convenience of people with full-time jobs. Because the courses are usually taught by working professionals, they are quite practical. These programs offer workshops on almost every craft within the field as well as seminars on topics that range from the basics of staying in business to the impact of cutting-edge technologies. Some programs are conducted with collaboration from an academic institution and offer continuing education units (CEUs), while others, like the International Communications Industries Association (ICIA), offer certification.

Before selecting a seminar or workshop, get as much information as possible from the sponsor. Find out about the instructor's credentials, about the course content, and try to get an outline of the topics or skills to be taught. Also inquire about prerequisites, who the course is designed for, and the format of the course (lecture, demonstration, hands-on, field trips). You will also need general information such as the course fee and whether this includes laboratory time, studio time, or materials. You will also want to confirm registration dates, the schedule, the location, and the cancellation policy.

Among the several types of nondegree programs available are:

- Product-specific skills training, usually sponsored by manufacturers and vendors of video hardware, software, and services.
- Specific skills training, usually offered by specialists in a specific area of production such as video editing or animation and also by academic institutions that have set up special programs in a specific skills area.
- General video production training, usually offered on a year-round basis by local chapters of national associations or by commercial enterprises such as magazine publishers.
- Workshops and seminars conducted on an annual basis in conjunction with annual conventions and trade exhibitions.

To get you started on your research on nondegree video and TV training, check the following organizations.

American Film Institute (AFI)
2021 North Western Avenue
Los Angeles, CA 90027
(800) 999-4AFI
www.afionline.org

The AFI offers a broad spectrum of courses in film, television, video, and new media arts and business. Specific courses cover writing, acting, producing, computer graphics, animation, and the business aspects of production. Its Enhanced TV (eTV) workshop pairs TV producers, directors, and creative executives with technology innovators to prototype the next generation of TV programming.

Avid Technology, Inc.
Metropolitan Technical Park
1 Park West
Tewksbury, MA 01876
(800) 949-AVID; (978) 640-6789
www.avid.com

Avid offers certification programs through authorized training centers nationwide and at two training locations, in Tewksbury, Massachusetts, and Burbank, California. Training is offered for all Avid products including Avid Media Composer, Avid Xpress, and Avid NewsCutter.

Bay Area Video Coalition (BAVC)
2727 Mariposa Street, 2nd Floor
San Francisco, CA 94110
(415) 861-3282
www.bavc.org

The BAVC offers more than four hundred workshops annually. Course categories include video production and postproduction, audio, graphic design, motion graphics, Web design and programming, and producing.

Digital Media Workshops
P.O. Box 200
2 Central Street
Rockport, ME 04856
(207) 236-8581; toll-free: (877) 577-7700
www.theworkshops.com

Digital Media Workshops are conducted at the same center in Rockport, Maine, as the well-known Maine Photographic Workshops and the International Film and TV Workshops. They are held in modern production facilities in a rustic New England setting. Course offerings include digital photography, 3-D animation and modeling, and digital postproduction. Training is also offered in subjects relating to the craft of film and video such as screenwriting, scene composition and camera operation, directing, editing, animation, and cinematography. The workshops range from one week to a summer-long program, depending on the area of study. A twelve-week film production program is available in Fall and Spring. Associate and MFA degree programs are also available.

dvcreators.net
2286 Ronda Vista Drive
Los Angeles, CA 90027
(323) 661-5626
www.dvcreators.net

This digital media training company conducts two- and three-day workshops in several cities and at national trade shows such as the NAB annual convention. Its *Making Awesome iMovies* CD-ROM offers excellent instruction on professional shooting techniques, proper lighting and exposure, and various editing styles. The company also offers CD-ROM–based instruction on other advanced software applications.

ICIA Academy (International Communications Industries Association)
11242 Waples Mill Road, Suite 200
Fairfax, VA 22030
(703) 273-7200
www.infocomm.org

The ICIA Academy offers high-quality technical training with certification. Throughout the year courses are offered on installation, design, rental, sales, and networking. The InfoComm Academy Online offers courses on topics such as "Essentials of the AV Industry" and "AV from A-Z for Sales Professionals."

MacAcademy/WindowsAcademy
102 East Granada Boulevard
Ormond Beach, FL 32176
(386) 677-1918, toll-free: (800) 527-1914
www.macacademy.com/indexmac.html

MacAcademy/WindowsAcademy offers training CD-ROMs and live seminars on a wide range of applications including After Effects, Dreamweaver, DVD Studio Pro, GoLive, InDesign, Illustrator, and Director.

Sony Training Institute
3300 Zanker Road SJ2A6
San Jose, CA 95134
(408) 955-5000
http://bssc.sel.sony.com/Professional/service/training/index.html

The Business and Professional Group of Sony Electronics conducts courses and workshops on the creative and technical areas of both analog and digital technologies. More than twenty intensive video workshop and operations course titles are offered for various levels of experience in all aspects of video operation and creation. Although most of the courses are held in San Jose, California, a few are held in other cities. Fees vary according to the type and length of the course. Among the hands-on courses, "Video Production Fundamentals: Producing Video for the Digital Age," a four-day class priced at $1,725, takes you through the video production process from concept to the finished production.

UCLA Extension
Entertainment Studies, Department E-6
10995 Leconte Avenue
Los Angeles, CA 90024
(800) 554-UCLA
www.uclaextension.edu

UCLA Extension's Entertainment Studies program offers single courses or an entire curriculum that includes interactive media, film, television, video, music, and the Internet. Every aspect, from preproduction through packaging and distribution, is covered. Through this program, you can study with top professionals in the field. The courses can also lead to a certificate program.

To continue your professional development, consider attending sessions on topical subjects hosted by the local chapters of professional associations in your area. Also, software companies such as Adobe offer free sessions to demonstrate the capabilities of new versions of their product. Often, value-added resellers (VARs) or equipment dealers and rental companies will host a free session or conference on a new technology. Take advantage of such programs to keep abreast of the technology and the industry. User group conferences such as the Macromedia Developers Conference also offer practical seminars.

AWARDS AND FESTIVALS

Landing your first job in the TV industry may not be easy—but holding onto that job, making the right career moves, and building a successful and rewarding professional career can be even more difficult. Once you make a start, your professional development must be a lifelong affair. The intensity of your desire to improve will determine how much time and energy you invest in continuing your media-related education and your participation in professional associations and other industry events.

Taking part in festivals and competitions, and networking with other professionals at seminars, conferences, and trade conventions can play a major role in promoting your ongoing professional development. The sponsors of festivals usually sponsor conferences too.

Pay attention to the fine print before sending in an entry. Eligibility may require that the program not have appeared on any national feed of a major network, including FOX and UPN, or may limit entries to programs produced within the previous two years. Some organizers charge a fee for converting a program to the accepted format. Non-English-language programs may require subtitles or a translation of the script into English. If the entry running times are specified, be sure you edit your program to that length if you want it to qualify.

The competitions described here, selected from among the many available, will give you an idea of the categories and the prestige that they command within the different media communities. And, for an extensive list of festivals in Canada, go to the website of Queen's University, Department of Film Studies at http://www.film.queensu.ca/Links/Festivals.html.

Hometown USA Video Festival. In community media and cable TV circles, this annual festival draws a great deal of attention. It is organized by the Alliance for Community Media. Entry forms can be downloaded from the website www.alliancecm.org.

The Association for Women in Communications. The AWC sponsors the Clarion Awards competition, which recognizes the best in all the communications fields, including television. For more information, go to www.womcom.org/clarion.

Cinema in Industry (CINDY) Competitions. These awards are held by the International Association of Audio Visual Communicators. Entries are accepted in several formats. Programs are judged in many categories including multimedia and best student work. For details, visit www .cindys.com.

The Telly Awards. This competition recognizes outstanding local, regional, and cable TV commercials and programs that have not appeared on the four major TV networks (ABC, CBS, NBC, or FOX). Still the most coveted award among advertising agencies and producers of commercials, the competition has been expanded to include nonbroadcast film and video productions and now draws more than ten thousand entries each year in all categories. Entry forms may be obtained from Telly Awards, 4100 Executive Park Drive, Cincinnati, OH 45241. For more information, visit http://telly.com.

The New York Festivals International Film and TV Festival. This festival features six separate competitions: design and print advertising; radio programming and promotion; interactive; TV programming and promotion; film and video; and TV, cinema, and radio advertising. You can enter and upload entries for many of the competitions, and sometimes even be judged online. You can also view the winning work and order duplicate awards online. For more information, call (212) 643-4800, write to New York Festivals, 7 West 36th Street, 14th Floor, New York, NY 10018, or visit www.newyorkfestivals.com.

Image Film & Video Center. This center produces the annual Atlanta Film Festival. For details, call the sponsor at (404) 352-4225, write to ImageFV at 75 Bennett Street, N.W., Suite N-1, Atlanta, GA 30309, or visit www.imagefv.org.

The U.S. International Film and Video Festival. This festival has been celebrating excellence in this field for more than three decades. It receives almost two thousand entries in categories that include more than three dozen application or special-interest areas such as agriculture, nature, history, and medicine, as well as media production categories. Gold Camera Awards, Silver Screen Awards, and Certificates for Creative Excellence are presented, usually in June. For an entry form, contact the sponsor at 713 South Pacific Coast Highway, Suite A, Redondo Beach, CA 90277, or visit www.filmfestawards.com.

UNIONS, GUILDS, AND ASSOCIATIONS

In major TV markets and at some TV stations in smaller markets, employees at broadcasting companies can benefit from collective bargaining agreements negotiated by labor organizations or professional guilds and associations. Here are a few that you should learn about.

The American Federation of Television and Radio Artists (AFTRA) (www .aftra.org). This national labor union is affiliated with the AFL–CIO and represents its members in four major areas: news and broadcasting; entertainment programming; the recording business; and commercials and nonbroadcast, industrial, educational media. The union negotiates and enforces more than four hundred collective bargaining agreements that guarantee minimum (but never maximum) salaries, safe working conditions, and health and retirement benefits.

The Directors Guild of America (DGA) (www.dga.org). Although most directors are not represented by a union, a few who work for television networks and some independent production companies are members of DGA. Several assistant directors and unit managers who work on TV network films are also represented by the DGA.

The International Alliance of Theatrical Stage Employees, Moving Picture Technicians, Artists and Allied Crafts (IATSE). The alliance (www.iatse-intl .org) represents a wide range of crafts in the entertainment industry, including film and videotape editors, and technicians and artists involved in video and motion picture production, computer graphics, AV, and related disciplines.

The National Association of Broadcast Employees and Technicians, the Broadcasting and Cable Television Workers Sector of the Communications Workers of America (NABET–CWA). NABET–CWA (www.nabet53.com) holds more than a hundred collective bargaining agreements that spell out wages, benefits, and working conditions for its members. Among the major employers of NABET–CWA members are NBC, ABC, and independent companies in the private and public broadcasting and teleproduction sectors.

NABET represents art directors and graphic artists who work in the broadcast industry, while many art directors and graphic artists who are not employed at TV stations but work on TV commercials and film promos are members of the Broadcast Designers Association (www.bdaweb.com).

The Screen Actors Guild (SAG). SAG (www.sag.com) represents its members to several creative communities, including filmmakers. SAG basic agreements cover contracts, wages, and working conditions for TV, theater, industrial, and educational productions as well as new media.

The Writers Guild of America (WGA). The WGA (www.wga.org) is the premier bargaining representative for writers in the broadcast, cable, motion picture, interactive, and new media industries. It negotiates minimum basic agreements with major producers of motion pictures and TV programs as well as contracts for writing staff at radio and TV stations.

There are no associations solely representing the interests of producers or assistant producers. Many executive producers are members of the National Association of Television Program Executives (NATPE), which represents the interest of content providers (www.natpe.org). Producers, technical, and creative personnel who work on corporate productions often belong to the Media Communications Association-International (MCA-I). For details, check www.mca-i.org.

SOURCES OF INFORMATION

Associations and Societies

A number of organizations serve the broadcast industry, and participation in one or more is essential for career advancement. If you are interested in the new media, check Chapter 7. If you want to pursue a career in broadcasting, check Chapter 5. More detailed contact information appears in the Appendix. For ease of reference, some of these listings appear here.

Alliance for Community Media (ACM) (www.alliancecm.org)
Association of Computing Machinery (ACM-SIGGRAPH)
    (www.siggraph.org)
Audio Engineering Society (AES) (www.aes.org)
Directors Guild of America (DGA) (www.dga.org)
International Communications Industries Association (ICIA)
    (www.infocomm.org)

National Association of Broadcasters (NAB) (www.nab.org)

National Association of Government Communicators (NAGC)
(www.nagc.com)

National Association of Television Program Executives (NATPE)
(www.natpe.org)

National Cable & Telecommunications Association (NCTA)
(www.ncta.com)

Radio-Television News Directors Association (RTNDA) (www.rtnda.org)

Society of Broadcast Engineers (SBE) (www.sbe.org)

Society of Motion Picture and Television Engineers (SMPTE)
(www.smpte.org)

Periodicals

Many of the new tools for capturing images, video editing, and animation
are used in both film and TV production. Trade magazines in both industries review new technologies and showcase current applications, so check
the list of periodicals in Chapter 4 on Film. Also check Chapter 7 on Multimedia for trade publications covering digital video. If you are unable to
subscribe to a publication of interest, you may be able to read it at a library
or borrow it from a production company or a media producer. Here is a
selected list of recommended current trade publications.

AV Video & Multimedia Producer (www.avvideo.com)

Broadcast Engineering (www.broadcastengineering.com)

Broadcasting & Cable (www.broadcastingcable.com)

Digital Video Editing (www.digitalvideoediting.com)

Post (www.postmagazine.com)

SMPTE's Motion Imaging Journal (www.smpte.org)

Video Systems (www.videosystems.com)

Videography (www.uemedia.com/cpc/videography)

Directories

Broadcasting & Cable Yearbook. New Providence, NJ: R. R. Bowker.

Canadian Production Guide. Toronto, Ontario: The Canadian Film &
Television Producers Association. Annual.

Digital Media Net Directories. Several databases serving this market and available online. (www.digitalmedianet.com).

Directory of Radio & TV News Awards. Washington, DC: Radio–Television News Directors Foundation.

Motion Picture, TV, and Theatre Directory. Tarrytown, NY: MPE Publications.

Television & Cable Factbook. Washington, DC: Warren Communications News.

Recommended Reading

Avgerakis, George. *Desktop Video Studio Bible: Producing Video, DVD, and Websites for Profit.* New York: McGraw-Hill/TAB Electronics, 2002.

Browne, Steven E. *Video Editing: A Postproduction Primer.* Woburn, MA: Focal Press, 2002.

Ferguson, Douglas A., and Susan T. Eastman. *Broadcast/Cable/Web with Infotrac: Strategies and Practices.* Belmont, CA: Wadsworth, 2001.

Freedman, Wayne. *It Takes More Than Good Looks to Succeed at TV News Reporting.* Chicago: Bonus Books, 2003.

Goodman, Robert M., and Patrick McGrath. *Editing Digital Video: The Complete Creative and Technical Guide.* New York: McGraw-Hill/TAB Electronics, 2002.

Jackman, John. *Lighting for Digital Video & Television.* Manhasset, NY: CMP Books, 2002.

Noronha, Shonan, F. R. *Opportunities in Television and Video Careers.* New York: McGraw-Hill, 2003.

Perry, Greg. *Digital Video in a Snap with Windows XP.* SAMS, 2003.

Poynton, Charles. *Digital Video and HDTV Algorithms and Interfaces.* Elsevier, 2003.

Smith, Dow. *Power Producer,* 3rd ed. Washington D.C.: Radio-Television News Directors Association, 2002.

Tuggle, C. A. *Broadcast News Handbook: Writing, Reporting, and Producing in a Converging Media World.* New York: McGraw Hill, 2003.

Whitaker, Jerry and Blair Benson. *Television Receivers and Cable/Satellite Distribution Systems.* New York: McGraw-Hill, 2002.

CHAPTER

MULTIMEDIA

No sector of communications has grown so rapidly or changed so much over the past few years as that amalgam of styles, technologies, and applications that we call multimedia. The term refers to any program with content that blends and integrates a variety of media elements including sound, video, and animation.

Multimedia programs are distributed on CD-ROM and DVD as well as through digital networks and the Internet. From boardroom presentations and product marketing programs to interactive computer games and distance learning, the applications of multimedia for mass-market or custom audiences have expanded rapidly in recent years. And, virtually every job in communications today will include some involvement with multimedia.

THE MULTIMEDIA LANDSCAPE

A snapshot of the industry shows a wide range of applications: business presentations, product marketing, entertainment, and education to name a few.

However, as is true for other areas in communications, the economic slump has had a negative impact on employment in the industry.

Entertainment: The Game Industry

The game industry has become a major player in multimedia production. Total revenues in the computer gaming industry in 2003 were $11.4 billion, down 4 percent from the record level of $11.7 billion set in 2002. This total reflected a gain in sales of software game titles and a slowing of demand for the consoles on which the games are played. Games are distributed on proprietary cartridges and on standard DVD discs for use on PC and Mac computers, and also via the Internet.

Three types of companies dominate this arena: manufacturers of game hardware such as Sony, Nintendo, Microsoft, and Sega; game production companies, like Acclaim, Electronic Arts, and LucasArts, that create multimedia content and titles; and publishing companies like Broderbund that finance, manufacture, distribute, and promote titles. Some publishing companies also have divisions that create content. Some smaller game development companies work as production arms of large publishers, while others create original games that are distributed through various channels including bookstores, computer stores, catalog companies, and the Internet. Some giant companies like Sony and Microsoft are involved at every level of the game industry.

One good place to begin learning about the world of computer games is through the website of *Game Developer* magazine at www.gdmag.com.

Education and Training

The production of interactive programs for education and corporate training is another significant part of the multimedia industry. A number of organizations are involved in creating and distributing multimedia programs for education and training. These organizations range from courseware giants such as PLATO Learning to small independent production companies, and from colleges and universities to traditional textbook publishing companies. The content may be intended for academic use, for corporate and industrial training, or for distribution to the consumer market for home schooling or as "edutainment" programs intended for the educational and entertainment market.

The Internet

The use of multimedia content on the Internet is expanding at a dizzying pace. As competition for Web audience share increases and more users get high-speed access to the Web, website proprietors and vendors are vying to provide the most exciting and stimulating content possible. Simultaneously, as the cost of multimedia hardware and software for the Web continues to fall, an increasing value is placed on creativity, technical proficiency, and solid audio and visual communication skills.

Multimedia Jobs

Content for multimedia programs, whether licensed or in the public domain, can be original, adapted, or repurposed from other media. Hence, many senior-level jobs require skills in business and legal areas such as marketing, distribution, licensing, and copyrights. Executive producers take on project management functions and work with several creative teams and business groups to bring all the elements together. Among the many newer production-related job titles are multimedia producer, Internet creative director, Web content writer/editor, interactive scriptwriter, interface designer, 3-D designer, animation artist, HTML programmer, website designer, Webmaster, database designer, and multimedia author.

CURRENT CHALLENGES

The incredible pace of growth and change in multimedia are both its greatest strength and the source of some of the biggest challenges for those who work in this field. On one hand, because the industry can respond almost instantly to customer needs with imaginative new solutions, it is the ideal medium for a world that is demanding ever better, faster, and more exciting ways of delivering important information. On the other hand, the resulting never-ending parade of new programs, platforms, and formats also make it difficult and expensive for multimedia creators and businesspeople to keep up with the latest technology.

Perhaps the greatest challenge for those seeking a career in multimedia is deciding how to invest their time and energy in learning and gaining mastery of the constantly changing software and hardware. Separating real trends from hype can be difficult, but the advice of working professionals is probably more trustworthy than the marketing-influenced "buzz" so prevalent in print, on TV, and on the Internet.

THE TECHNOLOGY ADVANTAGE

Many technologies, applications, and media comprise the megamedium generally referred to as multimedia. These include CD-ROM, DVD, video games, presentations for business, entertainment, and the Internet.

Despite a lack of universal standards, streaming video on the Internet, which allows users to view "TV" on their computers in real time, may be the fastest-growing segment of the video industry. The challenges are great, and include a maelstrom of incompatible and constantly evolving elements: compression schemes and business models, users with slow modems, local area networks (LANs) with limited bandwidths, and a raft of assorted technical and operational issues.

"Broadcast" video is used on news websites, corporate pages, and the promo websites of just about every TV and motion picture company. Check your favorite search engine or the websites of RealVideo, QuickTime, and Windows Media Player for Webcasts relevant to your interests. Good information on the latest in Internet video is usually available from Streaming Media World's website at http://streamingmediaworld.com. Information about the exciting possibilities of interactive multimedia videoconferencing on the Web can be found at www.cuworld.com, www.microsoft.com/windows/netmeeting, www.fvc .com, and www.imtc.org.

Multimedia reaches far beyond the World Wide Web. Although Internet applications are creating many opportunities, DVD, CD-ROM, kiosks, and even the production of coin-operated games are also growth areas. Many of the same skills and software are used to create and design both DVD and Web-based multimedia.

Production companies such as New York's 4-D Media Group are combining their visual expertise with powerful new software and hardware to push the multimedia envelope. David Campbell, a principal of 4-D Media Group, says: "We've seen an upsurge in new and innovative ways to get the word out. On the high end, we've been involved in 'film,' such as the promotional BMW Films and DKNY Films. These 'films' are created beautifully, with high production values. DKNY Films are actually shot and edited in HDTV. The final product is distributed on the Web and a DVD with full resolution and special interactive features is handed out free at retail outlets. Another innovative approach that we have used for marketing products allows customers to view the product from all angles. The program distributed through CD-ROM, DVD, and the Web, is created using tools such as QuickTimeVR and Macromedia Flash. Shooting product on our motion control animation stand from multiple angles, we then treat each angle and stitch together an object panorama with interactive options. Viewers can pan, tilt, and zoom an object to any desired angle on their computers. The treated files can also be repurposed for POP (point of purchase) presentation in the form of eye-catching 'lenticulars' (i.e., printed images that show motion or depth as the customer's point-of-view changes)."

The brave new world of multimedia even extends to the printed page. As Campbell reports: "An uncomplicated but cool offering we've been involved with is flip books using video and/or vector-based animation such as Flash. Each flip book contains sixty-four pages into which you can place four to eight seconds of motion, depending on the desired frame rate. Food companies, technology companies, and others use these addictive little flip books as packaging premiums cobranded with animated characters, or simply to depict their product in motion."

Other tools used by multimedia production houses include hypertext markup language (HTML), Shockwave, Director, and Flash. Shockwave from Macromedia optimizes interactive files from Director for Web use to create an efficient database that allows games and other interactive applications to be downloaded and experienced almost instantly on the Web. Flash allows immediate streaming of animation via Web browsers and is in addition a strong stand-alone cell animation application for TV and film projects.

Multimedia developments such as QuickTime, MPEG-2, MPEG-4, and the widespread availability of DVD hardware and software have greatly increased the ability of PCs to play back video and audio. This growth has spread from games and edutainment titles to mainstream business applications such as kiosks in stores and malls, and "video walls" in airports, exhibition halls, entertainment venues, and sports arenas.

The rapidly expanding business of multimedia production is opening up new opportunities for professionals with expertise in video production as well as interactive design skills such as information mapping, graphical user interface (GUI) design, and multimedia authoring. The interactive disc-based technologies currently in use include CD-ROM and DVD.

With the advent of DVD, the industry finally has a medium that combines the ease of use and economy of the CD-ROM format with the ability to store high-quality feature-length video. DVDs can store gigabytes of data, hours of MPEG-2 video, and CD-quality audio. Over the next few years, increasing DVD sales should fuel another upsurge in demand for employees with skills in multimedia production.

Before you invest a great deal of time and money toward gaining specialized expertise in a particular hardware or software system, it might be a good idea to get a reality check from those who are already involved. Most of the popular systems and programs have user groups and newsgroups. These groups, as well as trade shows, product demos, and workshops, are all good ways to acquaint yourself with developments in specific areas, but there is no substitute for hands-on training and practice. Hands-on experience is still the best way to really get into an application and to understand its potential and its relevance to your own objectives.

ABOUT MULTIMEDIA

When considering a career in multimedia, it is important to get an overview of the field. Explore websites in various sectors of the industry to get a broader view of the projects, people, tools and processes involved in the making of multimedia. The list at the end of this section offers several good starting points for your investigation.

A number of associations and publications also offer excellent information on their websites and are listed at the end of this chapter under "Sources of Information." In addition, you'll want to check the websites of vendors and production companies that serve this community because they often post career opportunities. Universities and various industry experts also offer useful information on their websites. Here is a selected list of useful sites.

General

Multimediator (Canada) (www.multimediator.com)

Northwestern University Multimedia Resource Center
(www.library.nwu.edu/media/resources)

Yahoo's directory of Internet Multimedia
(http://dir.yahoo.com/computers_and_internet/multimedia)

Tools and Technology Vendors

Adobe (www.adobe.com)

Alias (www.alias.com)

Apple Computer (http://developer.apple.com/macosx/gettingstarted)

Avid Technology (www.avid.com)

Macromedia (www.macromedia.com)

Microsoft (www.microsoft.com)

Philips (www.prodvd.philips.com)

Real Networks (www.real.com)

Silicon Graphics (www.sgi.com)

Game Production

Fun Kid Games (www.funkidsgames.com)

Game Developer (www.gdmag.com)

Game Developers Conference (www.gdconf.com)

Game Programming Academy (www.gameprogramming.org)

GameDev.Net (www.gamedev.net)

Havok (www.havok.com)

Online Commerce

Ecommerce Digest (www.ecommerce-digest.com)

Guidance Solutions (www.guidance.com)

Interactive CD-ROM/DVD Publishing Companies

Electronic Arts (www.ea.com)

The Learning Company (www.learningco.com)

WHERE THE JOBS ARE

There are two primary areas of employment for multimedia professionals: staff or freelance work for multimedia production houses and service companies, and in-house positions at corporations and organizations.

As a result of recent trends in downsizing and outsourcing, many opportunities for multimedia employment have moved from staff jobs to independent production companies. However, thousands of staff positions in corporations are still available, as well as freelance assignments with companies that have downsized their internal production and production management capabilities.

Temporary employment opportunities in this field are common and can often be located through temp agencies and services such as Net Temps (www.net-temps.com/jobs/internet). A recent search of that website showed twenty-two temporary or contract jobs available that required proficiency in Flash, Macromedia's popular animation program.

Independent Media Production Companies

If you believe that variety is the spice of life, then you should seek employment at an independent media production company. Since many of these companies have a fairly diverse client base, you will probably work on a constant stream of new and different projects. This can be very challenging because each project will bring new opportunities and new problems to solve.

It is not easy to get a foot in the door as a multimedia producer at an independent production company. A candidate for producer would be expected to have several years of experience and a list of awards and credits to prove talent and experience. Jobs tend to be more specialized at these facilities, which hire audio engineers, videographers, 3-D designers and animators, and HTML programmers all with skills in using specific software and hardware tools. Still, it is often possible to land an internship at one of these companies, and, if you prove to be very creative and capable, and they need you—well, you'll have yourself a job.

Advertising and Public Relations Agencies

Although a number of large advertising agencies are currently hiring creative people in multimedia and website positions, the long-term outlook for new positions is not very good, as agencies are now accustomed to outsourcing much of their film, video, and multimedia work to independent production companies.

On the other hand, many advertising and marketing firms offer multimedia consulting and creative services to their clients.

Advertising and PR agencies look for top-notch skills and want high-quality work. When an agency pitches a new client with a multimedia presentation, it wants to be perceived as the best in the business. This usually involves employing the latest in technology and design, with little concern for expense. Likewise, agencies take great care in the production of their websites, often contracting with top creative talent to design them because agencies are selling their expertise and want to appear in the best possible light.

Business and Industry

There are more multimedia career opportunities in business and industry than in any other market segment. Jobs are often located in corporate communications departments, which are responsible for both internal (company-wide) and external communication targeted at customers, shareholders, mass media, and other audiences.

Today, business graphics are used in multimedia presentation programs such as MS PowerPoint, which are displayed from computers via video/data projectors, are by far the most-used media, but some companies still use 35 mm color slides and overhead transparencies. Business graphics are typically used in presentations for speaker support and on company websites. While in the past these graphics were prepared as flat art and then photographed, today, computer-generated graphics are in general use. PowerPoint, Macromedia Director and Flash, and Adobe Photoshop and Illustrator are the primary tools used to create business presentations.

The Gartner Group has reported that the average manager spends 59 percent of her or his time in meetings. A Wharton School study reported that the use of visuals effectively reduces the duration of meetings by an average of 28 percent. Additional research has shown that 85 percent of those who both see and hear information remember it three hours later and that 65 percent remember it three days later. With the increases in productivity and information retention resulting from the use of well-prepared graphics, business executives now have bottom-line reasons for hiring and expanding their multimedia presentation capabilities. Working in a sophisticated facility to produce content for important business presentations can be a rewarding experience for multimedia professionals.

Some businesses have created special environments, both virtual and real, for displaying or showcasing their presentations. It is not uncommon to find boardrooms and conference rooms equipped with high-end projection systems and versatile multimedia control systems. These environments are ideal for making sales presentations to clients, for training, or for telling the company's story to the public. Organizations also use their intranets and the Internet to make presentations available to customers and employees. Webconferencing services such as WebEx also extend the power of live presentations all around the world.

Many large companies have training departments such as management development, sales support, and technical training that require multimedia materials. Some industries also support large customer training activities. A training department may have its own multimedia staff, although typically, video production is centralized, if not outsourced to independent production companies.

Marketing departments are major users of multimedia and other AV materials. At companies that participate in numerous trade shows, the AV and multimedia staff may not only produce the presentations, kiosk programs, and other visual material but also travel to the trade show, set up the presentation, and run it. This may be no easy task, because coordinating logistics at trade shows can be difficult and requires special skills. This type of work may require a lot of travel and time away from home, which may appeal to some but can cause considerable stress for others.

Large sales meetings, investor relations meetings, and similar events offer other significant multimedia production opportunities at some companies.

These kinds of programs give AV/multimedia professionals a chance to use virtually every production skill and tool available, often in coordination with outside vendors who specialize in event production. Lasers, dancers, musicians, singers, and comedians may all be used in conjunction with multi-image and video extravaganzas. The entire event may be transmitted via satellite or terrestrial digital networks to multiple locations across the country or even around the world.

Many media professionals are enjoying challenging and satisfying careers in corporate media departments, whether they are responsible for multimedia production and mounting sales meeting presentations or preparing a CEO's presentation to a small group of analysts. Good planning along with the ability to coordinate people, processes, and the various elements for successful implementation are the keys to success.

Whether you are working at a small company or a large one will usually determine if you will have the opportunity to specialize, or develop into an AV/multimedia generalist. A job at a smaller company often involves work with a wide range of technologies in a variety of environments, while a position in a larger organization may offer the opportunity to specialize in a specific area, such as video editing or the staging of special events. In either case, it will serve you well to hone your expertise in the most commonly used skills.

Health Sciences

You have only to look around the city nearest you to notice the number of hospitals and other medical facilities—and they all need multimedia communication skills. If you have an aptitude for or an interest in the medical field, a job at one of these institutions could be satisfying to you. Also, pharmaceutical companies as well as medical, dental, and veterinary schools use multimedia extensively and should not be overlooked.

The use of slides and digital photography is common in the health sciences. The use of videotape and optical media is also becoming common as medical institutions respond to the growing need for up-to-date patient, nursing and health care staff, and doctor education. To work in this field, you should be motivated by the challenge of capturing images and documenting processes and events as they occur without the temptation to alter them for aesthetic purposes. Many creative media professionals find work in the health sciences and, in particular, scientific documentation boring, because they would have to follow the routine established for the procedure that has to be photographed or videotaped. Special training in colorimetry and lighting is useful because the accuracy of color in the images presented is crucial for diagnosis and research.

Teaching hospitals are most likely to offer entry-level AV/multimedia jobs. These are generally good places to start your career because the department is usually small, so each member must become involved in all aspects of the production and presentation of programs. These jobs include shooting thousands of still images and hours of videotape for use in medical lectures and other presentations made by the institution. Because of confidentiality issues and the need for quick turnaround, many hospitals process their own film or use digital recording and image processing systems.

Government

Do not overlook federal, state, and local government departments when searching for a multimedia production job. The state and local government agencies most likely to use multimedia are agriculture; tourism; emergency services such as police and fire departments; environmental and conservation agencies; social service agencies that deal with health, education, and welfare; and highway and safety. Government agencies have been using videotape for many years and are now also using the newer communications media such as DVD and the Web. The more common application areas are information dissemination, marketing and promotion, and training.

JOB DESCRIPTIONS

Teamwork is critical to the success of any multimedia project. Jobs and responsibilities overlap and complement each other. Julie Thomas-Haskell, a multimedia professional at St. Vincent Hospital and Medical Center in Portland, Oregon, describes her facility: "We don't work alone. Medigraphics [the name of her department] is more than a roster of talented individuals, more than a list of skills and equipment." Her team, for example, includes a video specialist, a graphics coordinator, a graphic artist, a type-setter, a medical photographer, a photojournalist, a darkroom assistant, a surgical videographer, and a media clerk who all work as a team that handles projects from start to finish.

Multimedia Producer

The multimedia producer is responsible for the design, production, and evaluation of multimedia information and training programs for various audiences. Style, originality, and creativity are extremely important qualifications because the producer acts as resource person for organization members who have communication needs. Producers assist in achieving client objectives in a timely manner and using the appropriate system to best deliver the presentation, while staying within the budget. The ultimate job of the producer is to edit large amounts of information and visuals into a comprehensive and succinct program.

Whether preparing single presentations or websites, producers use managerial skills—planning, budgeting, leading others, and directing—as well as arranging for or carrying out a wide variety of technical skills that include research, scriptwriting and editing, storyboarding, photography, film processing, lighting, selecting music, recording and mixing audio tracks, designing graphics, programming, and operating all kinds of multimedia equipment.

Leadership and creativity are key to a producer's success, and interpersonal skills are crucial. Producers must be able to guide and bring excitement to the production team, to keep emotions and budgets under control in short-deadline situations, and to meet each client's objectives.

Producers must understand the capabilities of every kind of multimedia system including software, and be able to select the best equipment and ideal format for the project at hand. In addition to media production skills, excellent interpersonal skills are necessary.

Multimedia Writer

The work of a multimedia writer involves consultations with the producer and the client from program concept to completion. Writers must be able to develop innovative scripts, based on research and consultation, to generate quality programs that meet clients' stated objectives.

The multimedia writer must be able to perform the same tasks as any other writer: research, using both libraries and computer databases; face-to-face and telephone interviews; typing or word processing; and expert language skills, including a thorough grasp of grammar, spelling, punctuation, syntax, and sentence structure. Additionally, working in multimedia requires familiarity with a wide variety of presentation, videotape, multi-image, and website formats and capabilities, plus the ability to write narratives and dialogue in a lively and interesting way.

Writers are the unsung heroes of multimedia production teams. Although they are not as visible as most other members of the production team, their scripts are the visual and aural foundation of any project. As presentations and websites become more interactive, writers are expected to have expertise in information mapping and authoring programs such as Macromedia Director or Authorware.

Production Assistant

Production assistants are involved in every area of production including photography, lighting, audio, programming and presentation, and distribution of the program. Production assistants must have many of the skills required of producers, especially the mechanical ability to handle all the multimedia equipment available.

Production assistants must have a "team attitude," good interpersonal skills, and the flexibility and resourcefulness to deal with changing priorities during the course of a project. They must be willing to take direction from the producer and still have the self-confidence to offer creative suggestions and to work independently to get things done. This position is a stepping-stone to becoming a producer.

Multimedia Technician or Engineer

Multimedia technicians or engineers, who operate and maintain computing, photographic, audio, lighting, programming, and projection equipment, may be called upon to assist with any phase of production, postproduction, or distribution. Because they are responsible for maintaining high technical standards, they must also develop equipment maintenance procedures to keep all the equipment in the department or company performing at optimum levels. With multimedia hardware and software becoming increasingly complex, technicians must constantly be upgrading their skills and knowledge.

Multimedia technicians must have a basic knowledge of electronics and computer systems as well as strong mechanical ability. Experience operating all kinds of multimedia equipment, computers, and maintenance tools is the basis of the job. The ability to organize a work schedule, to set careful priorities, and to keep records of repairs and maintenance done on each piece of equipment is also important.

The job of a multimedia technician or engineer is crucial to the operation of a multimedia department or company. If equipment is not working properly, production schedules may be delayed or cancelled because it may not be possible to produce images or the quality of the images produced may be substandard. When multimedia technicians or engineers are doing their job properly, the members of the production team can focus on the creative side of the project and trust that the equipment will function properly.

Multimedia Manager/Director

The multimedia manager or director is responsible for establishing the budget and planning for the production and distribution of the programs. An effective multimedia manager has strong managerial skills including organization and communication as well as flexibility and leadership.

Managers of multimedia departments or companies are responsible for recruiting and developing a professional staff and for obtaining the equipment needed to produce quality content. They make the final decisions regarding all material produced and the purchases of equipment. Managers develop production schedules that make the most effective and efficient use of their human and technical resources, and they also evaluate operations for effectiveness. In an independent production environment, an executive producer often assumes this role.

Webmaster

The emergence of the Internet as a major vehicle for multimedia communications has resulted in the creation of many new types of specialized jobs. Foremost among these is the position of Webmaster. This term refers to the person who has the overall responsibility for the design, development, and maintenance of a website or group of websites. The Webmaster is responsible for ensuring that the website functions as required. Other duties typically include the development of website strategies, policies, and procedures, and recommendations on the selection of Internet products and services. Often the Webmaster is required to edit website materials to ensure ease of use and consistency.

Depending on the size of the organization, the Webmaster may work with various other departments to analyze website requirements and to provide expert advice regarding the presentation of material on the website. The Webmaster often develops marketing strategies to increase website traffic, and, in smaller organizations, may be required to implement these marketing programs. Some Webmasters create and format all the content for a website, while others manage their own creative and technical staff, work with other groups within a larger organization, or direct the activities of contract or freelance employees or production companies.

Website Designer or Developer

This job covers a number of specialties including HTML programmer, graphic artist, animator, database programmer, Internet analyst, among others. Depending on the size and complexity of the website and the organization, these essentially creative jobs may all be performed by a single person or be divided among many in-house or outsourced specialists. All these tasks require expertise in one or more specialized software applications ranging from Macromedia Dreamweaver and Flash to Adobe Photoshop and ColdFusion.

EDUCATION AND EXPERIENCE

The education requirements for multimedia producers, Webmasters, production assistants, writers, and designers are very similar. A bachelor's degree in mass communications, computer science, journalism, English, or another related liberal arts degree is helpful. A broad knowledge of the world, its technologies, and its cultures gives communicators in any field a strong foundation for their work. Some businesses and industries also look for employees with a strong technical background in the field involved. Writing skills are particularly important, not only for prospective multimedia writers but also for producers and others who work with writers. Many employers also expect new employees to have skills related to specific media or technologies, so training and/or experience in the basic creative and information management tools are necessary.

Internships can give you some practical work experience while you are still in college or technical school, and being able to say that you have hands-on experience with the widest possible variety of technologies will serve you well when you begin job hunting. AV conferences and seminars can also help because they will give you a feel for the industry as a whole and keep you abreast of the latest technologies and trends—not to mention opportunities to meet potential employers.

A multimedia manager or director needs the same basic skills and education required of any multimedia producer or writer, plus fairly extensive experience and a business-oriented approach to the work. Management skills, whether acquired through college coursework or through on-the-job experience, are key here. In some corporate environments, a master's degree in business may be important for advancement.

The training for multimedia technicians differs somewhat from that required for the other jobs discussed here. Technicians can get most of the required training for equipment maintenance by attending a technical school that specializes in electronics. A strong background in the theory of electronics and computer systems and knowledge of troubleshooting techniques are essential. Technicians must continue their education while on the job by attending seminars and training sessions sponsored by equipment and software manufacturers. Increasingly, technicians are also expected to be thoroughly familiar with operating systems and major applications such as Director, PowerPoint, Photoshop, and FrontPage.

Manufacturers' websites are a good place to start searching for useful training on specific applications and for information about multimedia technologies in general. For example, www.macromedia.com includes links to authorized hands-on training and it also serves as a portal for Macromedia

University, the company's excellent, cost-effective interactive training website for Flash, Director, and dozens of other applications. Several other manufacturers, including Apple, Avid, and Autodesk, have authorized training centers that are usually listed on their website. Some associations provide lists of educational resources, either in printed pamphlets or on the their website. For example, the Siggraph page that lists career education resources can be accessed at www.education.siggraph .org/docs/business.htm. Other possibilities include:

- InfoComm.org (www.infocomm.org). This website offers top-notch training and certification on the design, installation, operation, management, and maintenance of multimedia systems. Instruction is available online and at live training sessions in the United States and Europe.
- The American Film Institute (AFI) (www.afi.org). The AFI offers a broad spectrum of courses in the new media, television, and film. Specific courses cover topics including writing, acting, computer graphics, video editing, animation, and the business aspects of production. Classes are held both at the institute's main campus in Los Angeles and at other locations around the country.
- The Art Institutes. This consortium of thirty art institutes located in cities across North America offers master's degrees, bachelor's degrees, associate's degrees, and nondegree programs in a wide range of subjects including graphics, fashion, culinary, and media arts. Students can study in person or can learn online through The Art Institute Online, a division of the Art Institute of Pittsburgh. Visit www.artinstitutes.org for more information.
- Animation World Network (AWN) (www.awn.com). A comprehensive Web portal that includes news, employment information, and a database of more than four hundred schools that teach animation in thirty-four countries.
- The Interactive Media Technology Center (IMTC). A research, design, and education center that focuses on digital media processing applied to technology, education, culture, and medicine. IMTC is located in the Georgia Centers for Advanced Telecommunications

Technology (GCATT) on the campus of the Georgia Institute of Technology. For information, visit www.imtc.gatech.edu.

- San Francisco State University's Multimedia Studies Program (SFSU MSP). One of the most comprehensive multimedia training centers in the country. The SFSU MSP (http://msp.sfsu.edu) offers instruction in all aspects of multimedia, including the theory, history, and aesthetics of multimedia as well as its design, tools, and business practices.
- UCLA Extension's Entertainment Studies Department in Los Angeles offers single courses or an entire curriculum on the new media, film, television, and video that covers every aspect of multimedia from preproduction through packaging and distribution. Go to www.uclaextension.edu for more information.
- United Digital Artists (UDA) produces digital media events worldwide that include Flashforward, the world's largest gathering of Flash developers and designers. During these events, you can take training classes in specific skills and learn from experts in design and technology. Go to www.uda.com for the schedule.

Also check the listings in Chapter 4, "Film," and Chapter 6, "Television and Video."

SOURCES OF INFORMATION

Associations and Societies

Because multimedia is interdisciplinary, the associations that serve this market also serve the professional audio, video, animation, and computer industries.

Check Chapter 6, "Television and Video," because several of the organizations listed there also have special-interest groups that focus on the needs of new media producers. Also, the websites of these organizations will give you a broader picture of multimedia issues and concerns. More detailed contact information appears in the Appendix. For ease of reference, some of these listings appear in several chapters.

Academy of Interactive Arts and Sciences (AIAS) (www.interactive.org)

Association of Computing Machinery (ACM-SIGGRAPH)
(www.siggraph.org)

International Communications Industries Association (ICIA)
(www.infocomm.org)

Electronic Frontier Foundation (EFF) (www.eff.org)

Media Communications Association-International (MCA-I)
(www.mcai.org)

Software & Information Industry Association (www.spa.org)

Periodicals

New media technologies are continually evolving, and a number of new magazines and newsletters with technology-based or application-specific editorial niches serve this industry. Also, because multimedia is an interdisciplinary field, check the periodicals listed in other chapters, especially Chapter 6, "Television and Video." Here is a selected list of recommended trade publications at this writing.

AV Video/Multimedia Producer (www.avvideo.com)

Computer Graphics World (www.cgw.pennnet.com)

Digital Video (www.dv.com)

Macworld (www.macworld.com)

Presentations (www.presentations.com)

Wired (www.wired.com)

Recommended Reading

On Interactivity

Bolter, Jay David, and Diane Gromala. *Windows and Mirrors: Interaction Design, Digital Art, and the Myth of Transparency.* Cambridge, MA: MIT Press, 2003.

Glassner, Andrew S. *Interactive Storytelling: Techniques for 21st Century Fiction.* Natick, MA: AK Peters, Ltd., 2004.

On Presentations

Azarmsa, Reza. *Powerful Multimedia Presentations.* Belmont, CA: Wadsworth Publishing, 2004.

On Production

Chapman, Nigel, and Jenny Chapman. *Digital Multimedia.* 2nd ed. New York: John Wiley & Sons, 2004.

England, Elaine, and Andy Finney. *People and Processes* (Managing Multimedia: Project Management for Web and Convergent Media, 3rd ed, Book 1). New York: Pearson Higher Education, 2001.

Vaughan, Tay. *Multimedia: Making it Work.* 5th ed. Berkeley, CA. Osborne/McGraw-Hill, 2001.

On Digital Video

Austerberry, David. *Technology of Video and Audio Streaming.* Woburn, MA: Focal Press/Butterworth-Heinmann, 2002.

Rhodes, John. *Videoconferencing for the Real World: Implementing Visual Communication Systems.* Woburn, MA: Focal Press/Butterworth-Heinmann, 2001.

Symes, Peter D. *Video Compression Demystified.* New York: McGraw-Hill, 2000.

On Careers

Adams, Ernest. *Break Into the Game Industry—How to Get a Job Making Video Games.* Berkeley, CA: Osborne/McGraw-Hill, 2003.

Gardner, Garth. *Gardner's Guide to Internships in New Media: Computer Graphics, Animation, Multimedia.* Herndon, VA: Garth Gardner Company, 2004.

Hungerland, Elizabeth. *Marketing Your Creative Portfolio.* Englewood Cliffs, NJ: Prentice Hall, 2002.

Hunicke, Robin, et al. *Game Developer Magazine's 2003 Career Guide* (PDF format). Manhasset, NY: CMP Game Group, 2003.

Mencher, Marc. *Get in the Game: Careers in the Game Industry.* New York: New Riders, 2003.

On Specific Tools and Technology

Cohen, Luanne Seymour. *Adobe Photoshop CS Creative Studio*. San Jose, CA: Adobe Press; 2003

Goulekas, Karen E. *Visual Effects in a Digital World: A Comprehensive Glossary of Over 7,000 Visual Effects Terms*. San Francisco, CA: Morgan Kaufmann/Elsevier, 2001.

Page, Khristine Annwn. *Macromedia Dreamweaver MX 2004: Training from the Source*. 3rd ed. San Francisco, CA: Macromedia Press, 2003.

Weynand, Diana. *Apple Pro Training Series: Final Cut Pro 4*. Berkeley, CA: Peachpit Press; 2003

Williams, Richard. *The Animator's Survival Kit: A Manual of Methods, Principles, and Formulas for Classical, Computer, Games, Stop Motion, and Internet Animators*. London: Farber & Farber, 2002.

CHAPTER 8

ADVERTISING

Advertising is a multibillion-dollar industry geared to a single purpose: to persuade people to "buy"—to purchase a product or service, or to support a public cause or political stance. The advertiser, who controls the content, pays for the advertisement.

In the free enterprise economy of the United States, products and services abound. In fact, there is usually a greater supply of products than there is demand for those products. For instance, we have any number of choices or brands of even a basic necessity such as soap. In addition, products and services such as home electronics and leisure travel compete for our disposable income.

Today, even hospitals that are competing for patients are turning to advertising, which only a few years ago would have been dismissed as crass. Another recent trend is the advertising of prescription medication on television. Although this trend is expanding the opportunities for careers in advertising, it is putting new demands, such as knowledge of government regulations and consumers sensitivity to content, on advertising professionals.

Increasing globalization has resulted in heightened competition, and breaking into the business isn't easy. However, the enormous opportunities provided by the Internet and the growth of other media outlets are creating more jobs for both creative and strategic advertising and marketing professionals.

Manufacturers and service companies alike operate in an extremely competitive marketplace and must rely on advertising to help sell their products or services. To attract more business and increase their share of the market, they use traditional mass media—newspapers, magazines, radio, and television—as well as display outlets such as those provided in stores, movie theaters, exhibition halls, and at concerts and other special events. Outdoor media—billboards, skywriting, and blimps—are also used to increase consumer awareness of products and services.

In recent years, niche marketers have realized the benefits of advertising specialized products on cable TV. According to the Cabletelevision Advertising Bureau (CAB), the penetration of cable TV programming has grown to more than three-quarters of all U.S. households, and its growing emphasis on original programming in a wide variety of genres makes it an attractive choice for advertisers. The CAB forecasts that advertising revenues for local, regional, and network cable TV spots will reach $19 billion in 2004.

Direct mail and telemarketing have also proven highly productive in the past. However, the "do not call" initiative has thrown the telemarketing industry into disarray, and has almost limited this channel for advertisers. But the Internet has become a very successful marketing medium because it can carry both advertisements and publicity materials. Although the overuse of banner ads and pop-up messages is annoying to Web visitors, sophisticated media messages that feature audio, video, and animation continue to grab consumer attention. Improvements in technology are making it possible to run video smoothly through the Internet. Media buyers expect that before long online TV commercials will deliver broadband video footage at thirty frames per second, just as television does. The Internet also serves niche marketers well by providing opportunities for targeted marketing through E-mail.

Designing and producing an advertiser's message and presenting it in the various media requires the skills of many talented people—researchers, writers, illustrators, photographers, graphic designers, radio and TV producers, to name a few. Once an advertisement has been created or produced, specialists in media selection and placement ensure that it is delivered to its target audience through the selected media. The advertising industry holds out many job opportunities for creative people with diverse skills as well as for people with marketing and business acumen and training.

A number of corporations also have advertising departments that prepare, produce, and place company advertisements. These departments often use the services of freelance writers, graphic artists, and outside media-buying companies. They hire independent production companies to produce their radio and TV commercials. Some organizations establish an in-house ad agency, while others contract with full-service ad agencies. People interested in advertising as a career have many avenues of work to explore.

According to the U.S. Bureau of Labor Statistics, 439,700 people worked in advertising and related services in the United States in 2002, but the membership roster of the American Association of Advertising Agencies (AAAA) numbered only twelve hundred ad agency offices operating in the nation as of early 2004. Hence, getting a job with an advertising agency can be highly competitive. The recent trend toward the consolidation of media buyers, advertising agencies, and PR firms has resulted in downsizing. The past two years have been particularly challenging for advertising professionals seeking employment.

Job titles like Webmaster, website producer, and traffic coordinator/ Internet have now become commonplace in the evolving world of online marketing. Many agencies provide online marketing services and also subcontract various online tasks to specialized production facilities and service providers.

CURRENT CHALLENGES

Advertising has always been a part of the larger field of marketing. Recently, two trends have blurred the boundary between advertising and the other marketing disciplines.

The first is the growth and consolidation of agencies to serve worldwide markets with integrated marketing communications services while also providing economies of scale. Agencies increasingly offer a broad range of services that are no longer limited to conventional print and broadcast advertising but extend to direct and online marketing as well as PR services.

The second trend is the growth of new forms of "customer communications" that allow for a more direct relationship between advertisers and customers. Foremost among these is Web-based online marketing, which in just a few years has grown from a curiosity to a billion-dollar-a-year industry. The interactive nature and "targetability" of Web-based customer communications are changing the ways that marketers look at the process of selling goods, services, and ideas. Conventional applications in this area include banner ads on websites likely to be frequented by prospective customers and websites devoted entirely to touting the virtues of a particular product or company. But, as the advertising community learns more about the potential of this new medium, better use is being made of its unique character through the use of context-sensitive ads, "cookies" (i.e., activity-tracking files placed on user's computers by websites they visit), the creation of virtual communities, online sweepstakes, and other techniques

To succeed in interactive electronic advertising, it is important to be familiar with the specific media and their business mechanisms. A course in E-commerce and some serious study of publications such as *Internet World* and *Advertising Age* will put you in sync with these rapidly evolving media.

The AAAA, concerned that the value of advertising has been diluted by other marketing opportunities, has responded by attempting to educate marketers about the essential and major role that media advertising plays in creating, maintaining, or restoring the economic value of brand franchises. The books and tapes in its "Value of Advertising & Advertising Agencies" series are available to members and nonmembers alike. Visit the AAAA website (www.aaaa.com) for more information.

THE TECHNOLOGY ADVANTAGE

The Web, with its wealth of information about prospective customers and its potential for immediate market feedback, is a high-tech marketer's dream. Many agencies have established special divisions just to address these opportunities, and dozens of new companies have emerged to cater to the market's seemingly insatiable demand for online advertising expertise. Multimedia distribution formats such as CD-ROM and DVD are also employed by many advertisers, but increasingly the focus is on the World Wide Web and targeted "just-in-time" advertising.

The creation of online advertising campaigns includes development of the concept and creative content, tie-ins with campaigns in other media, links with other websites, and production of content to attract online audiences to the website. Online ads can be presented in the context of a special website devoted to that product or service, positioned as a section of an existing corporate website, or placed as banner ads on related specialized or portal websites.

The creation of integrated online marketing campaigns may include all the above plus the development of contests, chat groups, and online resources for the target audience as well as targeted market research and database marketing projects derived from online customer participation.

The development of E-commerce projects can include all the above tasks plus the creation of a structure that allows for the entire customer/ vendor relationship to be conducted online. This includes managing everything from the search for customers via direct E-mail to website advertising, online sales and order fulfillment, and follow-up database marketing.

WHERE THE JOBS ARE

All three of the participants involved in developing and executing advertising—advertising agencies, corporate advertising departments, and the media —offer job opportunities for those who have chosen advertising as a career.

Advertising Agencies

Creative young people and those who combine aggressiveness with business savvy often think that, to "make it" in advertising, they must move to New York City and tackle Madison Avenue. Many ad agencies have actually left Madison Avenue due to soaring commercial rents, but New York continues to be the advertising capital of the world. For example, BBDO Worldwide is headquartered in New York with nineteen offices and more than 3,400 employees in North America alone. The firm has 345 offices in 76 countries and more than twenty thousand employees.

You do not have to move to New York City to find a satisfying job in advertising. Several large agencies are headquartered in other major U.S. cities: Publicis & Hal Riney in San Francisco; TBWA\Chiat\Day in Los Angeles; Wieden & Kennedy in Portland, Oregon; Campbell Mithun in Minneapolis, Minnesota; Foote, Cone & Belding Communications in Chicago; Temerlin

McClain in Dallas; WestWayne in Atlanta; and Hill Holliday Connors, Cosmopulos in Boston, to name only a few. In addition, major European and other international agencies such as Saatchi & Saatchi have offices in several U.S. cities.

You can start your career and gain experience in a large agency environment by working at an office in any major city. Large agencies generally have a broad range of clients and can therefore provide you with a variety of work. Or, you can choose to start your career with a small agency in the city of your choice and specialize in a particular type of advertising or client.

The Red Books (formerly known as *The Advertising Red Books*) is an excellent research tool if you are looking for an agency job. It is available in print volumes, on CD-ROM, and online. Its "Agency Database" contains detailed profiles of more than thirteen thousand U.S. and international advertising agencies with information about regional offices, accounts, specializations, number of employees, and the names and titles of key personnel.

Corporate Advertising Departments

Many large corporations, and most very large ones, have advertising departments. Because corporations are the clients of ad agencies, corporate ad departments are often referred to as "client departments." A client department either acts as liaison between its company and the ad agency or produces the company's advertising and sales promotion material itself.

In its liaison function, a corporate ad department establishes advertising goals and ensures that the advertising prepared by the outside agency fits the company's sales and marketing objectives. Because this department is held responsible for the agency's performance, it is usually vested with the authority to approve or disapprove the agency's recommendations. At a very large corporation, for example, if the ad department is headed by a vice president, the decision to hire or fire an agency can be made at the department level. Depending on the size of the corporate ad department and the title of its highest executive, however, final approval may have to come from a higher level of management.

In some corporations, the advertising department is responsible for creating and producing advertising and sales materials including catalogs, brochures, and collateral materials. For instance, a major retail or department store such as Bloomingdale's or Macy's will maintain a large creative staff and ad department to handle daily ads and the continuous flow of new catalogs. Corporate departments responsible for the preparation and placement of materials are staffed in much the same way as ad agencies. They hire researchers, copywriters, graphic artists, creative directors, advertising assistants, and ad managers.

The Media

Every newspaper, magazine, radio, and TV station employs an advertising staff. Media advertising jobs are primarily sales jobs: Advertising salespeople sell ad space for their publications or time for their radio or TV station to agencies and advertisers. For job seekers who are not interested in selling, some sales support and creative jobs are available, especially at large media companies such as CBS or Murdoch Magazines. Sales support functions include market research and the production of collateral materials, as well as some ad materials.

An advertising sales manager or advertising sales director is usually in charge of a media ad sales department. Creative directors or art directors are generally responsible for the creative services staff. Large media conglomerates have research departments headed by a research director.

If you are interested in an ad rep sales position at a magazine, you should read *Folio:*, (Yes, the magazine's name is *Folio:*) which provides insightful articles on all aspects of magazine publishing. For sales jobs at radio and TV stations, refer to the *Broadcasting & Cable Yearbook*. If you are interested in the creative aspects of advertising, your best resource is a professional association such as The Society of Illustrators, which publishes the "Society of Illustrators' Career Guidance in Illustration and Graphics Design," a booklet that discusses portfolio preparation, gives detailed job descriptions of agency jobs, and offers hints on getting meetings with art directors.

JOB DESCRIPTIONS

Most ad agencies are organized into the following departments: administration or agency management, account management, creative services, media services, print production, traffic, finance, and bookkeeping. Large and medium-sized agencies may have specialists in each department as well as a separate department for research, TV production, and human resources or personnel.

Administration

Although agency management is always a crucial function, the trend toward mega-agencies is making it more so. The management function includes responsibility for establishing policies as well as planning, developing, and defining objectives to assure growth and profitability. At small agencies, the owner, president, or partners will carry out these functions. Super-large agencies may be structured like large corporations with a chief executive officer (CEO), a chief operating officer (COO), a chief financial officer (CFO), and an executive committee or board of directors.

Account Management

This department writes client marketing plans, presents plans, gets them approved by clients, coordinates the development of advertising programs, and ensures that the approved programs are implemented. These functions are executed by an account group that consists of a management supervisor, account supervisor, account executive, account coordinator, and account assistant. At a small agency, the account group may consist of fewer people, each of whom will carry more responsibilities.

The account group acts as liaison between the agency and the client. Every member of this group has a counterpart on the client side, and the higher up the account person, the higher up the contact on the client side. For example, a management supervisor will interact with the vice president of marketing, the account supervisor with the director of sales and advertising, and the account executive with the advertising manager.

Creative Services

The creative department conceptualizes and creates advertising. The creative team, which consists of art directors, copywriters, graphic artists, illustrators, photographers, TV producers, and layout and mechanical artists, works together to translate the marketing strategy into print advertisement and commercials to be broadcast. This group is also responsible for producing collateral materials such as logos and displays.

The function of the art department varies from agency to agency depending on the number of clients, billings, and the type of work required by the art department. For example, if the ad campaign being developed by the agency includes the production for all media, the art department will be responsible for conceptualizing and producing the ads for print and the commercials for broadcast media.

Once the department comes up with a concept and a plan that is "on target," it is presented to the client for approval. The department is then responsible for producing the ad.

The art director works with writers and the creative team to conceive and develop imaginative and persuasive print and TV advertisements. The art director prepares cost estimates relating to layout, illustration, photography, type, retouching, and pasteup as well as supervising all staff members involved in producing the various elements that make up the ad.

Entry into the creative department of an ad agency is extremely competitive. When applying for a job in this department, you must be able to present your portfolio to the art director. Creating a portfolio can itself be a very tough job.

However, most creative departments use the services of freelance writers, photographers, and graphic artists, so, if you have already done some freelance work, you can present a selection from those assignments.

Online Services

Although current spending on online advertising amounts to less than 2 percent of the amount devoted to print ads, knowledge of Web-based marketing is now essential for anyone entering the advertising business. Because the field is evolving at a breakneck pace, the best place to find up-to-date information is, of course, on the Web. Most agencies and online marketing companies have employment-related and job listing pages on their websites, and the online versions of publications such as *Internet World* and *AdWeek* will keep you abreast of the latest trends and buzzwords.

Media Services

This department analyzes, evaluates, selects, and recommends the appropriate media for a client's ads—the newspapers, magazines, radio, and TV stations best suited to meet the objectives of the advertising strategy. Job titles in this department include media director, media supervisor, broadcast media supervisor, media planner, media buyer, and media estimator.

The media director's key responsibility is to set internal policies regarding media planning and buying. This is a senior position that requires maintaining good relations with the media as well as developing new profit opportunities. Media supervisors develop and execute media plans that will meet clients' advertising objectives. They make formal presentations to both the agency's account group and to clients. Media supervisors guide the work of media planners.

Large agencies hire broadcast media supervisors to analyze and evaluate broadcast media, develop demographics and cost estimates, and negotiate "buys" of radio and TV time. The media planner's main task is to develop traffic and media schedules, which in turn entails media research and selecting a combination of media and appropriate advertising schedules.

Media buyers negotiate and purchase space and time. Because most print publications have a virtually unlimited amount of space for sale, buyers focus on negotiating position—getting the best position in the magazine for the client's ad.

In radio and television, buyers are given specifications for selecting the best spots for the client's commercial. Media buyers must find out what spots are available before negotiating purchases, and, because rates for spots are flexible, buying broadcast spots (known as "avails" because they depend on availability) requires both skill and experience.

Some large companies hire entry-level employees as media estimators. This work involves compiling rate and cost data for media buyers and planners. This is a good entry-level position because it offers on-the-job training that can lead to a promotion to media buyer.

Print Production

The print production department is responsible for the final creation of the advertisement. After the creative team has finalized and specified the various elements of the ad, the print production department purchases print elements such as color separations and type.

Print production managers are responsible for black-and-white and four-color printing, color separations, and the preparation of mechanicals. This department works closely with the traffic and creative departments in scheduling and coordinating production projects. It is also responsible for quality control of the final advertising materials to ensure that they conform to technical specifications and are produced on time. Entry into this department is not highly competitive, although it usually calls for some experience in production work. An entry-level position in this department is the best stepping-stone to greater responsibilities and better-paying agency jobs.

Traffic

Traffic department managers, supervisors, and assistants control and oversee the workflow to ensure that ads are conceived, produced, and placed as specified.

This department's primary function is to establish schedules and mediate among production staff, creative, and account groups. This department is also responsible for keeping complete records of projects, from the account group's first job order to completion. A traffic assistant's position requires little experience aside from basic organizational skills and is therefore an excellent entry-level job.

Finance and Bookkeeping

Ad agencies hire specialists in accounting, financing, and financial forecasting to monitor all financial transactions from collecting money from clients and paying the media and other creditors to meeting payrolls. Agencies receive frequency discounts from media when they make multiple unit buys; however, the agency must also pay the media company within a given period of time.

And, because clients rarely pay their ad agency in advance, the agency must sometimes lay out huge sums of money in the interim. Managing cash flow is therefore a critical function of the finance and bookkeeping department.

SALARIES IN ADVERTISING

Salary levels vary substantially depending upon location, firm size, level of managerial responsibility, industry, length of service, and education. A number of industry magazines publish salary survey reports based on data collected from readership studies.

Articles in magazines such as *Advertising Age* report ad agency salary levels as well as employment trends. In 2002, the www.adage.com Data-Center reported on executive pay at agencies including base salary plus bonus figures.

The average base salaries were: creative director, $116,000; associate creative director, $85,000; art director, $54,000; copywriter, $56,000; media director, $76,000; lead account planner, $79,000; and account executive, $50,000. The complete salary survey and report is available only to *Ad Age* subscribers.

According to the U.S. Bureau of Labor Statistics, median annual earnings in 2000 for advertising and promotions managers were $53,360; for marketing managers, $71,240; and for sales managers, $68,520. Earnings ranged from less than $27,840 for the lowest 10 percent of advertising and promotions managers to more than $137,780 for the top 10 percent of sales managers.

A 2003 corporate marketing salary survey by the American Management Association (AMA) reported on data collected from 11,461 marketing employees at 455 companies nationwide. For marketing employees, especially at the management level, there was evidence of a direct relationship between a company's return on marketing investment and the marketing employees' take-home pay.

For example, 74 companies that responded to applicable questions in the survey reported paying median total cash compensation of $197,900 for vice president of corporate communications, of which 17.6 percent or $34,800 was the typical bonus payout.

According to a recent survey by the National Association of Colleges and Employers (NACE), the average starting salary for marketing majors who graduated in 2001 averaged $35,000, while advertising majors averaged $29,700.

Education

Most major universities, colleges, and professional schools offer courses in the various aspects of advertising. For example, you can study writing, photography, broadcasting, advertising, and PR techniques as part of a communications program. Courses in graphic design, lettering, typography, pasteup and mechanical preparation, and illustration are usually offered by schools of graphic arts and design.

Business schools also offer courses in advertising, marketing, and magazine advertising sales. Knowledge of research, measurement, and statistical methodologies are also important for careers in advertising, and courses in those subjects are offered in many university and college economics and social science departments.

Advertising-related courses can be taken as part of a degree program or as noncredit courses. Professional societies and schools of continuing education also offer seminars and workshops in these areas.

One way to identify a strong program in advertising is by checking the website of the American Advertising Federation (AAF). Located at www.aaf .org, it lists the colleges that sponsor AAF college chapters by state and has active links to most of those institutions. AAF's college-chapter program has 210 affiliated chapters throughout the United States and abroad. The program includes 6,800 undergraduate student members and almost four hundred faculty advisers.

A strong foundation in written and oral communication skills supported by at least a high-school degree is a minimum requirement for entering advertising, but, because the marketplace is highly competitive, a college education in advertising, marketing, or journalism is becoming more and more of a necessity. However, some jobs in production and traffic do not require a college degree.

In addition to MBA and other graduate and doctoral programs for advanced studies in advertising and marketing at several universities, annual conferences and trade shows sponsored by publishing companies offer seminars for working professionals. The AAAA's Institute of Advanced Advertising Studies (IAAS) is a series of training programs developed with local colleges or universities and sponsored by AAAA councils in major cities. IAAS programs are comprehensive evening courses, thirteen to sixteen weeks long, designed for agency professionals with one to four years of experience. Students attend lectures each week and work in "mini-agency" teams to develop a total advertising program for a given product or service.

Experience

Agencies promote employees to management positions after they have attained several years of broad experience in advertising. Typically, top management jobs are acquired only after considerable managerial experience in high-level positions. The title of account management supervisor, which exists in large agencies, is usually granted to account supervisors with several years of experience. An account supervisor must have two to five years of experience as an account executive, and an account executive generally joins a firm as an assistant account executive with some management training. An MBA is preferred.

Creative directors and senior art directors are expected to have six to eight years of experience, most of it in art direction. Senior art directors must have three to five years of experience as an art director or as an assistant art director.

A top-level copywriter's job at a large agency would require three to eight years of copywriting experience. This job requires experience in managing a full team of writers. Some agencies hire junior copywriters without extensive experience if their portfolios look promising.

The job of media director calls for more than five years of experience in addition to several years of work in the business. Depending on the size of the agency and its organizational structure, this job can lead to an agency management position. The title of media supervisor is granted to media planners or buyers with two or three years of experience.

A traffic manager must have at least three to five years of experience specifically in traffic.

Most management titles at large and medium-sized agencies call for experience in supervising and managing a department.

Account Management The jobs of account executive and account supervisor require a thorough understanding of the advertising industry and a good business sense. A liberal arts education with broad experience is helpful in handling clients of diverse backgrounds. You must be self-confident and flexible, and have well-developed interpersonal skills. Agencies look for good business communicators with management qualifications. If you are planning on postgraduate education, an MBA would be appropriate. Professional associations such as the Ad Club of New York and the American Management Association offer a wide variety of noncredit courses on advertising and marketing.

Creative Services Jobs in this area require exceptional talent. Writers, illustrators, and photographers who work in this department are specialists in their specific creative fields and must have a thorough understanding of the advertising business as well. For example, a copywriter must have a sense of design in addition to being able to write imaginative and stimulating copy. As a creative person, you must be able to express your ideas in the context of the marketplace. You must know the client's product, its users, and its competition.

You must also have a good understanding of the media in which the advertising message will be presented and a clear understanding of the marketing plan and advertising strategy.

Ad agencies are always seeking out outstanding graphic designers because it is the visual element of an ad that grabs readers or viewers. If you are interested in the design aspects of advertising, you must know about different typefaces/fonts and sizes, and how to arrange images and type for maximum impact. As an art director, you will not actually be drawing the final graphic elements in ads (this is handled by the print production team), but you will need to be able to sketch ideas so clients can visualize the finished ad. Hence, training in the various aspects of design at an art or design school like the School of Visual Arts (www.schoolofvisualarts.edu) and Parsons School of Design (www.parsons.edu) in New York City is essential. Creative people should study publications of The Clio Organization, sponsor of the CLIO Awards for Advertising Excellence.

Print Production Whatever your title in the print production department, you will be expected to have a broad knowledge of all areas of graphic arts as well as a critical eye for color. As a print production manager, you must be well versed in scheduling and monitoring production jobs and able to work with vendors such as printers, typographers, engravers, and retouchers. You must also know each supplier's strengths and weaknesses. And, because you will be responsible for the production budget, you must also keep cost and efficiency considerations in mind.

Traffic Scheduling and coordinating people and projects are essential skills for traffic department employees. These jobs require an eye for detail, good organizational skills, and the ability to handle several tasks simultaneously. Because you will be dealing with the creative, print production, and account groups, you must have a pleasant personality and the ability to keep the work flow on schedule. As a senior person in this department, you will be responsible for preparing preliminary budgets and securing internal, as well as client and legal, approvals.

TRADE SCHOOLS

In addition to four-year colleges and graduate programs, a number of advertising trade schools offer real-world training that may make it easier to break into the industry or to make an upward career move. Some of these trade schools even partner with a university to offer a certificate program. At Creative Circus in Atlanta, for example, you can enroll in a six-week summer session and earn a one-hour-per-course credit through the University of Florida's Department of Continuing Education. Creative Circus offers a two-year program that has a strong reputation for giving students a solid foundation and helping them to build impressive portfolios in advertising art direction, copywriting, and graphic design. Go to www.creativecircus.com for more information.

At the Portfolio Center, also in Atlanta, the emphasis is on creation. The full-time two-year program includes comprehensive courses in design and media architecture, art direction, photography, illustration, and writing. In addition, every week a high-profile professional teaches a three-hour seminar. The center's career development office, which helps students to find jobs, does not charge a placement fee. Explore the center's design sensibilities at www.portfoliocenter.com.

The Miami Ad School also offers a two-year program in each of five portfolio programs including photo design and interactive design. It recently added a twelve-week course in account planning. For details, visit www.adschool.edu.

PROFESSIONAL ORGANIZATIONS

A number of industry organizations that encourage the growth of advertising professionals also offer useful resources for identifying opportunities. The major ones are described in brief below; for more detailed contact information, see the Appendix.

- The Advertising Council. As the leading producer of public service advertisements, the Ad Council (www.adcouncil.org) conducts extensive research and addresses crucial national social issues in America. Its Broadcast PSA Director Study ($30) details the factors considered by key personnel at TV and radio stations when reviewing, filing, and selecting PSAs to be aired.
- Advertising Educational Foundation (AEF). The website (www.aded.org) is an excellent resource and includes articles and commentary on current issues. It also offers comprehensive information about careers in advertising and employment opportunities such as a career guide and "Advice from the Pros."
- Advertising Research Foundation (ARF). The ARF research department champions key research initiatives in advertising, marketing, and media research. Its member companies receive the quarterly *Journal of Advertising Research* as a membership benefit. ARF's home page (www.arfsite.org) has a link to a glossary of digital media research terms that is available to website visitors.
- American Advertising Federation (AAF). In addition to its numerous college-chapter programs, which guide students in advertising curriculum and job placement, AAF's programs include more than a

thousand internships, plus scholarships, industry mentors, and opportunities to network with top agency and corporate recruiters. AAF is also an invaluable organization for advertising professionals. The online job bank on its website (www.aaf.org) features detailed job listings, confidential résumé posting, and search functions.

- American Marketing Association (AMA). The AMA's membership consists of 38,000 organizations and more than 750,000 marketing professionals. The association provides current and comprehensive information and training for professionals in advertising, all specialties in marketing including business-to-business (b2b), customer relationship management (CRM), and the Internet, media, marketing research, and public relations. Articles on many useful topics are presented in its publication, *The Source*, and on its website (www.ama.org). Its Web-based career center offers articles on job searches.

- Direct Marketing Association (DMA). DMA members include direct and interactive marketers, ad agencies, consultants, and industry suppliers. The DMA offers excellent career guidance, and its website (www.the-dma.org) hosts a job bank with lists of positions available as well as articles on preparing a résumé, interviewing skills, descriptions of jobs in various direct marketing and direct response fields, and professional development opportunities.

- Internet Advertising Bureau (IAB). The bureau's member companies include E-mail, wireless, and interactive broadcasting media companies. IAB's website (www.iab.net) presents standards and guidelines for "rich media" (i.e., large files with content such as video, animation, and interactive capability) presentation. Its various committees work on projects that include developing definitions, standards, and guidelines for areas such as advertising-based gaming.

- One Club. The One Club for Art and Copy (www.oneclub.com) is a nonprofit organization that recognizes and promotes creative excellence in advertising. It has several programs that focus on career development for art directors and copywriters, including portfolio reviews, a quarterly publication, competitions, annual exhibition of student work, and its prestigious annual events, One Show and One Show Interactive.

- Radio Advertising Bureau (RAB). If you work for a radio station that is a member of the RAB (www.rablcom), you can benefit from its training programs. RAB's Training Academy provides intensive on-site training in real-world skills for new radio salespeople and managers.

SOURCES OF INFORMATION

Associations

A number of associations have served the advertising industry over the years. With the advent of online marketing and advertising, new organizations are addressing some of the needs of professionals in this field. Here is a selected list of associations. More detailed contact information appears in the Appendix. For ease of reference, some of these listings appear here.

Advertising Council (www.adcouncil.org)
Advertising Educational Foundation (AEF) (www.aded.org)
Advertising Research Foundation (ARF) (www.arfsite.org)
American Advertising Federation (AAF) (www.aaf.org)
American Marketing Association (AMA) (www.ama.org)
Direct Marketing Association (DMA) (www.the-dma.org)
Internet Advertising Bureau (IAB) (www.iab.net)
The One Club (www.oneclub.com)
Radio Advertising Bureau (RAB) (www.rab.com)

Periodicals

Many magazines and newsletters serve the advertising industry. Some focus on a single medium such as print advertising, while others offer an industry-wide focus, including campaign strategies currently in use. Also, several publications that publish articles on marketing topics such as integrated marketing and multicultural issues are listed in Chapter 9.

Advertising Age: www.adage.com
Adweek: www.adweek.com

EMarketer: www.emarketer.com
Graphis magazine: www.graphis.com
Internet World: www.iw.com
Potentials in Marketing: www.potentialsmag.com

Directories

Adweek's three online directories:

> *The Adweek Directory,* the *Brandweek Directory,* the *Mediaweek Multimedia.* New York: VNU eMedia. $700/one directory; $1,150/two directories; $1,425/three directories.

Shoot Commercial Production Directory. New York: VNU. Annual. $100.

The Red Books. New York: LexisNexis.

Recommended Reading

On Branding

Gobe, Marc, Sergio Zyman, and Marc Gob. *Emotional Branding: The New Paradigm for Connecting Brands to People.* New York: Allworth Press, 2001.

Vaid, Helen. *Branding: Brand Strategy, Design and Implementation of Corporate and Product Identity.* New York: Watson-Guptill Publications, 2003.

Wheeler, Alina. *Designing Brand Identity: A Complete Guide to Creating, Building, and Maintaining Strong Brands.* New York: John Wiley & Sons, 2003.

On Broadcast Media

American Association of Advertising Agencies. *Broadcast Business Affairs for the Advertising Professional.* New York: AAAA, 2003.

Radio Advertising Bureau. *Radio Marketing Guide & Fact Book.* New York: RAB, 2003–2004.

Warner, Charles, and Joseph Buchman. *Media Selling: Broadcast, Cable, Print, and Interactive.* 3rd ed. Ames, IA: Iowa State University Press, 2004.

On Direct Marketing

Geller, Lois K., and Seth Godin. *Response: The Complete Guide to Profitable Direct Marketing.* Oxford University Press, 2002.

Hughes, Arthur M. *Strategic Database Marketing: The Masterplan for Starting and Managing a Profitable Customer-Based Marketing Program.* 2nd ed. New York: McGraw-Hill, 2000.

Stone, Bob, Ron Jacobs, and H. Robert Wientzen. *Successful Direct Marketing Methods.* 7th ed. New York: McGraw-Hill, 2001.

On Effectiveness

Kotler, Philip. *Marketing Management.* 11th ed. Englewood Cliffs, NJ: Prentice Hall, 2002.

Lewis, Herschell Gordon. *Effective E-Mail Marketing: The Complete Guide to Creating Successful Campaigns.* New York: AMACOM, 2002.

Schmitt, Bernd, David L. Rogers, and Karen Vrotsos. *There's No Business That's Not Show Business: Marketing in an Experience Culture.* Englewood Cliffs, NJ: Financial Times Prentice Hall, 2003.

On Media Planning

Avery, Jim. *Advertising Campaign Planning: Developing an Advertising-Based Marketing Plan.* 3rd ed. Chicago: The Copy Workshop, 2000.

Parente, Donald E. *Advertising Campaign Strategy: A Guide to Marketing Communication Plans.* 3rd ed. New York: International Thomson Publishing, 2003.

Percy, Larry, John R. Rossiter, and Richard Elliott. *Strategic Advertising Management.* Oxford Press, 2002.

Schmetterer, Bob. *Leap! A Revolution in Creative Business Strategy.* New York: John Wiley & Sons, 2003.

CHAPTER

9

PUBLIC RELATIONS

Public relations, or PR, describes the activities of organizations to communicate effectively with their various audiences. Public relations is a deliberate effort to build and maintain an image of the organization that will enable it to function smoothly and productively within society. A PR agent's primary responsibility is to develop and manage two-way communication processes between many types of organizations—corporations and businesses, nonprofits, and government agencies—and their publics. In the case of a corporation or business entity, for example, the public includes customers, employees, and stockholders. Nonprofit institutions that seek to influence specific groups of people to favor their cause or services may find that their publics include benefactors, members, and volunteers. And, government agencies may find their publics in different geographical locations or in specific industries related to their areas of responsibility.

Over the past few decades, the PR function has evolved and developed into a science and an art. Thanks to the experience and dedication of visionary practitioners and educators, publicists focus on the substance of their message as well as on its presentation. Working in this field involves not only media relations but also research; publicity campaign strategy, implementation, measurement, and evaluation; marketing communications; and even advising the management of the organization for which the PR agent is working.

CURRENT CHALLENGES

Ethical issues have been a concern in the PR profession for decades. Today, with the lines between types of content presented on the Internet becoming muddied in much the same way that advertorials and infomercials have blurred the lines between advertising and editorial content in other media, publicists are facing increasing challenges when it comes to maintaining integrity in material developed and presented on the Internet. The Public Relations Society of America (PRSA) has worked to develop and promote high standards of public service and conduct among its members. Toward that end, it has developed and adopted a code of professional standards that emphasizes a practitioner's ethical responsibility. Upon joining the society, members agree to adhere to its published code of professional standards.

Media and press relations are among the key responsibilities of PR professionals. With telecommuting gaining ground, and freelance writers and virtual workforces in media companies becoming commonplace, PR managers are facing increasing difficulty getting beyond media gatekeepers.

Cutting through the noise level caused by information overload is another challenge. Corporations and nonprofit organizations alike are finding it increasingly difficult to communicate effectively with their key audiences. One reason is information overload. Because today's desktop communication tools make it so easy to design and produce huge quantities of communication materials, many corporations are disseminating more information than ever before and using every medium of distribution from print and E-mail to CD-ROM and television. In this age of information proliferation, the responsibility of a PR staff to deliver information to the press, manage the client's reputation at a time of conflict and controversy, and build the organization's image has become even more crucial.

During this time of rapid social change and shifting values, organizations are turning more than ever to PR specialists to build trust with various publics because they realize that public understanding and support are crucial to achieving organizational goals.

However, the tools now available for the electronic delivery of information have expanded the reach of PR activities while, in fact, limiting the career opportunities in the field. For example, small businesses are lured by do-it-yourself offerings from news outlets such as PR Newswire's Small

Business Toolkit, which, for a nominal fee, offers member companies the ability to send a standard news release of about four hundred words to all the media in their state, plus trade publications, and to almost four thousand websites, online services, and databases.

SKILLS IN DEMAND

The Internet has expanded the reach of publicity messages. Consumers can now learn about products or services on the Web and read reviews by editors and customers as well as make purchasing decisions and concluding transactions, all online. That's why many companies have adopted an integrated approach to marketing products and services and are making PR activities an integral part of their marketing strategies. PR professionals must be familiar with the online opportunities available for publicity and be able to prepare press releases and other information for various types of electronic delivery.

The ability to work with website producers to create "killer" online newsrooms that will deliver information that journalists are looking for when visiting a corporate website is in high demand. As more companies adopt integrated and interactive marketing strategies, the demand for PR pros with experience in this area will increase.

Research skills, especially for entry-level positions, are also in great demand. Proficiency in the use of Internet-based and commercial database electronic information resources such as Lexis-Nexis, Dow Jones/Factiva, GaleNet, and First Search will prove useful.

Another skill involves monitoring and measuring the effectiveness of cyber-media content, just as it is necessary to scour traditional media to determine the effectiveness of PR content. Although the task may seem daunting—given that there are an estimated three billion Web pages—a number of commercial services will monitor a large number of websites daily, identify when an organization is mentioned, and send the stories by E-mail. You can also develop online research skills using search engines such as Google. A useful article on this subject, "A Primer in Internet Audience Measurement" by Bruce Jeffries-Fox, is downloadable at www.instituteforpr.com.

A deeper understanding of the factors that influence different ethnic groups, and fluency in other languages, especially in Spanish, is in high demand. As the U.S. population becomes increasingly multicultural, and corporate diversity initiatives that address the changing workforce and the multicultural marketplace expand, the need for bilingual PR specialists is increasing, especially in major metropolitan areas. Several major advertising agencies and PR firms include specialties in Hispanic, African American, and Asian American consumer marketing, among other areas. The key skill required is the ability to develop customized campaigns with tailored messages and events that will resonate with each audience.

Throughout the United States, the number of small and midsized businesses of all kinds is growing rapidly, and this should be viewed as increasing the opportunities for PR practitioners. Owners of microbusinesses with one to nineteen employees typically handle PR functions, as well as marketing and other responsibilities, themselves. However, a study conducted by the research foundation of the International Association of Business Communicators (IABC) revealed that CEOs at microbusinesses are aware of the strategic communication skills of professional publicists and the relationships they develop with writers and editors. PR professionals should gain a better understanding of the culture of small companies, the special needs of their markets, and the challenges of the business environment within which they function. The communications departments of large corporations usually have guidelines that define specifications for visual material. In small companies, it might take special skills to discover the owners' preferred communication style and to then develop useful guidelines.

Corporations and institutions are striving to understand the forces of change and are constantly adapting their activities to new aspirations. As they turn to PR practitioners to win public support and trust, the profession is gaining greater respect and prominence. PR practitioners are interpreters of an organization's policies, programs, and practices to the public, and are in turn interpreters of public attitudes toward the organization.

INSIGHTS OF WORKING PROS

Working publicists are the best sources for insights on careers in public relations. Carrie Lombardi is an independent publicist and president of Madison House Publicity, based in Boulder, Colorado. She currently handles public relations for such clients as The String Cheese Incident, Steve Winwood, Keller Williams, Charlie Hunter, and Steve Kimock, among others. She says: "For entertainment publicity, in addition to strong communication skills, both written and oral, creativity in developing artists' careers and well-rounded people skills play a large role in one's success. It helps to have good intuition, especially at media events and in setting up and managing in-person celebrity interviews." When it comes to day-to-day challenges, she says: "It can be difficult to feel creative and be patient while working in a high-pressure environment. It's important to be able to work with speed and efficiency, as well as to be able to learn fast and enjoy a busy and creative work life." According to Lombardi, success requires developing many skills that are not taught at school: "These include: how to gracefully accept criticism and not take business personally, general professionalism, how to accept responsibility and be a team player, and how to see a project through and know what tasks will be needed to get there."

Scott Heath is a media relations consultant for a major international digital imaging equipment manufacturer. His experience includes employment as an internal PR manager at Yamaha Motors and setting up and operating an office in the Orange County area of Southern California to represent Mitsubishi Motors, among other accounts. He says: "I don't see public relations for high-tech clients as any different than for those in other industries. The essentials in any PR effort in addition to solid written and oral skills are: knowing your client's services, products, or messages; knowing what the media in the category or sector need to create a story on your client; knowing your client's competition so you can speak intelligently on where your client fits in the marketplace; and being a resource to the media at all times, not just when you are pitching your specific story. Also, since public relations is a service industry, a service-oriented personality helps."

Heath, who majored in public relations and psychology at Pepperdine University in Malibu, California, says that training in PR basics—the ability to craft a message, write an exceptional press release or pitch letter, and to be articulate in a succinct way—is a necessity, and adds, "In the undergraduate PR courses, I learned the basics, but what they didn't teach was enough of the service attitude or how to deal with different client personalities and needs. Courses in psychology helped me with a better understanding of people and situations."

Debra Mercado, president of Debra Mercado Public Relations in New York City, has orchestrated publicity and event management for more than three hundred entertainment artists and is a leader in the Latin community. According to Mercado, "Public relations is an exciting profession, in part because it requires one to network successfully, especially with the news media to get exposure for your clients. Since event planning is part of entertainment PR, you also have the opportunity to network with other groups, which in turn can lead to new clients." Mercado says that the challenges of working with Latin artists include the language barrier and arranging interviews with non-Spanish-speaking reporters or writers. Read more about Mercado's insights in Chapter 11.

Sofia Alayon, also in New York City, recently started her own firm, A-PRmedia Group, which also specializes in Hispanic markets. Her publicity experience includes Sony Music's Latin division, where she created successful tour publicity for such stars as Ricky Martin and Shakira. Alayon says: "Good publicists build solid relationships with the press. In the Latin community, it's like having an extended family. Essential ingredients in these relationships are honesty and trust. When promoting music, media relations extends to radio and TV outlets as well as to DJs and record pools." According to Alayon, unfavorable reviews or exposés of an artist's personal life can present major challenges. "It's important not to get upset and not to take it personally," she says. "There isn't a set solution, so you have to explore various avenues."

SPECIALTY AREAS

Today's PR professional, whether a sole practitioner or working in a multinational agency, would also do well to master the specific skills required to provide services in a specialized area of practice. Although some practice areas or functions are specific to industries such as health care and technology, others, like the three listed below, are common to many organizations.

- Reputation Management. Many organizations have not yet realized that reputation is an important asset that requires careful building and maintenance. Companies' and institutions' business practices are under greater scrutiny from the government, the media, and analysts today than ever before. Reputation management is one of the newer practice areas. It focuses on the strategic planning, design, and implementation of long-term initiatives targeted to both internal and external audiences.

- Crisis Management. An organization is particularly vulnerable when experiencing a crisis situation. At such times, it depends on its PR professionals to implement damage control or crisis management strategies to protect its public image. During any emergency, it is essential that organizations communicate with news media, employees, and the public at large in an intelligent and forthright manner.

- Event Marketing. Smart corporations have realized the value of sponsoring events that will nurture a positive image of the company and its products among consumers. Many major sports events are cosponsored by several companies. Some PR firms and advertising agencies specialize in sports and event marketing. They offer comprehensive services in this area that include event development and management; contract negotiations and sponsorship recruitment; and media relations.

- Other PR practice areas include financial and investor relations, public affairs, community relations, and government relations. A more comprehensive picture of the various practice areas can be gleaned from a look at the eighteen special-interest areas identified by members of the Public Relations Society of America (PRSA). This list is included in the section "Where the Jobs Are," later in this chapter.

THE TECHNOLOGY ADVANTAGE

As in other careers for professional communicators, emerging technologies are providing new impetus for growth in the area of public relations. Practitioners and the industry at large are benefiting from the new tools for opinion research, audience measurement, and related metrics as well as from the digital production and electronic delivery of press releases and related information.

Many PR firms and advertising agencies have set up a practice in inter-active communications. They have invested in high-end production facilities so they can offer their clients full-service production and distribution of information that takes advantage of the new media technologies. Although it is not expected that publicists will have high-end media production skills, it is necessary for them to know what media are available and to guide decisions regarding their use. These services include:

- Home page and website production. Some firms offer services aimed specifically at shaping the client's image as it is presented to Internet audiences.
- Website promotion. This service focuses on arranging links with other websites to increase viewership as well as promoting the client's website on other websites and through other media.
- Online marketing. This service uses the Web, E-mail, and other online media tools to achieve the client's communication objectives, whether to increase product sales, acquire feedback, or present new information.
- Internet monitoring. This services focuses on surfing the Internet and tracking information on the client on not only commercial news websites but also newsgroups, chats, and E-zines related to the client's business interests.
- CD-ROM. Because CD-ROM and DVD are ideal for content-rich multimedia communication such as product catalogs, these services focus on program design, production, and packaging.
- Interactive kiosks. These services generate program design, computer programming, and media production for such applications as customer education and feedback. Examples of these are found in retail stores, doctors' offices, museums, and convention centers and exhibition halls.

Specialty areas such as opinion research and public issues analysis also require technical knowledge and skills.

Surfing the websites of the PR industry's major sectors is an excellent way to learn more about the profession and its many dimensions.

Public Relations Firms

The websites of PR firms will give you an idea of how companies position themselves as well as their practice areas. Some firms offer case studies of challenges presented by clients, strategies employed, and campaigns they have designed and implemented. The websites of Edelman Public Relations Worldwide (www.edelman.com) and Hill & Knowlton (www .hillandknowlton.com) will give you a useful overview.

You should also check the websites of other PR firms and the major advertising agencies referred to in Chapter 8; some of them offer comprehensive information on PR course offerings as well as links to resources.

News Outlets

These services handle the electronic delivery of press releases and also publish news on the Web and update E-news and information throughout the day. The following websites will give you a feel for the kinds of information sent to the press by electronic distribution companies and the different presentation styles.

Business Wire (www.businesswire.com)
NewsLink Associates (http://newslink.org)
PR Newswire (www.prnewswire.com)

PR practitioners use news outlets to disseminate information about their clients and to track information published about their clients by the news media.

Online Portals

A number of companies, including the ones listed below, provide information that is useful in the day-to-day activities of PR practitioners. In addition, most print publications for PR professionals have an online presence. A couple of websites run by PR insiders present useful how-to articles and links to resources; check "Sources of Information" later in this chapter for a list of periodicals. Here are three websites that provide valuable information and links.

> All About Public Relations (www.aboutpublicrelations.net)
> ClickZ Network (http://clickz.com)
> PRStrategy.net (www.prstrategy.net)

Associations

This chapter discusses some of the programs of the two primary associations for publicists, Public Relations Society of America (PRSA) and the International Association of Business Communicators (IABC); their websites (www.prsa.org and www.iabc.org) offer more comprehensive information. The Appendix contains further contact information.

WHERE THE JOBS ARE

According to the U.S. Bureau of Labor Statistics, PR specialists held about 158,000 jobs in 2002. Employment of PR specialists is expected to increase faster than the average for all occupations through the year 2006. PR professionals work in many types of organizations including banks, hospitals, religious organizations, public utilities, labor unions, and colleges and universities, to name only a few.

Almost every organization or enterprise can use the service of a PR specialist to promote an idea or to help sell a product. Because opportunities for PR functions exist in every organization that must communicate with people, job opportunities are available not only at PR firms and advertising agencies but also in the communications departments of corporations, institutions, associations, and government organizations.

PRSA Professional Interest Sections

Association	Health Academy
Corporate	Independent Practitioners Alliance
Counselors Academy	International
Counselors to Higher Education	Military & National Security
Educators Academy	Multicultural Communications
Employee Communications	Public Affairs & Government
Environment	Strategic Social Responsibility
Financial Communications	Technology
Food and Beverage	Travel & Tourism

In corporations, many PR functions are handled by the corporate communications department. However, because investor relations are a critical practice area, in larger corporations, a senior executive with the title of vice president of external affairs or public affairs may be named to manage PR functions. At government agencies, the job is typically located in the office of public information. At nonprofit institutions, PR functions can be located in a PR department, in the communications department, or in the office of public affairs.

Many newcomers seek out job opportunities at PR firms or advertising agencies instead of positions at PR departments of corporations and nonprofit institutions, so that they can gain broader experience while working with a variety of clients.

PR Firms

PR firms, like advertising agencies, handle accounts from a number of different client organizations. A good starting point for locating PR firms is the *O'Dwyer's Directory of PR Firms*, which is updated and published annually. The current edition lists more than seventeen hundred firms in the United States and five hundred more in fifty-five countries, but not all firms are listed, and the real number of PR firms in the United States is much higher.

PR firms vary in size depending on the number of clients they have and their total annual billing. Staff size can range from one-person consultancies to a few PR generalists hired at small agencies, and from more than a hundred employed at larger firms to several thousand at multinational firms.

Most larger firms have a variety of clients, but some specialize in certain practice areas. For example, Edelman Public Relations Worldwide offers its clients specialized services in seven different practice areas, whereas Madison House Publicity, a much smaller agency, focuses on music entertainers on tour. Job descriptions also vary from agency to agency. In a small agency, for example, you may have the title of account supervisor but be called upon to do the job of an account executive or, at times, even that of a writer.

Advertising Agencies

Some large advertising agencies now offer their clients integrated services and have established subsidiary PR companies or firms so they can offer their major corporate accounts a full slate of marketing services.

Government Agencies

The U.S. Department of State's Bureau of International Information Programs is just one of many government bureaus, commissions, and departments that employ public information officers to disseminate information on policies and activities. The U.S. government is perhaps the single largest employer of press secretaries, information officers, public affairs experts, and communications specialists who work out of national, state, regional, county, and district offices. The United States Information Agency (USIA) is perhaps the most far-reaching public communications arm of the federal government.

Corporations

Business and industry spend literally billions of dollars annually on public relations. Almost every corporation has a department of communications that carries out PR functions intended to maintain employee relations in-house as well as promoting the company's product and services externally.

In a corporation, PR tasks will vary according to the size of the company and the type of industry. In a public utility company, for example, the job will be geared to developing good customer and government relations. In an industrial or consumer company, the PR job would focus on developing strategies to promote the product or service as well as the corporate image.

Nonprofit Institutions

The PR function in nonprofit organizations such as the American Red Cross is directed primarily toward fund-raising by creating a favorable climate for the activity or cause. There are more than fourteen thousand national nonprofit associations nationwide. Information bureaus, institutions, councils, and foundations also engage in PR activities that relate to matters of public concern such as environmental protection, safety, and nutrition. In addition, voluntary agencies in the health and public service sectors provide varied job opportunities in press, community, and patron relations as well as fund-raising.

JOB DESCRIPTIONS

PR Firms and Public Relations Departments of Ad Agencies

In a PR firm or the PR department of an advertising agency, PR practitioners typically carry the general job titles and functions described below. However, PR job descriptions can vary depending on the size of the firm and its types of clients. Large PR firms often hire account executives with special expertise such as investor relations.

PR Director PR director or director of PR services at an advertising agency is a top-level job that requires management experience and extensive knowledge of advertising and PR techniques. This person has full responsibility for setting objectives and overseeing projects, establishing policies and budgets, and setting fees for accounts. The job also calls for maintaining contact with clients.

Account Supervisor The account supervisor is the primary link between an individual client and the agency, and performs a managerial role by integrating PR plans with the client's marketing efforts. Many PR firms also need account supervisors with specialized expertise in particular industries such as entertainment, finance, and community relations.

Account Executive The account executive participates in developing PR plans and is specifically responsible for implementing them. Account executives must be good coordinators. The job involves contact with the press to gain editorial coverage for clients. Training or experience in journalism or public relations is a plus for this job.

PR Writer The PR writer's main task is research and writing, and assignments include writing press releases, speeches, reports, and product information.

PR Researcher The PR researcher's job involves information gathering and fact-finding to be used in preparing speeches and news releases. It also involves opinion research and audience surveys that provide data to be used in designing PR programs.

Production Supervisor Large PR firms hire production supervisors to oversee printing, graphics, and other production work. Production supervisors also maintain production records on all PR accounts.

PR Assistant This job, which entails offering basic support services to all PR personnel, provides a mix of all the functions basic to PR and is therefore a good position for launching a PR career. Daily tasks include following up on production schedules, research, some writing, coordinating special events, and maintaining records.

Corporate Public Relations

In a corporation, the PR staff may be located in the public affairs, communications, or media department. It is often part of the marketing and advertising department. In smaller companies, one person will carry out all PR functions. Large PR departments have a person responsible for each function. The director of public relations is in charge of the PR staff.

The main purpose of corporate PR activity is to gain publicity, promote a product or service, develop community relations, and maintain government relations. Publicity calls for planning and developing campaigns that involve selecting the information to be disseminated and the media to be used. The most important and frequently used tools are press releases, feature articles, newsletters, press conferences, press kits, and interviews between corporate management and reporters.

Speech writing is regarded as a coveted function in corporate PR departments because it wins writers recognition from top management. PR promotion activities reinforce advertising, sales, and marketing programs. Promotion experts are required to be highly creative because they must conceive, develop, and execute unique and novel methods of influencing consumers.

Community Relations Most corporations seek to achieve community acceptance by highlighting their contributions to the welfare of the community, so PR in this area will focus on recommending sponsorship of cause-related or cultural events.

Government Relations Corporate PR specialists who handle government relations strive to improve communications with government personnel and agencies, to monitor the activities of legislators and regulatory agencies and, most importantly, to influence legislation that affects the company and the industry at large. PR practitioners in this field must understand the structure and operation of the various levels of government, have access to government communications channels, and maintain contacts with government staff.

Nonprofit Institutions Public relations for most nonprofit organizations such as churches and hospitals focuses primarily on fund-raising activities. Fund-raisers must be good letter writers, brochure writers, and public speakers. They must have a thorough knowledge of the sources and procedures for obtaining funding from foundations and government grants.

SALARIES IN PUBLIC RELATIONS

According to the U.S. Bureau of Labor Statistics, in 2002, 158,000 PR specialists were employed and earned a median salary of $42,000 annually, while 69,000 PR managers earned a median salary of $69,000 annually. The bureau projected that, between 1998 and 2008, public relations would be one of the fastest growing fields that does not require a master's degree or higher.

Research firms, trade associations, and publications also publish salary information for the PR field. Among the periodicals, *PR Week* conducts an annual salary survey and makes the information available to its subscribers.

EDUCATION

A PR specialist must have knowledge and skills in a wide range of areas including journalism, speech, and communications techniques as well as political science, sociology, and psychology. Top-level jobs require managerial experience and often training in business administration and finance. Writing, counseling, and good judgment are at the core of all PR functions.

A liberal arts background is arguably the best undergraduate preparation for a PR career. Some experts advise that writing and communication skills are crucial for entry into the field and that graduate studies in finance, marketing, and business administration are necessary, if not essential, for future career progress.

Anyone considering a career as a publicist or a PR specialist must be a people person. Public relations is a function of the process of persuasion, so strong interpersonal skills and the innate ability to sell are prerequisites for success.

Writing

Because writing is the primary task in public relations, you must be able to write easily, clearly, concisely, coherently, and quickly. The most essential writing skill is versatility in style. Although a press release calls for a good writing style, you must also be able to write application story briefs to pitch to magazine editors. Likewise, you must know the difference between writing for the eye and writing for the ear. Writing a speech, for example, calls for an introduction that will grab the audience and hold its interest, whereas a business style is appropriate for white papers, proposals, or annual reports.

Not everyone is a born writer, but most people can learn to write with training. Good writing, like any other skill, can only get better with practice. Once you have mastered the fundamentals, the more you write, the better you'll write. Practice also builds writing speed, which is vital in the fast-paced PR environment. Typing and word processing skills are essential supplementary tools of the trade.

The importance of editing for breathing life into dull copy can hardly be overstated. Strong editing skills will ensure that all your written material has the desired impact.

Journalism and communications schools teach writing and editing. A journalism or communications degree is a good basis for entry into the PR field.

Research

PR practitioners use informal research on a daily basis, while larger PR firms often conduct formal qualitative or quantitative research for clients. Informal interviews and opinion surveys are often used in the preparation of speeches, press releases, and proposals. Formal, analytical research is usually conducted with specific objectives, for example, to determine the basic attitudes or awareness levels of certain audiences or to test-market campaign themes. In the PR environment, the most widely used methodologies are fact-finding research, attitudinal studies, and opinion surveys.

Library and survey research skills are considered a plus for entry-level job candidates. A basic undergraduate course in social research or research methods will prove useful, as will courses in online research and statistical software.

PR executives are finding that "futures research," which continually monitors the world for bits of information that indicate that something different is happening, is an important factor in strategic planning. In futures research, you scan newspapers, magazines, polls, reports, and studies for items that might ordinarily escape notice but that indicate future trends and directions.

The process reveals information about the competition and consumer acceptance of new products and services. This research method, it is believed, will indicate areas of need that are not yet being met.

If you aspire to a position at the policymaking levels of an organization, become involved in futures research. It will equip you to be an "early warning system" for your employer, and that in turn will open new possibilities for professional advancement.

Oral Communication Skills

Because PR people are spokespeople for the organizations they represent, they must be able to address audiences and present information in an honest, straightforward, and interesting manner. Most important is the ability to communicate financial and technical information in a clear and comprehensible fashion. As a spokesperson, you must be articulate and thoroughly knowledgeable about the subject you are presenting. Handling questions and controlling an audience are equally important skills. Training in public speaking can help enhance oral and presentation skills.

Management

Managing time and people are perhaps the most essential skills required by a PR practitioner who has supervisory responsibilities. In addition, senior-level PR professionals must be good at financial planning and budgeting. In a corporate environment, knowledge of legal and financial affairs will undoubtedly enhance the opportunities for upward mobility.

You must start developing time and people management skills with your first steps in the PR field. In this high-pressure environment, you must consciously manage your time and your clients' time carefully. You will find yourself constantly juggling and coordinating schedules and budgets, and you must be able to do this with sensitivity to everyone involved in the project. And, while effectively managing time and people on a project-to-project basis, you must continue to maintain good interpersonal relationships with all your clients and your staff.

If you want to make it to the top, you must acquire business and administrative skills. You will need them if you plan to work with an agency and even more so if you are in corporate communications. Your need for finance and business skills will be greatest if you launch out on your own and start a PR firm. Business school is the best place to learn good management skills and practices, but you can learn much from reading the many books and magazines on management topics. Trade associations such as the American Management Association (AMA) conduct workshops on every aspect of management—attend them. If your goal is an upper-level corporate position, your chances will be best if you have an MBA. So start working toward it right now.

To achieve excellence and to truly stand out in the highly competitive and visible PR field, you must master the basic skill of effective communication at the outset. The next important ingredient is a thorough knowledge of the business or field in which your organization operates. If your company is in the travel industry, for example, it is imperative that you keep abreast of developments in that field.

Leadership qualities and management techniques will help you to broaden the dimensions of your job and to achieve the highest levels of professional excellence. In addition, a successful career depends on the following personal characteristics.

Intellect

Identifying problems and providing immediate solutions calls for a keen intellect. In today's environment of accelerated social change, PR people must keep up-to-date on all issues by reading everything they can and learning constantly.

Integrity

Truth and credibility are the cornerstones of good public relations. PR professionals must have the highest level of integrity and be able to command credibility on behalf of the organizations they represent. Pressure from government agencies and advocate groups obligates organizations to tell the truth in areas such as product labeling and financial reporting. PR professionals must have the courage of their convictions and stand up to clients or employers when they are in the wrong.

Perspective

To project a positive image of a company, you must view all its activities in the larger social, political, and business context. In addition, PR practitioners must maintain an appropriate balance between client needs and agency priorities.

Interpersonal Skills

Before you can persuade people to believe your message, you must win their confidence and trust. Good interpersonal skills are the key to effective communication. Social scientists have studied and written extensively on how interpersonal relationships are formed and what it takes to develop and maintain them. A study of sociology and psychology will give you an understanding of how to create and sustain trust, interpersonal influence, and mutual expectations.

You must be adaptable, so that people of varying levels of ability and intelligence feel comfortable communicating with you. Because you will be dealing with every level of employee, from clerical staff to line managers to top management, you must be able to treat everyone with equal respect and confidentiality. This can be achieved by emphasizing even little things that affect another person's self-esteem. You must maintain respect for the dignity of each individual at all times.

For example, being able to listen without interrupting when another person is speaking is essential to building interpersonal relationships and trust. Good listening demands involvement. A good listener observes the speaker attentively and actively participates in giving feedback. The art of active listening can be acquired with training and practice.

Empathy

Understanding clients' needs requires sensitivity to all the issues, concerns, and people involved. A PR professional must have the ability to listen and to grasp clients' needs quickly.

Creativity

Imagination and creativity are the magic ingredients—the product, if you will that the PR industry "sells." The entire PR package, from planning to presentation, calls for creativity.

Initiative

Of necessity, PR people must be self-starters, so the ability to identify problems and come up with solutions quickly is an asset.

Because PR work covers many varied tasks, there is no typical background or set of "ideal" qualification for PR professionals. An undergraduate degree is a common entry qualification and is necessary for higher than entry-level jobs.

Although newcomers may come from a wide variety of college majors or backgrounds, courses or workshops in writing are expected. Most firms require that you have strong writing skills. Many of today's senior PR professionals started in journalism. PR practitioners with graduate degrees in communications or business usually command higher salaries than those who have only bachelor's degrees.

Some firms hire employees who have specific PR experience. For example, an agency that specializes in investor relations may consider only job applicants with experience in that area. Some corporate public affairs departments require at least minimal experience in a communications job. Senior positions at agencies require several years (often four to seven) of varied PR experience. When hiring for a management position, corporations often look for a PR generalist with an MBA degree, several years of experience, and accreditation by the Public Relations Society of America (PRSA), as described immediately below.

PRSA Accreditation

The PRSA (www.prsa.org) has accredited about one-third of its members through a standardized examination. Any individual who has devoted a substantial portion of time over at least five years to the paid professional practice of public relations, or to the teaching or administration of PR courses at an accredited college or university, and who is currently so engaged, may apply for the accreditation examination. Candidates must be a member of one of the eight organizations that participate in the APR (Accredited in Public Relations) program.

As of July 2003, the APR examination has been reengineered and is now computerized. The written portion of the new examination is in multiple-choice question format and takes three hours to complete. Candidates must complete a readiness review prior to taking the written portion, which replaces what had been known as the oral examination. The readiness review will include a portfolio review and an assessment of the candidate's readiness to take the examination.

Most accredited candidates find that the process of demonstrating their knowledge and competence in the practice of public relations is a rewarding experience. Passing it gives them the right to use "PRSA Accredited" or "APR" in business contacts and also enhances their professional confidence.

Internships

An internship is one of the best ways for students to gain hands-on experience in the PR field. Educators view internships as a bridge between the fundamentals learned in school and the demands of the real-world job environment.

Employers view internships as opportunities to develop new talent and as a way to prescreen potential new employees. For the student, the time spent learning while working in a professional environment provides an opportunity to build confidence, earn college credits and often even a stipend, and make contacts.

Many universities have well-established internship programs that offer placement and faculty supervision. The University of Texas–Austin for example, sets up student-run PR companies in which the students go through the process of actually setting up an agency, "hiring" staff, seeking clients, and entering into contracts. Their clients are usually nonprofit organizations.

The Public Relations Student Society of America (PRSSA) is the student arm of PRSA. It is a preprofessional organization made up of more than 8,000 members in 243 chapters at colleges and universities nationwide. The PRSSA JobCenter is an online career resource that allows society members to search for jobs and internships nationwide. Members can post their résumés and take advantage of the many career resources offered on the website (www.prssa.org). PRSSA also offers more than $20,000 in scholarships and awards annually to its members.

Associations

The Public Relations Society of America (PRSA) and the International Association of Business Communicators (IABC) are the primary associations for PR practitioners. The following list mentions selected organizations that represent areas of practice in which PR agents and agencies specialize; their websites give a broader picture of the issues and concerns within each industry. More detailed contact information appears in the Appendix. For ease of reference, some of these listings appear here.

American Association of Advertising Agencies (AAAA)
(www.aaaa.org)
American Marketing Association (AMA) (www.ama.org)
Canadian Public Relations Society (CPRS) (www.cprs.ca)
Financial Management Association (FMA) (www.fma.org)
International Association of Business Communicators (IABC)
(www.iabc.com)
Institute for Crisis Management (ICM) (www.crisisexperts.com)
National Investor Relations Institute (NIRI) (www.niri.org)
Public Relations Society of America (PRSA) (www.prsa.org)

Periodicals

A number of magazines and newsletters have served this industry over the years. However, the publishing industry is constantly changing, with new owners, new magazines and newsletters, and often new subscription rates. If you are unable to subscribe to a publication of interest, you may be able to read it at a library or borrow it from a PR firm or a practitioner. Here is a list and short description of recommended publications at this writing.

- *Bulldog Reporter* This semimonthly (24 times per year) newsletter offers updates on media placement opportunities and personnel changes. Subscription: $549/year.

- *Communication World* This journal, published six times a year by IABC, focuses on communication management and covers trends, issues, and the latest in communication research, global perspectives, technology, and best practices. Subscription: $270/year.

- *Jack O'Dwyer's Newsletter* This eight-page weekly covers up-to-the-minute news and tips that can lead to jobs, new accounts, and media placements. Subscription: $295/year; website subscription: $14.95/month (cancelable at any time). Other publications include the biweekly *O'Dwyer's Washington Report*, $125/year; the monthly *O'Dwyer's PR Services Report*, $60/year; and *O'Dwyer's PR MarketPlace*, free with the purchase of the previous two publications, or $24/year if purchased separately.

- *PR News* This weekly newsletter covers the PR industry, media trends, and technology. Subscription: $597/year. PBI Media also publishes the *PR and Marketing Network Catalog*.

- *PR Reporter* This weekly publication is dedicated to the behavioral aspects of public relations, public affairs, and communication strategies, and includes trends, issues, research, and case studies. Subscription: $250/year.

- *PR Week* This weekly publication serves as a watchdog of the PR industry and is written for opinion leaders in the public, business, academic, and media sectors. Subscription: $128/year.

- *Public Relations Review* Published five times a year, the review features articles based on empirical research undertaken by professionals and academics in the field. Each issue contains a half-dozen major articles, notes on research in brief, book reviews, and concise summaries of new books in the fields of public relations, mass communications, organizational communications, public opinion formations, social science research and evaluation, marketing, management, and public policy formation. Subscription: $137/year (personal); $386/year (institutional).

- *The Public Relations Strategist* This quarterly PRSA publication aims to present fresh perspectives and new ideas related to the strategic importance of effective public relations at the management level. It examines changing concepts and occasionally challenges current wisdom about PR practice. Subscription: free to members; $100/year (U.S. nonmembers); $110/year (Canada nonmembers); $120/year (international nonmembers).

- *Public Relations Tactics* PRSA's monthly newspaper publishes news, trends, and how-to information about the practice of public relations. Written by seasoned professionals who know how to make public relations work, it is designed to help PR practitioners improve their job skills and stay competitive. Subscription: Free to members; $75/year (U.S. nonmembers); $85/year (Canada nonmembers); $95/year (international nonmembers).

- *O'Dwyer's Media Placement Guide* This publication discusses how to work with editors and enjoy it. Its media placement tactics and strategies include tips on pitching and working with reporters to attain successful media placement. $25.

- *Ragan's Media Relations Report* This is a monthly guide to the most influential U.S. business and consumer journalists. Subscribers receive three E-zine updates per month in addition to the monthly print newsletter. Subscription: $347/year.

Directories

Bacon's Media Directories. Chicago: Bacon's Information. Annual.
Bowker's News Media Directory. New Providence, NJ. Annual.
O'Dwyer's Directory of Corporate Communications. New York: J. R. O'Dwyer.
O'Dwyer's Directory of PR Firms. New York: J. R. O'Dwyer. Annual.
The Green Book: A Guide to Public Relations Service Organizations. New York: Public Relations Society of America. Annual.

Recommended Reading

Andreasen, Alan, and Philip Kotler. *Strategic Marketing for NonProfit Organizations*. 6th ed. Englewood Cliffs, NJ: Prentice-Hall, 2002.

Breakenridge, Deirdre, and Thomas J. DeLoughry, *The New PR Toolkit: Strategies for Successful Media Relations*. Englewood Cliffs, NJ: Financial Times/Prentice Hall, 2003.

Carstarphen, Meta G., and Richard A. Wells. *Writing PR: A Multimedia Approach*. New York: Pearson Allyn & Bacon, 2003.

Laermer, Richard, and Michael Prichinello. *Full Frontal PR: Getting People Talking About You, Your Business, or Your Product*. New York: Bloomberg PR, 2003.

Newsom, Doug, Judy V. Turk, and Dean Kruckeberg. *This Is PR with Infotrac: The Realities of Public Relations*. 8th ed. Belmont, CA: Wadsworth Publishing Co., 2003.

O'Keefe, Steve. *Complete Guide to Internet Publicity: Creating and Launching Successful Online Campaigns*. New York: John Wiley & Sons, 2002.

Ries, Al, and Laura Ries. *The Fall of Advertising and the Rise of PR*. New York: HarperBusiness Essentials, 2002.

Seital, Fraser P. *The Practice of Public Relations*. 9th ed. Englewood Cliffs, NJ: Prentice Hall, 2003.

Sterne, Jim. *World Wide Web Marketing: Integrating the Web into Your Marketing Strategy*. 3rd ed. New York: John Wiley & Sons. 2001.

Williams, Louis C. *Communication Research, Measurement and Evaluation: A Practical Guide for Communicators*. San Francisco, CA: International Association of Business Communicators, 2004.

10

JOB SEARCH

Effective communication is the most important job search skill you can possess. Being able to express yourself clearly, in both writing and speaking, is essential for the two crucial steps in landing a job: preparing your résumé and speaking at interviews.

Every basic communication skill comes into play when you look for a job. You will need to research the job market, write a résumé and cover letters, create a portfolio, sell your skills (if necessary, by using advertising media), and be your own publicist. Although the field of communications is growing at a rapid pace, so too is the number of trained people trying to enter the field. The marketplace is fiercely competitive, especially during national economic downturns. Nevertheless, you can get the job you are looking for if you go about it in a succinct manner and with the required tenacity. Be prepared for hard work—and some disappointments too. Looking for a job can in itself be a full-time job.

EMPLOYMENT TRENDS

The landscape for those with careers in communications is always changing. The good news is that many marketable skills are transferable from one specific media industry to another. Professional communicators has another major career advantage: Even during a recession, when companies shrink their communications departments, the work continues but is usually outsourced to employees who have been laid off. Also, the field offers abundant opportunities for working as an independent or freelancer.

In the last few years, the overall U.S. job market for professional communicators has been tight due in part to the consolidation of media ownership and, more importantly, to the national economic slowdown. Although some specialty areas declined more steeply, others picked up the slack. The preceding chapters have detailed specific issues and challenges in each of the communications careers. You may find it useful to read the chapter on your career interest as well as some of the others to get a handle on where employment shifts are taking place. In addition, the resources in each field will give you ideas about where to start if you are planning a career shift within the larger communications industry.

For example, although at one time the job market for journalists was limited to national newspapers, the tremendous growth of regional and local newspapers has opened up new opportunities for today's journalists. In broadcasting, the market that was formerly limited to networks and affiliates has now expanded to independent stations and a growing number of cable TV channels. In film, although multimillion-dollar productions continue to employ a large number of trained people, the growth of small-budget documentaries as well as corporate and educational films has expanded the job market.

You must keep track of changing employment trends. The birth of new technologies also gives rise to new job titles. For example, the job of "interactive media designer" came about when more corporations' communications departments started producing interactive media. Other examples are jobs for "infomercial producers" and "Web content editors." The need for media people to design and produce programs that can inform as well as "sell" the image or product of a sponsor came about with the growth of cable and low-power TV stations.

Reading trade journals is an important way to keep abreast of changing trends in the work world. You should also invest some time talking with practitioners in fields closely related to your area of work. For example, if you are a corporate video producer, it may prove useful to follow developments in technologies that integrate video and computers.

Your ability to stay on the leading edge of new occupational developments will depend in part on how well you keep up with national business and economic trends. Publications such as the *Wall Street Journal* and the business sections of national newspapers are crucial to this task.

RESEARCH

The most critical factor in job hunting is research geared toward targeting a job market. Once you have determined your area of interest and your career goals, you should make a list of potential employers. Each chapter of this book lists the main directories for the specific communications field; these will give you leads to specific employers. Use the directories to develop your target list. In addition, use the membership rosters of associations in your field to identify the hiring executives at companies that interest you. Also, read trade publications that report on personnel moves within the industry to keep your list up to date.

Your research should also include profiles, especially the needs, goals, and philosophy, of the organizations where you seek employment. The Dun & Bradstreet directories, Moody's manuals, and Standard & Poor's *Register of Corporations, Directors, and Executives* are good sources of information about specific companies. They provide addresses, telephone numbers, information about the nature of the company's business, annual sales figures, and the names of officers and directors. These directories are available in the reference section of public and university libraries.

JOB POSTINGS

The lowest-tech entry-level job posting service continues to be the bulletin board, usually found in a central location in the telecommunications or media studies department at a college or university. In addition, placement offices at some campuses are active in seeking out employment opportunities and succeed in making a good number of placements each year. For a nominal fee, some campus placement offices maintain résumés on file as a service to their graduates. These résumés are updated periodically and are available for employers to review.

The local chapters of professional communications associations usually offer some type of job posting either through their bulletin board, newsletter, or website.

Most national associations offer job posting services, often at no charge to the job seeker. For example, the NAB's Career Center is the best gateway to broadcast and journalism job banks. In addition to job banks sponsored by associations of broadcasters in each state, the center includes links to job banks hosted by radio and TV stations.

Many cable TV stations post job openings online. Through Cox Communications' Career Network on the Web, for example, you can view job postings and search for jobs by category, title, and state. It presents information about corporate culture and the benefits of working with the company as well as comprehensive information about campus recruiting and special events. Check it out at www.cox.com/coxcareer.

Some organizations, like Canadian Women in Communications (CWC), make their service available at no cost to any company that wants to post a job, but access to those postings may be available only to members in good standing.

CAREER INFORMATION ONLINE

The Internet has created a revolution in the job market. Nowhere is this more evident than in high-tech industries like video, multimedia, and television. Up-to-date information about virtually every job, internship, and volunteer opportunity in TV and video is now just a few mouse clicks away. Although the surest path to the right job may still be through your network of friends, teachers, and colleagues, the Web offers major shortcuts to identifying specific opportunities.

Sources for employment information on the Web fall into four categories: trade organizations, job search databases, corporate websites, and recruiter websites.

Trade Organizations

The Radio–Television News Directors Association (RTNDA) is one of dozens of professional and trade organizations that offer job listings. It operates a job website with available positions in electronic journalism. Searching for jobs is free. The association posts additional resources, including research on salaries and articles to help those committed to a career in news. Noteworthy among its resources is "Life in News," an area with articles for novice and veteran newspeople. Go to www.rtnda.org/jobs.

Job Search Databases

Some online job directories or job search databases are general, while others specialize in the various communications industries. The two most popular general job search databases are CareerBuilder.com and Monster.com. By using the advanced search engines on CareerBuilder.com, for example, you can identify jobs by company, industry, or country. You can also conduct your search in Spanish. This website has a comprehensive advice and resource section for every level of employment seeker. It even has a salary calculator. Among its featured resources is a career assessment center that helps you to identify a career that's right for you.

Monster.com also offers comprehensive career advice and has an additional feature, "Network Now," that enables you to connect with other professionals within a defined geographic location. Monster.com is one of the best resources for finding jobs and job information online. This massive website lists thousands of jobs, provides free help with résumés and job searches, serves as a platform for career networking, and provides access to a variety of useful tools and services.

Many industry-specific job websites also offer a wealth of information and assistance. TalentZoo.com serves the advertising industry and, in addition to specific employment opportunities, provides up-to-date articles, advice, message boards with topics such as a salary monitor, and a special "Rookie Scene" for those just starting out.

If you're looking for a production job in film or television, you'll want to go to *Mandy's International Film & Television Production Directory* at www.mandy.com. Its latest database, "Casting Calls," lists jobs for actors in TV, film, theater, and radio, and is searchable for locations all over the world.

Corporate Websites

Almost all TV stations, production facilities, and other corporate citizens of the media world have pages on their websites that list employment and internship opportunities. Once you have identified a specific company or even types of organizations where you would like to work, their home pages are the place to start. Frequently, the job opportunity link may not be listed on the home page. More often than not, you'll find it on the page that contains the company's basic information. Or, simply use the search engine and type "jobs" as the keyword. Macromedia, for example, does not have a link from its home page, but if you go to "Company," you'll find access to "Job Opportunities."

Recruiter Websites

A number of headhunters or recruiters who specialize in media job placements also provide good information for job seekers. Birschbach Recruitment Network at www.mediarecruiter.com lists media sales positions nationwide across all media.

Broadcast Employment Services at www.tvjobs.com is an excellent website replete with the latest employment information and professional development opportunities. Freelancers might want to consider paying a nominal fee to be listed in its database of freelance talent, access to which is provided at no charge to those looking to hire.

INTERNSHIPS

One of the best ways for students to gain hands-on experience in the media is through an internship program. According to Professor Alan Richardson of the Department of Telecommunications at Ball State University, Muncie, Indiana, "Our university considers the internship program one of the most valuable learning experiences possible during a student's college career." He identifies these primary benefits to interns:

- They learn to relate to the business environment and to understand the performance criteria expected of employees.
- They learn to relate to their peers on a professional level, often for the first time, because interns are not treated like students in the work environment.
- They make contacts that sometimes lead to a job upon graduation.
- They can add a valuable reference to their résumé.
- During an internship, students may learn that certain jobs or environments are not suited to them.

Many colleges and universities have well-established internship programs that provide placement and faculty supervision. If your school does have such a program be sure to take advantage of it. If not, take the initiative and contact your local cable or network TV station. Ask if you can intern there. You may also be able to set up an internship program for yourself by contacting associations and organizations that sponsor internships.

David Ostroff, professor of journalism and communications at the University of Florida at Gainesville, offers the following suggestions for students seeking internships:

- Your school may have eligibility rules for internships. For example, you may have to complete a minimum number of credits within your major or have reached a certain class status, such as being a sophomore. Either your school or the internship site may require that you have completed certain courses.
- Organizations with established internship programs seek candidates by contacting appropriate academic departments or placement offices. Some select interns through formal interview procedures, while others will accept the first qualified applicant. You might also contact sites where students from your school have previously had successful internships. Faculty members or other students can tell you about the quality of the experience, whom to contact, and what

to expect. Some organizations, including government, nonprofit agencies, and smaller companies, may never have considered interns but may be willing to do so, once approached.

- Searching for an internship is like seeking a regular job. Identify geographic areas where you would like to work, and determine potential internship sites using resources such as the telephone directory, directories from trade and professional organizations, and your network of contacts. Write to or call the site to determine if it takes on interns. If necessary, arrange for an interview. Check with your academic department to see if there are rules about internship registration, whether you must submit a report after the internship, or other requirements.

- If you are seeking a summer internship, remember that many other students will have the same idea. If you are seeking an internship at a particularly attractive site, you may be competing with students from all over the country, so start your search early!

Ostroff also offers insights on how to get the most from an internship. An internship should help to prepare you for a professional career. It may also allow you to explore professional options by working in or observing many different jobs. Get a written statement from the internship supervisor at the site that describes your specific responsibilities. Sometimes organizations agree to take on interns without thinking about what they want them to do. Sitting around with nothing to do is frustrating for both the intern and the employees at the site.

This does not mean you shouldn't expect to do some menial tasks. Someone has to make photocopies, pick up lunch for the executives, or carry the heavy gear, and interns are at the bottom of the pecking order. The important thing is to carry out your job efficiently and enthusiastically. If you impress your supervisor and coworkers, you will be given more responsibilities.

An internship with a major film studio or a TV network might seem more appealing than one with a local production company or a small-town TV station. Not necessarily! Because of union rules, or the level of expertise required for many jobs, interns at "glamorous" sites may sit around with little to do, whereas an intern at a smaller site may get more opportunities for hands-on experience.

Most interns are not paid, but you must receive some compensation, either pay or academic credit, to comply with wage and hour laws. The amount of time you work on your internship will be determined by many factors—your class schedule, the rules of your school, and the needs of the internship site. Try to arrange your internship so that you work for the longest possible blocks of time. You will gain more from an internship if you work once a week for a full day than by working one or two hours several days a week.

Finally, if your circumstances allow, take an internship at the end of your academic career. That way, when you do a great job and impress your supervisors, you will be able to accept the job they offer you at the end of your internship!

If you are considering a newsroom internship, you should read the online article on "Internships in TV and Radio News: Paid and Unpaid—They're Becoming the Rule," by Vernon Stone, professor emeritus at the University of Missouri School of Journalism. He discusses how the unpaid have taken over many newsrooms, how interns are favored in entry-level hiring, and how to play by the rules. Go to www.missouri.edu/~jourvs/index.html and select "Internships" and scroll down for the link to the article.

CONTACTS

Many jobs in the communications industry are obtained by word of mouth. That is why it is very important to start making and maintaining contacts—"networking"—with people in your profession at an early stage of your career. You can make contacts with working professionals by joining trade associations.

Most national and international trade associations have local chapters that meet frequently. The more you attend these chapter meetings, the greater your opportunity to meet people and learn about new job openings. Other good places to make contacts are trade fairs, conventions, communications congresses, and conferences.

RÉSUMÉS AND COVER LETTERS

Your résumé must show that you meet the specifications of a particular job. A résumé is your way of presenting or "selling" your skills to a potential employer. Therefore, it should contain all pertinent information regarding your education, skills, employment experience, and career goals. A résumé can have many different formats. The format you choose must be one that will set you apart from other applicants, as well as one that is attractive enough that the hiring executive will grant you an interview. Here are some suggestions for designing your résumé:

- Your résumé should contain your name, address, telephone number, work history, education, awards and honors, professional appointments, associations, and other activities.
- A résumé should not exceed two typewritten pages. Leave enough margin and white space that it looks uncluttered and is easy to read.
- List your work experience first, before your education and training. In most production jobs, work experience is more valuable than higher education without any experience. List all items in each category of your résumé in reverse chronological order, with the most recent information presented first.
- Emphasize the links between your skills and the responsibilities of the position for which you're applying.
- Use action words to indicate your competence.

A number of the books listed in the recommended reading section in the earlier chapters of this book contain sample résumés.

Every cover letter should be personalized and targeted to the individual company executive. It should specify the job or type of work for which you are applying. Keep the cover letter as brief as possible. Because the cover letter is your first sales pitch, it should get the reader's attention by being creative, yet professional, as well as straightforward, lucid, and informative—without repeating the contents of your résumé. Use the cover letter as an opportunity to highlight the ways in which your experience and training match the job requirements. End by saying that you will call to set up a personal interview.

The main purpose of a portfolio is to display the full range of your skills, abilities, and accomplishments. Like a résumé, it should be concise and selective, yet representative of your work. If you are a journalist, don't include clippings of every piece you have written. Rather, select the ones that match the writing style of the publication where you are applying. Photographers should read Chapter 3 on "Photography," which has a section on how to put your portfolio together.

Multimedia and video producers' portfolios can include scripts, photographs, slides, floor plans, and lighting schemes. In the video industry, a short videotape of your clips is a good way to demonstrate your skills. Your video résumé should showcase excerpts of programs in which you played a key production role. This will suggest what you are capable of doing as well as provide some insight into your personality. But remember, video résumés should be short—five to six minutes in length is best.

Read the career guidance literature from professional associations and pay attention to suggestions on how to put a portfolio together and market your skills. A good portfolio will put you several steps ahead of other job candidates.

THE INTERVIEW

The two essential elements to a successful interview are these: Be yourself, and be prepared. Your dress and manner should be appropriate for the position you are seeking. You should come across as confident and self-assured. Be at ease, and answer questions in a direct, accurate, and brief manner. Don't try to please, Use your responses to emphasize your strengths.

Being prepared involves thoroughly researching the organization beforehand. If you can, find out something about the person who will interview you. Starting out with some mention of common interests will set the tone for a warm and productive interview. Use what you have found out about the company and its clients to discuss the company's needs and your abilities to help meet them. This should impress the interviewer. It will demonstrate your interest in and enthusiasm for the organization and will establish an image of you as a bright and intelligent person.

You may ask questions as the interview progresses. It is customary, however, to wait to be asked if you have any questions. Be careful not to control the interviewer or to talk too much; interviews should be interactive.

Books on careers and employment are full of information on how to handle interview questions. A wealth of articles on interview techniques are also available. Interview Mastery is a software program, available on CD-ROM and online at www.interviewmastery.com, that enables job seekers to develop interview skills in an interactive environment. The starter interview quiz evaluates your interview skills, highlights your strengths, and identifies areas you can improve so you can get hired faster.

Follow up every interview with a letter of thanks. It should be brief and include a sentence that reinforces your interest in the job.

RECOMMENDED READING

A job search can be very demanding, but many books are available to guide you in your endeavors so you can find a position that will best suit your abilities. Here are some suggestions.

Bolles, Richard. *What Color Is Your Parachute?, 2004: A Practical Manual for Job-Hunters & Career-Changers*. Berkeley, CA: Ten Speed Press. 2004

Gagliardi, Gary, and Sun-Tzu. *Sun-Tzu's The Art of War Plus The Art of Career Building*. Seattle, WA: Clearbridge Press, 2003.

Moses, Barbara. *What Next? The Complete Guide to Taking Control of Your Working Life*. New York: DK Publishing, 2003.

Wilson, Robert F.. *Executive Job Search Handbook: All You Need to Make Your Move—From Marketing Yourself with a Master Résumé to Networking, Targeting Companies, and Negotiating the Job Offer*. Franklin Lakes, NJ: Career Press, 2003.

Wood, Lamont. *Your 24/7 Online Job Search Guide*. New York: John Wiley & Sons, 2002.

CHAPTER

11

WOMEN AND MINORITIES

During the last few years, the pace of progress toward equality of employment for women and minorities in the media has slowed. The sluggish economy is often blamed, but mainstream media opportunities for women and minorities have been further limited by the consolidation of broadcast companies, which has resulted in downsizing and layoffs, as well as politically motivated reductions in funding for public media. Keen competition is expected for many jobs, particularly in large metropolitan areas. Job prospects will be best for applicants with a college degree as well as relevant work experience. Many entry-level positions remain available at specialty media companies that serve smaller markets.

The good news is that now there is much more news and cultural programming that represents various minority groups in the print media and on commercial TV stations than ever before. There is more Spanish language programming on all program outlets, and more Italian, Chinese, and Indian programs on cable TV channels. Public access and community media programs are encouraging minority community involvement, and this means more career opportunities for women and minority professionals. A look at the bylines in print and on the Internet, as well as the credits on TV programs, reveals the increasing ethnic and gender diversity represented in the media.

Widespread access to new media technologies is also nurturing a new generation of visual communicators. Desktop publishing systems, the Internet, low-cost camcorders, nonlinear video editing systems, and affordable DVD-recorders are just a few examples of the tools that are democratizing electronic communications and enabling media professionals to set up their own enterprises. New employment opportunities are opening up at small and medium-sized media companies.

WHAT THE NUMBERS SHOW

National statistics are good indicators of trends and a general consciousness regarding significant issues. In the past, the Federal Communications Commission (FCC) released five-year reports on trends in minority and female employment for the broadcast and cable industries based on data prepared by its Equal Employment Opportunity (EEO) unit. The FCC report, which is no longer published due to budget cuts, often served as a wake-up call to media organizations and as a reminder of the nation's obligation to further gender and ethnic diversity in employment. However, several trade associations have started initiatives to increase diversity in hiring.

A number of organizations conduct annual salary surveys, but only a few track and report data regarding minorities and women in media organizations. The data presented here should provide you with a broad picture.

The American Society of Newspaper Editors (ASNE) conducts an annual census of diversity in the newsrooms of American daily newspapers. Of the 1,423 daily newspapers surveyed, 935 responded to ASNE's 2003 employment survey. The results show that even in the midst of budget cutbacks over the previous two years, diversity is increasing. Table 11.1 shows the numbers for the three-year period from 2001 to 2003.

Asian Americans made the greatest gains, growing by 152 journalists to 2.62 percent. African Americans have the largest total numbers in newsrooms, with 5.33 percent.

The two highlights of the 2003 survey were:

1. Minorities account for 9.9 percent of all supervisors in newsrooms; 19 percent of all minorities were supervisors, a slight decrease from the previous year.

TABLE 11.1 Ethnic Diversity in the Newsroom*

Year	Asian Americans	African Americans	Hispanics	Native Americans
2003	2.62 (1,435)	5.33 (2,919)	4.04 (2,212)	0.53 (289)
2002	2.36 (1,283)	5.29 (2,879)	3.86 (2,098)	0.56 (307)
2001	2.30 (1,299)	5.23 (2,951)	3.66 (2,064)	0.44 (249)

*Percentage of total newsroom population

Source: American Society of Newspaper Editors

2. For the first time, ASNE reported on the number of newspapers that achieved parity with their communities. The result is that 134 newspapers have met or exceeded parity (i.e., the percentage of minorities working at the newspaper equals the percentage of minorities in the community they serve).

Regarding television, the Directors Guild of America (DGA) reported in mid-2003 that there had been no progress in the hiring of women and minority directors in the previous three seasons of Top 40 prime-time drama and comedy series TV programming. The DGA report showed that, for the third year in a row, white males directed more than 80 percent of episodes and that women and minority directors continued to be missing from some of the best-known series lineups. The report also revealed that in the 2002–2003 season, thirteen of the Top 40 shows had not hired minority directors, ten had not hired women directors, and three had hired neither women nor minority directors.

In TV news, figures from the 2003 RTNDA/Ball State University Annual Survey, conducted in the fourth quarter of 2002, showed the largest percentage of women TV news directors ever, at 26.5 percent. But the numbers for minorities in both radio and television were down. In television, the minority workforce dropped to 18.1 percent, and all minority groups lost ground except for Native Americans, who remained the same. The percentage of minority news directors fell from 9.2 percent to 6.6 percent, with all minority groups dropping except Asian Americans. In radio, the percentage of minorities continued the general slide that started with the elimination of the EEO guidelines.

The RTNDA survey also polled all 1,421 operating nonsatellite TV stations and a random sample of 1,490 radio stations. Valid responses were received from 890 TV stations and 272 radio news directors as well as the general managers of 445 radio stations. The article "Women & Minorities: One Step Forward and Two Steps Back" in the July/August 2003 issue of *Communicator* can be downloaded free at www.rtnda.org/diversity/Diversity2003.pdf.

In November 2002, the FCC adopted new Equal Employment Opportunity (EEO) rules and policies for broadcasters that are expected to boost the hiring of minorities and women. In addition to prohibiting discrimination, the new rules require that broadcasters publicize each full-time opening and give notice about of each full-time opening to recruitment organizations that request it. In addition, broadcasters must complete two or four (depending on company size) longer-term recruitment initiatives within a two-year period. These initiatives can include job fairs, scholarship and internship programs, and other community events related to employment opportunities. There are also new record-keeping requirements, and compliance with the new EEO rules will be reviewed and enforced at license renewal time.

From time to time, trade publications include articles on salaries and job satisfaction among women and minority employees who work in corporate media departments. That more and more women are holding media positions at corporate and independent production companies is evident from the membership figures of many trade associations. However, the progress of minority groups in this area is more difficult to track.

Perhaps the most thorough study of salaries at ad agencies is *The 2003 Ad Age Salary Survey: Who Makes What in the Advertising Industry*, prepared by *Ad Age* and the market research firm Broh & Associates, based in Des Plaines, Illinois. Table 11.2 breaks down base salaries by gender for each job title within four categories of agency size, as defined by gross annual income.

INSIGHTS OF WORKING PROS

Articles in trade magazines occasionally focus on minority and women professionals in specific media industries. For example, the RTNDA article

Table 11.2 Average Base Salaries by Agency Size and Gender

| | Agency Size* | | | | | | | |
| | <$3.6 | | $3.7–$7.5 | | $7.6–$15 | | $15.1–$457.5 | |
	Male	Female	Male	Female	Male	Female	Male	Female
CEO	$118,000	$120,000	$202,000	$189,000	$250,000	$259,000	$269,000	187,000
Creative director	92,000	85,000	121,000	119,000	120,000	109,000	154,000	138,000
Chief financial officer	81,000	64,000	108,000	80,000	125,000	113,000	119,000	200,000
Chief technology officer	55,000	63,000	65,000	70,000	78,000	60,000	163,000	70,000
Associate creative director	66,000	60,000	87,000	80,000	79,000	90,000	108,000	113,000
Art director	49,000	46,000	56,000	54,000	55,000	52,000	68,000	70,000
Copywriter	51,000	40,000	62,000	53,000	56,000	52,000	68,000	66,000
Media director	70,000	56,000	80,000	74,000	87,000	90,000	100,000	92,000
Management supervisor	81,000	76,000	101,000	83,000	104,000	93,000	116,000	97,000
Lead account planner	76,000	70,000	97,000	71,000	117,000	79,000	156,000	109,000
Account executive	55,000	47,000	53,000	48,000	61,000	52,000	61,000	51,000
Media planner	40,000	42,000	49,000	44,000	57,000	49,000	46,000	45,000
Account planner	64,000	38,000	53,000	59,000	50,000	62,000	84,000	68,000

*Gross income in millions of dollars.

Source: Reprinted by permission of Advertising Age. Copyright 2003 Crain Communications.

on "Women & Minorities" includes the opinions of several minority and women radio and TV news directors.

Associated Press photojournalist Bebeto Matthews credits his mentor for helping him break into a highly competitive field: "Robert Jones, my professor for an elective photojournalism class, recognized my potential. His encouragement and industry contacts made it possible for me to start a career immediately after college. I don't believe that I could have done it on talent alone. Two decades ago, the opportunity just didn't seem to be there for a young black man like me. When I started at the *Patriot Ledger*, a midsized daily in Quincy, Massachusetts, I hit the ground running, feeling the pressure of being the only black in the newsroom who had better not screw up."

Matthews identifies other key factors that could help the careers of minority photojournalists: "One needs to understand and remember at all times that one brings their creative sensibilities to bear on what is observed without any self-involvement that rearranges the truth other than observed. It is also necessary to develop a visual intellect that enables distinctive journalism."

Although it's not an obligation, Matthews says that minorities should try to open doors for others, especially those for whom the door remains shut. His advice for freelancers is to invest in digital technology such as cameras and computers because, in today's competitive marketplace, these can make the difference between working and not working.

In the field of public relations, women have made strides to achieving top management positions at large corporations in recent years. Additionally, corporate downsizing has led many women to set up their own practice, often with their former employer as their first client. Women PR practitioners frequently attribute their success to their pleasant personalities. But Debra Mercado, president of her own PR firm in New York City, says that although an amiable personality is essential to all PR activities, it takes a lot more than that for women to succeed. Mercado, who has managed publicity for such Latin music celebrities as Marc Anthony, says: "In addition to language skills, a deep understanding of the culture and its nuances and the ability to fit are key factors in being accepted. It's all part of building and maintaining a durable relationship. And then, you've got to be able to keep your femininity, but think the way men do." She believes that women have a natural flexibility that enables them to multitask with ease: "We are always juggling—schedules, tasks, and work and family responsibilities. Event management is increasingly becoming part of entertainment publicity, and so you need those skills, which include the ability to juggle schedules and tasks." Mercado also wants women to be aware that because PR activities are time intensive and make demands on one's personal life, they can be challenging for women with young children.

CAREER PLANNING

Any well-qualified and capable person should not fear discrimination on the grounds of sex or minority status. The law provides for equality of opportunity. In addition, a number of organizations and many prominent individuals are helping to build awareness of the need to increase the representation of women and minorities in media organizations.

Nonetheless, your experience could vary, based on individual circumstances. As you may have gathered from the statistics presented in this chapter, the pace at which women and specific minority groups make strides does vary. Although these national statistics provide an overall picture, they should not unduly inflate or hinder your enthusiasm if you wish to break into mainstream media.

In addition to the career preparation steps discussed throughout this book, experts offer the following suggestions:

- Develop the qualifications and competencies you need to work in this business. You must be both competent and qualified.
- Be willing to go wherever a job is available. Do not limit yourself to major markets or to certain regions of the country.
- Demonstrate your talent and dependability. Be willing to take on responsibility.
- Demonstrate your ability to learn. Be willing to start at the bottom, and do the work assigned with enthusiasm.
- Do not anticipate special consideration—or discrimination.
- Take advantage of the assistance offered by organizations that are specially geared to serving the needs of women and minorities.
- Acquire broad-based experience and skills. If you want to move up

into management, move from specific tasks or job areas to general administration.

- Be patient. Do not expect to move into management too soon.
- Blow your own horn, but modestly. Promote yourself, your skills, and your unique abilities.
- Be ambitious, and set your goals high.

Women and minority employees who have already distinguished themselves in the TV and video industry have had a positive influence on management and have paved the way for those just starting out on their careers. Study the successes of those with whom you share a commonality of background or ideals. If you are fortunate enough to find mentors, hang on to their coattails.

INDUSTRY INITIATIVES

A number of new industry initiatives, several of which are described below, are geared toward promoting diversity in the media, both in coverage and in employment. In addition, the associations mentioned in this chapter have programs especially designed to develop and support women and minorities who have chosen to work in media professions.

The Emma L. Bowen Foundation was established by the media industry to increase access to permanent job opportunities for minority students. The foundation's program is a work-study type of internship that enables students to work for a partner company during summers and school breaks from the end of their junior year in high school until they graduate from college. During that five-year period, students learn many aspects of corporate operations and develop company-specific skills. Corporations guide and develop minority students and have the option of hiring them permanently after they obtain their college degree. Students in the program receive an hourly wage as well as matching compensation to help pay for college tuition and expenses. Mentoring by selected staff in the sponsoring company is also a key element of the program. Between forty and forty-five new students are added to the program each year. The foundation also maintains a talent bank that media companies can use to recruit minority employees. Go to www.emmabowenfoundation.com for details.

The Katz Media Group sponsors an annual Women's Career Summit for women and men in the broadcast and advertising industries. The program addresses key career advancement skills, workplace diversity, and issues of life–work balance. Its program includes keynote addresses, industry panel discussions, workshops, an awards ceremony, and a networking reception. Go to www.katzwomenscareersummit.com for more information.

Unity: Journalists of Color is a strategic alliance comprised of four national associations, the Asian-American Journalists Association, the National Association of Black Journalists, the National Association of Hispanic Journalists, and the Native American Journalists Association. Unity represents more than seven thousand journalists of color. One of its goals is to stem the exodus of working professionals of color from the industry by encouraging fairer promotion practices, more representative media leadership, and the development of role models. Unity's mentor program matches dozens of aspiring journalists with experienced journalists. Go to www.unityjournalists.org for more information.

NURTURING ORGANIZATIONS

A number of organizations identify opportunities and encourage the professional growth of women and minorities working in the media. A brief description of only a few are included here. The Appendix contains a more comprehensive list as well as complete contact information for the following associations:

- The Society for Professional Journalists (SPJ) provides an open forum for the discussion of diversity issues in journalism. SPJ's Diversity Committee prepares *The Whole Story,* an electronic newsletter with tips and tools for diversifying news content. SPJ urges all journalists to take steps against racial profiling in their coverage of the war on terrorism and has made its "Guidelines for Countering Racial, Ethnic and Religious Profiling" available online (www.spj.org). Its "Rainbow Sourcebook and Diversity Toolbox," a database searchable by common news topics, features qualified experts from demographic groups underrepresented in the news.

- The Associated Press Managing Editors (APME) sponsors Time-Out for Diversity and Accuracy, which encourages newsroom staff and managers to pause and consider the diversity of their staffs, their communities, and their coverage (www.apme.org).

- The American Society of Newspaper Editors (ASNE) sponsors a variety of initiatives and projects including job fairs directed at young journalists of color (www.asne.org). ASNE's Diversity Mission has set a goal of achieving racial parity in newsrooms, so that the percentage of minorities working in newsrooms nationwide should equal the percentage of minorities in the nation's population by 2025.

- The California Chicano News Media Association (www.ccnma.org) promotes diversity in the news media by offering encouragement, scholarships, and educational programs for Latinos who are pursuing careers in the news media. It also fosters accurate and fair portrayals of Latinos in the news media as well as promoting the social, economic, and professional advancement of Latino journalists.

- The Directors Guild of America (DGA) has committees that serve the minority groups within its membership. These committees explore how members can advance their careers, enhance their job opportunities in both the English and other language media, and improve their skills within the TV and motion picture industry. The DGA's African American Steering Committee plans events throughout the year to celebrate the achievements of African Americans and takes an active role in meeting with industry executives to address the issue of hiring more African Americans (www.dga.org).

- Women in Cable and Telecommunications (WICT) focuses on serving the needs of women who work in the cable TV industry. Its stated mission is to develop women leaders. The WICT Foundation undertakes initiatives that include advocacy, research, and educational programs. Its PAR Initiative measures cable and telecommunications companies against three standards: pay equity, advancement opportunities, and resources for work/life support (www.wict.org/WICT/Foundation/PAR/). The foundation has also developed the *CableForce 2000 Resource Handbook*, a compilation of work/life programs being instituted throughout the industry.

- Another organization dedicated to advancing the presence of women in the electronic media is American Women in Radio and Television (AWRT), a national, nonprofit, professional organization of women and men who work in the electronic media and closely allied fields. More than thirty AWRT chapters provide an opportunity for regular local meetings with peers in your area to discuss common issues and plan local activities. According to AWRT, it is through local, regional, and national programs that members discover how to do their jobs better: how to make technology work for them, how to function effectively in a diverse workforce, and how to become a valued source of information. Student membership is available. AWRT's CareerLine is an online listing of job openings across the country, compiled and updated biweekly (www.awrt.org).

- The Black Broadcasters Alliance (BBA) was formed to better educate and assist African Americans seeking career opportunities in the radio, and cable industries, and to push for increased representation by African Americans in the broadcast industry's ownership, management, engineering, and sales sectors. Its membership is primarily comprised of African American broadcasters who represent the interests of both employees and owners in the broadcast communications industry (www.thebba.org).

- The Native American Journalists Association (NAJA) addresses issues and challenges that face Native American journalists. Its programs are designed to improve media coverage of Native Americans, to offer training and support to Native Americans already in the field, and to increase the number and quality of Native American journalists. Membership includes a student category for Native Americans, and non–Native American journalists or media instructors can join NAJA as associate members. NAJA maintains a job bank and referral service for Native American journalists seeking employment (www.naja.com).

- The National Asian American Telecommunications Association (NAATA) was founded in 1980 by producers and community activists to further awareness of the issues and concerns of the growing Asian American minority population. Its mission is to advance the ideals of cultural pluralism in the United States and to promote better understanding of Asian-Pacific-American experiences through film, video, radio, and new technologies (www.naatanet.org). The Corporation for Public Broadcasting has helped NAATA with financial assistance as well as program distribution.

SCHOLARSHIPS AND AWARDS

Scholarships, internships, and other tuition assistance programs are offered by several organizations, including:

- The Foundation of American Women in Radio and Television (AWRT) honors and encourages the positive and realistic portrayal of women in entertainment programs, commercials, news, feature films, and other programs with the Gracie Allen Awards, which recognize current and future leaders in the electronic media (www.awrt.org).
- The Native American Journalists Association (NAJA) offers scholarship and internship programs to outstanding Native American college students who are pursuing communications-related degrees. Scholarship recipients receive financial assistance for books, tuition, and other education costs. Internship participants obtain on-the-job learning opportunities with Native American and mainstream media organizations (www.naja.com).
- The National Association of Black Journalists' (NABJ) Salute to Excellence Awards honor outstanding coverage of people or issues in the African diaspora. The competition covers print, television, radio, and new media coverage, with awards in thirty-one categories. NABJ has made a major commitment to honor excellence and outstanding achievements by African American journalists and the media

industry, particularly when it comes to balanced coverage of the black community and society at large (www.nabj.org).

- The Radio–Television News Directors Association (RTNDA) sponsors several annual competitions, awards, and scholarships. Its RTNDA/UNITY Award honors outstanding achievements in the coverage of diversity issues. The purpose of the award is to encourage and showcase journalistic excellence in covering issues of race and ethnicity. It is presented annually to news organizations that have shown an ongoing commitment to covering the diversity of the communities they serve (www.rtnda.org).

- Women in Cable and Telecommunications (WICT) has established the Betsy Magness Leadership Institute, which accepts up to twenty-five fellows each year. The year-long program is designed to help fellows hone their leadership skills through self-assessment, mentorship, and industry involvement. In addition, WICT's annual Women in Technology Award recognizes the achievements of a female technology professional who has made significant contributions to the industry. The WICT Foundation awards three scholarships to the annual WICT Forum: the Lucille Larkin Fellowship, the Cheryl Greene Scholarship, and the June Travis Scholarship (www.cwc-afc.com).

NORTH OF THE BORDER

Awareness of the need to nurture the careers of women and minority media professionals extends into Canada as well.

- Canadian Women in Communications (CWC) believes that the future success of the Canadian communications industry demands the involvement of skilled, experienced women. CWC works to ensure that future by identifying employment opportunities, creating professional development strategies, and serving as a forum for networking and the exchange of ideas. CWC is a national, bilingual, not-for-profit organization dedicated to advancing the involvement and impact of women in the converging communications industries.

It works with all sectors of the industry including broadcasting, telecommunications, cable, film, print, and the new media, and with representation from all work areas including human resources, programming/production, creative/design, engineering/technical, sales/marketing, on-air, general administration, and legal. CWC has chapters in British Columbia, Calgary, Edmonton, Greater Toronto Area, Ottawa, Quebec, Halifax, Manitoba, National Capital Region, New Brunswick, Southwestern Ontario, and Winnipeg (www.cwc-afc.com).

- St. John's International Women's Film and Video Festival in Newfoundland will hold its 15th Annual Festival in 2004. For more information, contact the Festival at P.O. Box 984, St. John's, Newfoundland, A1C 5M3, Canada; voice: (709) 754-3141; fax: (709) 754-3143 (www.womensfilmfestival.com).

- Women in Film and Television–Toronto (WIFT–T) is an internationally affiliated industry organization that recognizes, trains, and advances women in screen-based media. WIFT–T offers a year-round slate of skills development courses, networking events, and industry awards that provide the tools needed to succeed in Canada's global entertainment industry. WIFT–T serves more than seven hundred women and men in Canadian screen-based media by connecting them to almost ten thousand leading film, television, and new media professionals worldwide. Unique among its Web-based industry resources is a list with links to funding sources (www.wift.com).

- Women in Film and Video Vancouver (WIFVV) is a nonprofit association of professional women founded to support, advance, promote, and celebrate the professional development and achievements of women involved in the British Columbia film, video, and TV industry. Among its many programs is WIFVV Breakfast Club, where members and nonmembers network and share stories each month. Its website is an excellent resource and includes a Great Women database as well as links to funding and financial support websites (www.wift.com).

The associations mentioned in this chapter are good sources of information about the current status of women and minorities working in the media. Many of these organizations publish newsletters, magazines, and journals that contain information of specific interest to minority professionals. In addition, some offer pamphlets and booklets on career topics. More detailed contact information appears in the Appendix. For ease of reference, some of these listings appear here.

Directories

Recruiting for Diversity: A News Manager's Guide. New York: Radio Television News Directors Foundation, 2004.

2003 Resource Directory. McLean, VA: American Women in Radio and Television, 2003.

Recommended Reading

American Women in Radio and Television. *Making Waves: 50 Greatest Women in Radio and Television.* Kansas City, MO: Andrews McMeel Publishing, 2001.

Foster, Gwendolyn Audrey. *Performing Whiteness: Postmodern Re-Constructions in the Cinema* (SUNY Series in Postmodern Culture). New York: SUNY Press, 2003.

Rashkin, Elissa J. *Women Filmmakers in Mexico: The Country of Which We Dream.* Austin, TX: University of Texas Press, 2001.

APPENDIX

PROFESSIONAL ASSOCIATIONS AND SOCIETIES

Academy of Canadian Cinema and Television (ACCT)
    172 King Street East
    Toronto ON M5A 1J3
    (416) 366-2227; (800) 644-5194
    www.academy.ca

Academy of Interactive Arts & Sciences
    9343 Culver Boulevard
    Culver City, CA 90232
    (310) 441-2280
    www.interactive.org

Academy of Motion Picture Arts and Sciences
    8949 Wilshire Boulevard
    Beverly Hills, CA 90211-1972
    (310) 247-3000
    www.oscars.org

Advertising Council
    261 Madison Avenue, 11th Floor
    New York, NY 10016-2303
    (212) 922-1500
    www.adcouncil.org

Advertising Educational Foundation
220 East 42nd Street, Suite 3300
New York, NY 10017-5806
(212) 986-8060
www.aded.org

Advertising Photographers of America (APA)
PO Box 361309
Los Angeles, CA 90036
(323) 933-1631; (800) 272-6264
www.apanational.org

Advertising Research Foundation
641 Lexington Avenue
New York, NY 10022
(212) 751-5656
www.arfsite.org

Alliance for Community Media
666 11th Street, N.W., Suite 806
Washington, DC 20001
(202) 393-2650
www.alliancecm.org

American Advertising Federation
1101 Vermont Avenue, N.W., Suite 500
Washington, DC 20005-6306
(202) 898-0089
www.aaf.org

American Association of Advertising Agencies
405 Lexington Avenue, 18th Floor
New York, NY 10174-1801
(212) 682-2500
www.aaaa.org

American Film Institute
   2021 North Western Avenue
   Los Angeles, CA 90027-1657
   (323) 856-7600
   www.afi.com

American Marketing Association (AMA)
   311 South Wacker Drive, Suite 5800
   Chicago, IL 60606-5819
   (312) 542-9000
   www.marketingpower.com

American Society of Composers, Authors and Publishers
   One Lincoln Plaza
   New York, NY 10023
   (212) 621-6000
   www.ascap.com

American Society of Media Photographers (ASMP)
   150 North Second Street
   Philadelphia, PA 19106
   (215) 451-2767
   www.asmp.org

American Society of Newspaper Editors
   11690B Sunrise Valley Drive
   Reston, VA 20191-1409
   (703) 453-1122
   www.asne.org

American Women in Radio and Television
   8405 Greensboro, Suite 800
   McLean, VA 22102
   (703) 506-3290
   www.awrt.org

Associated Press Managing Editors
50 Rockefeller Plaza
New York, NY 10020
(212) 621-1838
www.apme.com

Association of Computing Machinery (ACM-SIGGRAPH)
1515 Broadway
New York, NY 10036
(212) 869-7440
www.siggraph.org

Association for Education in Journalism and Mass Communication
234 Outlet Pointe Boulevard
Columbia, SC 29210-5667
(803) 798-0271
www.aejmc.org

Association of Independent Video and Filmmakers
304 Hudson Street, 6th Floor
New York, NY 10013
(212) 807-1400
www.aivf.org

Audio Engineering Society (AES)
60 East 42nd Street, Room 2520
New York, NY 10165-2520
(212) 661-8528
www.aes.org

Black Broadcasters Alliance (BBA)
3474 William Penn Highway
Pittsburgh, PA 15235
(412) 829-9788
www.thebba.org

Cabletelevision Advertising Bureau (CAB)
830 Third Avenue, 2nd Floor
New York, NY 10022
(212) 508-1200
www.cabletvadbureau.com

California Chicano News Media Association (CCNMA)
USC Annenberg School of Journalism
3800 South Figueroa Street
Los Angeles, CA 90037
(213) 743-4960
www.ccnma.org

Canadian Association of Journalists (CAJ)
Algonquin College
1385 Woodroffe Avenue, B224
Ottawa, Ontario K2G 1V8, Canada
(613) 526-8061
www.caj.ca

Canadian Public Relations Society
Suite 346, 4195 Dundas Street West
Toronto, Ontario M8X 1Y4, Canada
(416) 239-7034
www.cprs.ca

Canadian Women in Communications
372 Bay Street, Suite 804
Toronto, Ontario M5H 2W9, Canada
(416) 363-1880; (800) 361-2978 (in Canada only)
www.cwc-afc.com

Center for Photography at Woodstock (CPW)
59 Tinker Street
Woodstock, NY 12498
(845) 679-9957
www.cpw.org

Cinema Audio Society (CAS)
12414 Huston Street
Valley Village, CA 91607
(818) 752-8624

Direct Marketing Association (DMA)
1120 Avenue of the Americas
New York, NY 10036-6700
(212) 768-7277
www.the-dma.org

Directors Guild of America (DGA)
7920 Sunset Boulevard
Los Angeles, CA 90046
(310) 289-2000
www.dga.org

Education Writers Association
2122 P Street, N.W., Suite 201
Washington, DC 20037
(202) 452-9830
www.ewa.org

Electronic Frontier Foundation
454 Shotwell Street
San Francisco, CA 94110
(415) 436-9333
www.eff.org

Evidence Photographers International Council (EPIC)
600 Main Street
Honesdale, PA 18431
www.epic-photo.org

Financial Management Association International
   University of South Florida
   College of Business Administration
   Tampa, FL 33620
   (813) 974-2084
   www.fma.org

Institute for Crisis Management
   950 Breckenridge Lane, Suite 140
   Louisville, KY 40207-4687
   (502) 891-2507
   www.crisisexperts.com

Institute of Electrical and Electronics Engineers (IEEE)
   3 Park Avenue, 17th Floor
   New York, NY 10016-5997
   (212) 419-7900
   www.ieee.org

Intercollegiate Broadcasting System
   367 Windsor Highway
   New Windsor, NY 12553-7900
   (845) 565-0003
   www.ibsradio.org

International Association of Business Communicators
   One Hallidie Plaza, Suite 600
   San Francisco, CA 94102
   (415) 544-4700
   www.iabc.com

International Center of Photography (ICP)
   1114 Avenue of the Americas
   New York, NY 10036
   (212) 857-0001
   www.icp.org

International Communications Industries Association (ICIA)
   11242 Waples Mill Road, Suite 200
   Fairfax, VA 22030
   (703) 273-7200
   www.infocomm.org

International Fire Photographers Association (IFPA)
   146 West Caracas Avenue
   Hershey, PA 17033-1510
   (717) 533-4133
   www.ifpaonline.com

Internet Advertising Bureau (IAB)
   200 Park Avenue South, Suite 501
   New York, NY 10003
   (212) 949-9034
   www.iab.net

Investigative Reporters and Editors (IRE)
   Missouri School of Journalism
   138 Neff Annex
   Columbia, MO 65211-1200
   (573) 882-2042
   www.ire.org

Media Communications Association-International (MCA-I)
   401 North Michigan Avenue
   Chicago, IL 60611
   (312) 321-5171
   Fax: (312) 673-6716
   www.mca-i.org

National Asian-American Telecommunications Association (NAATA)
   145 Ninth Street, Suite 350
   San Francisco, CA 94103
   (415) 863-0814
   www.naatanet.org

National Association of Black Journalists (NABJ)
    University of Maryland
    8701-A Adelphi Road
    Adelphi, MD 20783
    (301) 445-7100
    www.nabj.org

National Association of Broadcasters (NAB)
    1771 N Street, N.W.
    Washington, DC 20036
    (800) 342-2460; (202) 775-4970
    www.nab.org

National Association of Government Communicators (NAGC)
    10366 Democracy Lane, Suite B
    Fairfax, VA 22030
    (703) 691-0377
    www.nagc.com

National Association of Latino Independent Producers (NALIP)
    2425 East Olympic Boulevard, Suite 600E
    Santa Monica, CA 90406
    (310) 857-1657
    www.nalip.org

National Association of Photoshop Professionals (NAPP)
    333 Douglas Road East
    Oldsmar, FL 34677
    (813) 433-5000
    www.photoshopuser.com

National Association of Television Program Executives (NATPE)
    2425 Olympic Boulevard, Suite 600E
    Santa Monica, CA 90404
    (310) 453-4440
    www.natpe.org

National Cable & Telecommunications Association (NCTA)
   1724 Massachusetts Avenue, N.W.
   Washington, DC 20036
   (202) 775-3550
   www.ncta.com

National Investor Relations Institute (NIRI)
   8020 Towers Crescent Drive, Suite 250
   Vienna, VA 22182
   (703) 506-3570
   www.niri.org

National Press Photographers Association (NPPA)
   3200 Croasdaile Drive, Suite 306
   Durham, NC 27705
   (919) 383-7246
   www.nppa.org

National Stereoscopic Association (NSA)
   P.O. Box 86708
   Portland, OR 97286
   www.stereoview.org

Native American Journalists Association (NAJA)
   555 North Dakota Street
   Vermillion, SD 57069
   (605) 677-5282
   www.naja.com

North American Nature Photography Association (NANPA)
   10200 West 44th Avenue, Suite 304
   Wheat Ridge, CO 80033-2840
   (303) 422-8527
   www.nanpa.org

Photo Marketing Association (PMA)
   3000 Picture Place
   Jackson, MI 49201
   (517) 788-8100
   www.pmai.org

Photographic Society of America (PSA)
   3000 United Founders Boulevard, Suite 103
   Oklahoma City, OK 73112
   (405) 843-1437
   www.psa-photo.org

Professional Photographers of America (PPA)
   229 Peachtree Street, N.E., Suite 2200
   Atlanta, GA 30303
   (404) 522-8600
   www.ppa.com

Public Relations Society of America (PRSA)
   33 Maiden Lane, 11th Floor
   New York, NY 10038
   (212) 995-2230
   www.prsa.org

Radio Advertising Bureau (RAB)
   261 Madison Avenue, 23rd Floor
   New York, NY 10016
   (212) 681-7211
   www.rab.com

Radio–Television News Directors Association (RTNDA)
   100 Connecticut Avenue, N.W., Suite 615
   Washington, DC 20036
   (202) 659-6510
   www.rtnda.org

Society of American Business Editors and Writers (SABEW)
  University of Missouri School of Journalism
  134 Neff Annex
  Columbia, MO 65211-1200
  (573) 882-7862
  www.sabew.org

Society of Broadcast Engineers (SBE)
  9247 North Meridian Street, Suite 305
  Indianapolis, IN 46240
  (317) 846-9000
  www.sbe.org

Society of Motion Picture and Television Engineers (SMPTE)
  595 West Hartsdale Avenue
  White Plains, NY 10607
  (914) 761-1100
  www.smpte.org

Society for Photographic Education (SPE)
  110 Art Building
  Miami University
  Oxford, OH 45056-2486
  (513) 529-8328
  www.spenational.org

Society of Professional Journalists (SPJ)
  3909 North Meridian Street
  Indianapolis, IN 46208
  (317) 927-8000
  www.spj.org

Society for Technical Communication (STC)
  901 North Stuart Street, Suite 904
  Arlington, VA 22203-1822
  (703) 522-4114
  www.stc.org

Software & Information Industry Association
1090 Vermont Avenue, N.W.
Washington, DC 20005
(202) 289-7442
www.spa.org

Sundance Institute
P.O. Box 3630
Salt Lake City, Utah 84110-3630
(801) 328-3456
http://institute.sundance.org

Traffic Directors Guild of America (TDGA)
27270 Nicolas Road, Suite C-112
Temecula, CA 92591
www.tdga.org

University Photographers' Association of America (UPAA)
SUNY College at Brockport–Photo Services
350 New Campus Drive
Brockport, NY 14420-2931
(585) 395-2133
www.upaa.org

Wedding and Portrait Photographers International (WPPI)
1312 Lincoln Boulevard
P.O. Box 2003
Santa Monica, CA 90406-2003
(310) 451-0090
www.wppinow.com

White House News Photographers' Association (WHNPA)
P.O. Box 7119
Ben Franklin Station
Washington, DC 20044-7119
(202) 785-5230
www.whnpa.org

Women in Cable and Telecommunications (WICT)
P.O. Box 791305
Baltimore, MD 21279
www.wict.org

Women in Film and Television–Toronto
2300 Yonge Street, Suite 405,
P.O. Box 2386
Toronto, Ontario M4P 1E4
(416) 322-3430
www.wift.com

ABOUT THE AUTHOR

Award-winning producer, writer, educator, and internationally recognized authority on mass media communications, Shonan F. R. Noronha is president of Media Resources, a consulting firm based in White Plains, New York, that serves the media, corporations, and educational institutions. Her essays and articles on television and the new media have been published in journals and magazines all over the world.

She formerly held the position of vice president and chief content officer for Learning Technologies Group, where she was responsible for the design and delivery of Web-based courses for NYIF Online, an E-learning environment of the New York Institute of Finance. She has also designed courses for ChaseExecTech, a technology training program for the bank's senior management.

Her broadcast experience includes production work with PBS New York; RTE Dublin, Ireland; and All India Radio & Television. She was also TV host of the International Youth Program during the early days of cable television in New York.

She has written and produced training and marketing programs for distribution on a variety of media, for a broad spectrum of corporate and institutional clients. She wrote the interactive script and served as executive producer for the popular CD-ROM title *The Orvis Fly Fishing School*.

Noronha was awarded an Ed.D. in educational technology by Teachers College, Columbia University. She also earned M.A. and M.Ed. degrees from

Columbia University. She completed her media studies from the Xavier Institute of Communication Arts in Bombay after receiving a B.A. with a major in economics from the University of Bombay, India.

Most recently, Noronha was editor-in-chief of *Radio City Entertainment Headliner* magazine. Previously, she was editor of *Teleconferencing Business* and editorial director of *AV Video, Multimedia Producer, Computer Pictures,* and *Tape/Disc Business* magazines at Knowledge Industry Publications (KIPI). She was also responsible for the company's conference and seminar programs, and she designed and launched KIPI's website.

Earlier in her career, she was editor-in-chief of *Tour & Travel News: The Newspaper for the Leisure Travel Industry* at CMP Publications as well as *International Television: The Journal of the International Television Association* (ITVA) for Ziff-Davis Publishing Co. Prior to joining Ziff-Davis, she was technical director of the EPIE (Educational Products Information Exchange) Institute.

Noronha was assistant professor at Iona College in New Rochelle, New York. She was adjunct associate professor at the Graduate School of Corporate and Political Communication, Fairfield University, Connecticut. For several years, she chaired the Mid-Career Scholarship Committee of the ITVA Foundation.

She is frequently invited by universities and corporations to speak on the applications of new media technologies, and her research work has been the basis of design decisions made by several communications hardware and software companies. Shonan Noronha is also frequently invited to serve on judging panels of domestic and international video competitions.